T0360834

A WORLD OF STANDARDS

A World of Standards

Nils Brunsson and Bengt Jacobsson
and Associates

OXFORD
UNIVERSITY PRESS

This book has been printed digitally and produced in a standard specification
in order to ensure its continuing availability

OXFORD
UNIVERSITY PRESS

Great Clarendon Street, Oxford OX2 6DP

Oxford University Press is a department of the University of Oxford.
It furthers the University's objective of excellence in research, scholarship,
and education by publishing worldwide in

Oxford New York

Auckland Cape Town Dar es Salaam Hong Kong Karachi
Kuala Lumpur Madrid Melbourne Mexico City Nairobi
New Delhi Shanghai Taipei Toronto
With offices in
Argentina Austria Brazil Chile Czech Republic France Greece
Guatemala Hungary Italy Japan South Korea Poland Portugal
Singapore Switzerland Thailand Turkey Ukraine Vietnam

Oxford is a registered trade mark of Oxford University Press
in the UK and in certain other countries

Published in the United States
by Oxford University Press Inc., New York

Oxford is a registered trade mark of Oxford University Press
in the UK and in certain other countries

Published in the United States
by Oxford University Press Inc., New York

ISBN 0-19-925695-0

Preface

During the last few decades students of organizations have demonstrated a strong interest in how organizations are affected by general beliefs and rules in the wider society. Some of these beliefs and rules strongly influence how organizations talk and often how they act. Many studies have examined how organizations adapt to beliefs and rules.

We think that it is also important to study how beliefs and rules arise. In particular many of the underlying processes in relation to rules are organizational. Many rules that become important in society at large are created in and by organizations. They can at least partly be understood through concepts, theories, and methods of organization research. The production of rules for others should be an item high on the agenda of students of organizations.

In this book we discuss standards, in particular how standards are produced and propagated. Standards constitute a special kind of rule, but a common and very important one. Most standards are produced by organizations. We argue that standardization is a fundamental form for governance and co-ordination in societies, and a form to which social science has paid far too little attention.

In the course of producing this book, we have had the privilege of co-operating with a number of eminent scholars representing several social science disciplines: Göran Ahrne, Staffan Furusten, Christina Garsten, Roger Henning, Håkan Hydén, Kerstin Sahlin-Andersson, and Kristina Tamm Hallström. We have also learnt much from the participants in the seminar on standardization held in Arild in September 1997 and from our colleagues at Score. John Meyer gave valuable comments on several chapters. We would like to thank all these colleagues, as well as all the standardizers who allowed us to interview them, or who helped in other ways. The Swedish Council for Research in the Humanities and Social Sciences partially financed this research effort.

Nils Brunsson
Bengt Jacobsson

Contents

Part II Producing and Distributing Standards

Part III Adopting Standards

List of Contributors

Göran Ahrne is professor of sociology, Stockholm University.

Nils Brunsson is professor of management, Stockholm School of Economics.

Staffan Furusten is research fellow in management, Stockholm School of Economics.

Christina Garsten is research fellow in social anthropology, Stockholm University.

Roger Henning is associate professor of political science, Stockholm School of Economics.

Bengt Jacobsson is professor of public management, Lund University and Stockholm School of Economics.

Kerstin Sahlin-Andersson is professor of management, Stockholm University.

Kristina Tamm Hallström is Ph.D. candidate, Stockholm School of Economics.

All the authors are at the time of writing working at Score, Stockholm Center for Organizational Research.

Acknowledgement
Part of chapter 11 comprises a revised version of the following journal article, printed with permission from Elsevier Science: Brunsson, N., 1997, 'The Standardization of Organizational Forms as a Cropping-up Process', *Scandinavian Journal of Management*, Vol. 13, No. 3, pp. 307–20.

1

The Contemporary Expansion of Standardization

NILS BRUNSSON AND BENGT JACOBSSON

There are plenty of people in the modern world who know what is best for everyone else. Self-appointed experts and pressure groups abound, all with their own good causes and all trying to convince states, corporations, and individuals how much better off they would be, if only they would follow certain specific rules of behaviour. There is hardly a field of human activity, from the management of companies to the management of our own health, that does not have its experts and its pressure groups. The pundits of the Worldwide Fund for Nature (WWF), the International Womens' Rights Watch, the International Standards Organization (ISO), the International Football Association (FIFA), the International Labour Organization (ILO), OECD and many more cannot perhaps force us to follow their rules, but they still often manage to get us to do so. Even powerful organizations like states and large corporations go by rules that others have provided about how to organize, what policies to pursue, what kind of services to offer, or how to design their products.

These rules are described as voluntary. They are standards, not mandatory directives. In modern life standards flourish. Standards may refer to the design and qualities of telephones, how companies should report their financial transactions, how contracts should be worded, what environmental policies states should pursue, how organizations should be structured, how children should be brought up and educated, how tennis should be played, and a host of other matters.

In this book we discuss standards and standardization—the production of standards—as a form of regulation. We argue that standards generate a strong element of global order in the modern world, such as would be impossible without them. People and organizations all over the world follow the same standards. Standards facilitate co-ordination and co-operation on a global scale. They create similarity and homogeneity even among people and organizations far apart from one another. They are instruments of control. Standardization is a form of regulation just as crucial as hierarchies and markets, and relative to which it can be said to be more, or less, beneficial: it can be seen as involving too much regulation, for example, or too little, of not being sufficiently democratic or of leading to undesirable rules. Either way standardization has important consequences. And yet it seems to have been a much neglected area of social science, attracting far less attention than it deserves in view of its importance to society. To understand the modern world, we have to know a great deal more about standardization. Here, we look at a number of aspects of standardization, at how standards are created, and what their consequences are. First we give some examples of standardizers and standards, and of those who adopt the standards.

Standardizers, standards, and adopters

In modern nation-states we are used to seeing the state as the main rule-making body for a great many people. State legislators possess considerable hierarchical authority: they are regarded as having the right to regulate certain matters within the national borders. In addition, they and the public bodies subsumed under them have access to sanctions of various kinds, which means that people have a further incentive to follow their directives.

Standardizers, too, provide rules for the many, but in most other respects they differ from the nation-state. Standardizers cannot claim hierarchical authority, nor can they impose sanctions. They offer standards—which could be described as pieces of general advice offered to large numbers of potential adopters. And since standards are presented as voluntary, standardizers often have to expend considerable effort convincing other people that it is in their interest, either now or in the long term, to accept the standards.

Most standardizers are private sector organizations or private persons. They are particularly common and important on the global stage, where they meet less competition from other rule setters; there is no world state with legislative power.

Many organizations refer to themselves as standard setters. Standards organizations such as the American National Standards Institute (ANSI), the Association Française de Normalisation (AFNOR), the British Standards Institution (BSI), and Deutsches Institut für Normung (DIN) were founded in the first decades of the twentieth century. Their importance in providing standards has diminished, however, as the importance of the international standards organizations has increased. CEN (Comité Européen de Normalisation), ETSI (European Telecommunications Standards Institute), and ISO (International Organization for Standardization) are examples of international standard-setting organizations, most of them founded just after the Second World War. They are private organizations, their major activities being financed by companies that belong to committees for developing standards of various kinds. These organizations develop standards for the way things should be named and for the qualities that various products should possess. Within the last few decades ISO has also begun issuing standards for administrative processes, such as the series of standards called ISO 9000.

There are also a great many other international non-governmental organizations (INGOs) that issue standards, for instance organizations such as the International Handball Association, the International Chamber of Commerce (ICC) and the International Committee on Bird Protection (ICBP). These organizations issue standards on such diverse subjects as how handball should be played, how advertisements should be designed, and how threatened bird species should be protected. Large corporations operating in a global market sometimes co-operate in creating standards applying to their particular line of business.

A number of less well-organized actors also issue standards. In the administrative field there is no dearth of consultants or other people writing books or articles for the media on how firms should be organized or how marketing should be conducted. Books on the best way to run our lives belong to the same kind of publication.

Academic researchers and scientists are often active standardizers: a conspicuous number of economists have felt called upon to advocate standards for the way governments should manage their economies (Hugemark 1994). In a similar manner students of government, either at their own behest or that of others, have created standards for how democracy should be maintained and safeguarded. In the field of management research there is also a long tradition of providing prescriptions for the way organizational matters can best be dealt with.

Although these standardizing organizations or people are not themselves public bodies, many of them have close contact with such bodies at the national or international level. Rather than being controlled by states, many standardizers want to influence and control state policies (Sassen 1998; Hirst and Thompson 1996). A variety of women's organizations try to influence social and labour policies, environmental organizations try to establish and influence environmental policies, and so on. Many of these standardizers are also highly successful.

But not all standardizers are private. The governments of various countries also issue standards. The law often contains many optional elements (Hydén 1997). Laws pertaining to purchasing or the drawing up of contracts, for instance, contain certain rules that those involved can adopt or not, at will. Such optional laws represent standards in our sense of the word. Similarly, various public agencies may not just issue directives within their particular area of responsibility, but also assume the role of friendly experts and provide general advice to other public bodies or to citizens and private organizations. In this way they become standardizers.

Various international governmental organizations such as the United Nations, OECD, UNESCO, or the European Union, which have sovereign states as their members but often lack enough authority to issue binding directives, create a great number of standards instead. They issue huge numbers of recommendations, white books and the like—what is sometimes called soft law. The increasing importance of such standards compared with directives, has produced a kind of 'neo-voluntarism' (Streeck 1996): the capacity of the EU to impose binding obligations is low, and various voluntaristic approaches are used instead. In addition to producing standards itself, the EU has actively delegated much rule making to various standards organizations: instead of issuing directives for a particular area, it often refers to existing standards or suggests that new standards be developed (Jacobsson 1993; Bundgard-Pedersen 1997).

Standards

However much such organizations and individuals may differ from one another, they all issue standards. On a general and abstract level, standards constitute rules about what those who adopt them should do, even if this only involves saying something or designating something in a particular way. More specifically, three types of standards can be distinguished: standards about being something, about doing something, or about having something.

Standards about being something classify things or actors in a standardized way. There are standards telling us what a telephone or a facsimile machine is. Classificatory standards include standards for measuring, such as the metric system or the Celsius temperature scale. Scientific classifications are also standards for what certain things are, ranging from the Linnaean system for classifying plants to systems in the information technology field. Statistical standards prescribe how to measure a country's gross national product, its unemployment rates, or pollution of various kinds. There are general and technical dictionaries that set standards for what words and technical terms mean and for how they are spelled.

Standards for what we do

There are many standards applying to what we do, in the narrow sense of the word. For centuries books have been written on etiquette, on the conventional rules of individual behaviour in social contexts (Elias 1939). Many people also claim to know how organizations should behave. There are standards regarding the service that organizations offer to their customers or clients, standards saying what should be included in different types of educational programme, and standards for what states should do about their financial problems. Other standards specify the design of the products that a company can manufacture and offer for sale: there are standards for building materials, paper of various formats, loading pallets for storage and transport, or the requirements that potatoes or telephones should fulfil.

Standards can also apply to various processes—the production process for instance—within an organization. They may pertain to the effects of production on the external environment or the internal work environment. Or they may concern the processes for the planning and control of the production process. These last are one example of the administrative standards that are legion today: they include standards that describe how leadership should be exercised, how organizational processes should be designed and controlled, and how accounting should be conducted.

Many standards are primarily concerned with procedures and presentations rather than with production, products, or the effects of these. A number of standards concerning the work environment refer not to the work environment itself, but to the plans and procedures organizations should develop for dealing with related issues (Jacobsson 1993). Quality standards refer not to the quality actually achieved, but to the types of administrative processes that are supposed to lead to high quality (see Chapter 8). Standards referring to the requirements a product should fulfil in order to be safe are being abandoned in favour of standards for the routines that the producer should employ for testing the products.

Standards for what we have

Standards can also refer to things we should have. People are advised to have a plan for their careers. A modern state is subject to standards, designed by various UN bodies or by OECD, for example, about the need to have democracy, a constitution, an educational system, or unemployment statistics. According to some standardizers, companies or government agencies should have clear goals and departments for personnel questions (where personnel should preferably be referred to as human resources).

There is a steady increase in the number of standards regarding what organizations should have. A university department, for instance, should have a strategic plan, equal-opportunity groups, a quality system, and course evaluations. Such structures have emerged from a multiplicity of standards and standardizers, ranging from women's organizations to management gurus. Various other INGOs also propose and support structural elements for states, which should thus provide themselves with both agencies and policies for such things as research, administration, employment, and so on.

But standards do not necessarily refer to things we should have; they can also refer to persons—to those with certain qualifications, knowledge, or skills. Organizations should, for example, hire both chartered accountants and certified translators.

What we have may not necessarily entail what we do. Organizations may have strategic plans without planning strategically, or plans for job equality without these affecting equality as such, or quality systems without altering the quality of the relevant activities. States can have research policy programmes without any research being conducted (Finnemore 1996), or administrative policy programmes without any particular administrative policy being pursued.

Sometimes, however, it becomes necessary to show that we are doing what we say we are. Organizations may want to obtain certification for their processes and products from some certifying body, which is supposed to check on whether organizations actually live up to the standards to which they allegedly subscribe. Not all certification, however, involves a direct check on what the organization does, of what it produces, or of its results—all aspects that are of interest to the outside world. Instead it may simply be a matter of checking that the organization has some regulatory or documentation system which is believed to produce good results. Prizes for 'best quality' are conferred not upon those companies whose products are of the highest quality, but upon those which are considered to have the best processes in terms of management, leadership, and working organization (see Chapter 8).

Adopters of standards

Standardization is based on the hope that some organizations or individuals will adhere to the standards concerned, or will at least consider doing so. Standardizers have no role unless there are people who adopt their standards. Standardizers' more specific reasons for needing adopters, and the kind of adopters that are most important to them, will vary from one standard maker to the next. Some standardizers, such as management gurus, make money out of their standards and related activities. They need buyers.

Other standardizers want to improve and reform what they see as important aspects of life; they want to change others, and so they need to reach these others. Most standardizers lack the resources, authority, or power necessary to achieve any actual changes in the behaviour of others by their own direct efforts. Consequently they need intermediaries, some more powerful agent—often a state or a large corporation—to do the job for them, and their own efforts are directed mainly towards these. States may be persuaded to change their legislation to comply with a standard. Corporations may be persuaded to make a certain standard a binding rule within their own organization or to require their suppliers to follow a certain standard. Or standardizers may succeed in convincing public opinion that a certain standard is highly justified, and this may compel states and corporations to follow it.

Still other standardizers develop standards that they themselves are going to adopt, but they are dependent on others also adopting them. Industrial companies are often interested in establishing certain product standards in their own line of products, if they can get others to do so too.

Regardless of who the adopters may be, it is necessary that they can in fact act in accordance with the standards. They must also have the freedom to choose. If they do not have that freedom, or if they are compelled to comply, then the standardizers have no immediate interest in trying to influence them. In other words, standardization presupposes an ability on the part of the adopter to act independently. In the social sciences entities that have this ability are often referred to as actors. An actor is a separate and distinguishable entity with definite boundaries, enjoying a certain degree of independence, and possessing resources of its own (Meyer and Jepperson 1996). There are two types of actor in the modern world: individuals and organizations (including states), and it is at these actors that standards are aimed.

The compass of standardization

The reader may wonder at this point how much can be included in the concept of standardization. We have covered a fairly extensive area of the social landscape, indicating a wide range of actors either issuing standards or adopting them. Many rules and types of advice—although by no means all—can be described as standards. Is our conception of standards perhaps too comprehensive? We would argue that, at least for the purposes of this book, the broad sweep of our definition is justified.

Standards and standardizers come in a vast range of types, but we feel it would be an unfortunate decision to limit ourselves from the start to certain kinds only. They also have much in common and it is on these shared aspects that this book focuses. The fact that standardization apparently encompasses much, seems to us to indicate its extreme pervasiveness in modern society.

Perspectives on standardization

In light of the abundance and importance of standards, standardization might be regarded as an underdeveloped area in the social sciences, at least compared with other forms of regulation, such as markets and organization. However, it has not been completely neglected. Several branches of social science have addressed various aspects of standardization, or have at least touched upon the subject.

In economics, standards have been considered largely in connection with the pros and cons of markets or formal organizations. An established way of doing things can emerge as a result of market processes or it can be suggested by standardization bodies or by the state. When there are interdependencies between consumers of a product, market processes may lead to suboptimal technical solutions due to 'lock-in processes'. If some people start using PCs, it may be difficult for one of them, wanting to use a better technical solution, such as the MacIntosh computer, actually to do so, since all the computers need to be able to interact. In such cases it may be wise to make a rule instead, prescribing the best technical solution. In practice, such rules often come in the form of standards.

The mixture of markets and organization has also been discussed by students of globalization and internationalization. For example, studies have been made of ways of regulating global markets in the absence of an authoritative body at the world level. The emergence and development of international regimes, such as the Bretton Woods Agreement and the GATT have often been studied as a kind of governance without government. Regimes have been seen as 'sets of governing arrangements' that include 'networks of rules, norms, and procedures that regularize behavior and control its effects' (Keohane and Nye 1977) and as 'sets of implicit or explicit principles, norms, rules, and decision-making procedures around which actors' expectations converge in a given area of international relations' (Krasner 1983). Such regimes contain many standards. These standards will not necessarily always be fully consistent with each other or with other aspects of a regime, that is, it is far from certain that all aspects will in fact 'converge'. It is therefore important to study standards and the other aspects separately, as well as in combination.

How rules are created and implemented in organizations has been a classical theme in organization studies. The main focus has been on rules issued by the leadership of an organization. Over the last few decades, however, this theorizing has begun to follow new paths. Researchers are now giving greater weight to the fact that organizations are embedded in society, which makes them susceptible to rules that come from their environment rather than from their own management. Studies are undertaken of how organizations are affected by institutions, by ideas, rules, and legitimate patterns of action that are generally taken for granted (Meyer and Rowan (1977) and DiMaggio and Powell (1983)).

Institution is a broad concept, used to describe ideas and patterns of action as well as formal rules (Jepperson 1991). Some standards become institutionalized in the sense that, in practice, actors take it for granted that they should be followed. However, there are also many ideas, patterns of action, and rules in modern societies that actors do not necessarily take for granted, in other words that are not institutionalized. Most standards belong to this category. Even though such elements in the environment do not fully determine what we should do in a given situation, they can still be important since many actors may choose to act in accordance with them.

Standards may not explain as much of individual and organizational behaviour as institutions do. The mere existence of a standard does not guarantee that it will be followed either by individuals or by organizations. To understand what happens to standards, we obviously have to examine specific situations and details of the reception processes involved.

There has been growing interest in how organizations receive ideas and models that arise and then spread round the world (Powell and DiMaggio 1991; Czarniawska and Sevòn 1996; Røvik 1998). We know a considerable amount about how such ideas and models spread, and what happens as organizations try to translate them, adjust to them, and implement them. The focus has often been on change processes in certain sectors of society or in organizational fields, that is, among organizations that 'constitute a recognized area of institutional life: key suppliers, resource and product consumers, regulatory agencies, and other organizations that produce similar services or products' (DiMaggio and Powell 1983, p. 148).

According to the above definition, standardizers are also part of some organizational field. The financial accounting field consists not only of companies that produce accounts but also of organizations like parliaments and governments, international standards organizations, the European Union, and so on, that create and issue rules. Some of these regulators lay down rules that are binding, while others work with standards. Although standardizers and other rule setters have been seen as part of organizational fields, more interest has been paid to the way specific actors adapt to rules than to how the rules are created. In this book we look not only at the adoption of standards, but also—and primarily—at their production.

But who are these self-appointed experts who do not act themselves, but who seek to create rules for others to follow? In an attempt to classify these 'others', Meyer (1996) singled out successful organizations perceived as models for other organizations, associations of organizations (for instance INGOs), social movements, science, and the various professions, and he recognized—as we do—the importance of these creators and transmitters of models and ideas, and of trying to discover the kind of attributes that tend to enhance the potential of such ideas for travel.

Compared with Meyer (1996) and Czarniawska and Sevòn (1996), we focus more narrowly here on standards and standardizers. Standards are related to other ideas and rules, but they have characteristics requiring special attention. Standards possess some qualities that can affect the ease with which they travel between and within organizations and organizational fields: they consist of explicit statements and they are presented as being voluntary.

Naturally, we do not regard standardization as a field that can be cheerfully left to technicians and engineers. We have already seen just how many people are engaged in standardization activities apart from those who, like standards organizations, actually call themselves standardizers. But the product standards set by these organizations also deserve more extensive interest on the part of the social sciences. Some case studies have already been conducted of the development of standards for a variety of products, such as colour televisions, video recorders, electricity-production systems, or telephone systems. The fundamental task, according to these studies, has been to create some kind of compatibility between the different parts of a system: for instance, what is needed for people to be able to take a train from Paris to London, in terms of tracks, timetables, signal systems, and so on.

Historical studies of technological development such as those of the struggles between Edison and Westinghouse ('the battle of the systems'), or between different standards for colour television, or of the triumph of the qwerty keyboard (David 1986) show that standards sometimes evolve gradually in the interplay between companies, public organizations, and standardizers on the one hand, and more market-driven processes on the other (Hughes 1987; Schmidt and Werle 1998).

In this literature the proliferation of standards is often explained in terms of new needs. Globalization, for instance, creates an increase in the demand for worldwide standards. The studies also show that the creation of standards can seldom be seen as a natural, straightforward or harmonious process. Rather, many factors are important: which actors are able to participate or allowed to do so, how the decision processes are designed, and so on. Although the standards involved are often called 'technical', they are constructed in processes that appear to be anything but technical (Guillet de Monthoux 1981; Schmidt and Werle 1998). Technological development is not linear, nor does it automatically mean that the best standard wins (Pinch and Bijker 1984; Hawkins, Mansell, and Skea 1995).

Standardization and standards have also been seen as a question of strategy (Grindley 1995). Standards can be strategically important to individual actors such as manufacturing firms, for which the standardization of products and production processes is often a vital matter. A company may be very eager for its own particular solution to be accepted as the general standard: if it succeeds, it will have a great advantage over its competitiors in the market-place; if it fails, it will have to make costly and time-consuming changes to its products. Not surprisingly, companies are often ready to invest considerable effort in standardization processes.

Large industrial corporations are often participants in committees for product standardization. Individual companies try to get approval for standards that are desirable for themselves or to prevent any standards at all being accepted in certain areas. The resources available for participating in standardization committees of this kind represent a decisive strategic advantage, and one which small companies do not usually possess. In such cases standardization may reflect and even increase differences in the power possessed by firms of different sizes.

Also, for a large company seeking to introduce a new product, standardization can be an important means to success—if, for example, the company can use its influence to get a standard adopted that will favour the use of its own product, such as a standard saying that the company's type of product should be a component of certain other products. Even if other companies try to introduce similar products that comply with this standard, they may find it difficult to reduce the lead that the first company has achieved. In this way, a standard can provide a far more effective method of ensuring sales than acquiring a patent or launching a marketing campaign would have done.

Suppose, for example, that a company invents a new safety device for use in cars. Although a patent would ensure the company's position as the sole manufacturer of the device, it would by no means guarantee good sales. To establish a market for it the company would have to convince customers that they needed such a product. Although doing this is a traditional way of creating a market for a product, and one that is described in detail in the marketing literature, it also obviously requires ample resources, and the results can be very uncertain. Hence, it may well be more effective to set about establishing a standardizing committee for the relevant type of product, perhaps within CEN or ISO. This can result in the safety device becoming the standard for cars in general, suddenly providing the company with an enormous market as well as a clear lead over its competitors.

Standardization as regulation

In this book, we address the topic of standards and standardization as part of a wider discussion of regulation. To regulate is, in our view, to create and propagate rules. We do not view regulation as something narrow and largely technical, although some standardizers would have us believe that it is. On the contrary, regulation should be seen as rule-making in a broad sense, as a form of organized governance. Standardizers and standards are more important than is often thought by students of society, and even by those who claim to be standardizers themselves. We believe that considerations regarding the significance and effects of standards should be related to the broader issue of the significance and effects of rules generally. The alternative to standards is seldom a situation without rules; rather, it is a situation in which rules other than standards obtain. It will thus be interesting to investigate how, compared to other rules, standards are produced and supplied, as well as how they are received.

Viewed as a form of regulation standardization is a core aspect of society. Society is possible because there is a certain degree of regularity in people's actions. People behave and can be expected by others to behave, in specific ways in certain situations, and these expectations are generally met. Social processes become predictable. Not only do we know what to do in most situations, but we also think we know what others will do and we can therefore adapt to their actions in advance. We do not need to wait until after they have acted. There is less need for information about specific cases. Co-ordination and co-operation are facilitated.

Regularity may be interpreted as the result of people following rules—rules that are more or less explicit, written or unwritten, and more or less consciously considered before or after the relevant action. A rule tells us what to do in certain situations. It indicates what is appropriate or permitted or, in negative terms, what we should not do. Rules are conceived as applying on more than one occasion, and most rules apply to more than one person. Rules are essential to provide social order and to prevent anomie or anarchy (Durkheim 1906; Parsons 1937; Coleman 1990).

When we follow rules we are displaying a specific kind of intelligence. Different rules apply to different people and different situations. So, explicitly or implicitly, we have to answer three questions in order to know which rule to follow (March and Olsen 1989): Who am I? What sort of situation am I in? What is appropriate for a person like myself to do in a situation like this? In other words, we must define ourselves and the situation, deciding on the category under which we, and the situation, should be subsumed.

This is a different type of logic than the logic we use when employing other kinds of intelligence. It has often been contrasted with intentionality and rationality, to the idea that it is our intentions and our assessment of the future that steer our actions. The questions to be answered then are the following: What will I like or prefer in the future? What action alternatives are open to me? What would be the future consequences of each of these alternatives? The consequences of which alternative will best fit my future wishes and preferences? If we ask and answer all these questions properly, we can also be said to be rational. But while the logic of intentions and rationality looks ahead at what will occur, the logic of following rules is based on history and on something that already exists, namely rules.

The following of rules can also be compared with other forms of intelligence such as imitation and learning. Imitating means basing our actions on what we think others have done, said, or thought. Learning means making experiments: we act first and think later: we repeat actions whose outcomes we like, or try new ones when we do not like the outcomes of our previous attempts. In practice all these forms of intelligence need not exclude all the others. We may follow a rule that says people should be rational. Or we may choose to follow the rules that we feel best fulfil our intentions and preferences. We might imitate others by following the same rule that they do, or we might follow various rules experimentally to see which we like best.

Rules are directed towards social actors, individuals or organizations of various kinds, such as associations, companies, or states. We are confronted daily with a plethora of rules. Much of what we do, in fact, can be interpreted as the following of rules. Rules guide our getting to work at 9.00 a.m., stopping at red lights when we are cycling to work, greeting our colleagues when we get there, as well as the way we perform most other activities at our place of work. Since rules can co-ordinate activities they tend to abound wherever activities occur, the co-ordination of which is important. Traffic flows much better, for example, if there is a rule telling us which side of the road to drive on.

Since the co-ordination of activities is important in organizations—some would say it is their very *raison d'être*—it is essential that rules obtain there (Weber 1964 ch. 1) . Organizations such as our modern industrial firms or our nation-states are, after all, at least sometimes very efficient and effective actors. And state legislation can have important co-ordinative effects in society. Rules are also important in markets, where they concern such essentials as ownership rights, the drawing up of contracts, and the role of money.

Some rules gain easy acceptance, on the grounds of the co-ordination that can benefit us all. Other rules can be appreciated because they prescribe behaviour that we think is morally correct or that would favour ourselves. Other rules may be perceived as expressions of inequality in power: some have the power to set rules for others and to see that the rules are followed, without the followers necessarily seeing the rules as moral, justified, useful, or in their interests.

Norms, directives, and standards

Standards represent a specific type of rule alongside two other types, namely norms and directives. Most rules are social norms that we rarely find in written form but that we have learnt to accept as natural in the society we to which we belong (Durkheim 1906; Coleman 1990). Norms are internalized rules that we can follow without having to reflect on them. Of the three types of rule, norms can be seen as the most self-evident and least problematic, both for those who follow them and for those who see them being followed, at least if both parties belong to the same culture. Attention is seldom drawn to norms, except when someone is violating them. That we should not steal, and that we should help one another in various situations, are two examples of norms. Social norms have no obvious source, appearing instead to be a part of us. Norms are compelling, in the sense that it is difficult to violate them; and they are voluntary, in the sense that we appear to be following them because we want to, and not because we are exposed to any outside pressure to do so.

Then there are other more explicit rules, this time generally in written form. Many such rules are issued by persons or organizations to whom we have given, or been forced to give, the formal authority to create rules for us and for others. These rule setters are often able to combine their rules with sanctions, that is, to punish those who do not obey them and, perhaps, rewarding those who do. The rules are mandatory. Here, we refer to such rules as directives. It is not uncommon for directives to be justified on the grounds that they are good for others apart from those who are supposed to follow them.

An organization contains a centre with the authority to issue directives (Weber 1964, ch. 1). The leadership of a formal organization has a mandate to issue even quite detailed directives about what the organization members should or should not do. The members are often individual people, such as the employees of a company or public agency, the members of an association, or the citizens of a state. But organizations, too, can be members of other organizations. Companies can belong to a trade association or they can form a cartel. States can belong to international government organizations such as the UN or the EU. Membership of an organization is generally voluntary (states being one exception), but once one is a member one has to follow the directives of the leadership. Members of an organization have to give up some part of their right to decide for themselves.

Standards are explicit rules issued without reference to the kind of authority that the leaders of organizations enjoy. Individuals can issue standards for others, and organizations can issue standards for others apart from their own members. Sometimes the leadership of an organization may choose not to exploit its formal authority when it issues rules, thus issuing standards rather than directives. Those who issue standards are unable or unwilling to make others follow them, at least not by exploiting any formal authority they may possess.

Standards resemble directives in two ways that distinguish them from norms: they are explicit and they have an evident source. They also differ from directives, however, in that they are claimed to be voluntary. The standardizers do not have access to sanctions against those who do not comply with their standards. Whether or not a standard is adhered to depends primarily not on the hierarchical authority or power of the issuing source, but on whether the standard appeals to the adopters for other reasons. Standards can be said to provide a kind of recipe or advice for many others regarding what they should do. Since standardizers present their standards as voluntary, they cannot be sure that anybody will in fact follow them. They must convince potential adopters that they would benefit from following the standards.

Complex standards

In reality it is not particularly easy, and not always necessary, to distinguish between our three types of rule. The same content can appear in norms, directives, and standards. That we should not steal is both a social norm and a directive included in our criminal law. That we should sometimes greet each other by shaking hands is a norm, as well as a standard recommended in books on etiquette. The way in which organizations are to report their economic transactions is regulated by national law as well as by international standards. Moreover, rules may turn up in various guises in different social settings. A certain content may turn up as a norm in some settings and as a directive or a standard in others. Certain groups of people, for example, may embrace norms for behaving in an environmentally 'sound' way; at the same time there are also many environmental standards intended for individuals and organizations; and again, many industrial firms issue environmentally driven directives as to how their employees should act, for example in handling hazardous material. And something that is a standard in society at large becomes a directive for the members of an organization whose management has decided that the organization is to follow the standard. A standard clause used in an agreement form, perhaps between a buyer and a seller, becomes a directive for the parties to the agreement.

In the course of time an existing rule may become a directive, a norm, and a standard. Legislation based on existing norms can also affect social norms. Standards can be created as specifications of social norms. When states 'deregulate', abolishing some of their directives, ideas similar to those inherent in the directives may turn up in standards.

Standards can also give rise to norms or directives. Standardizers may note a strong need for a standard where there is no similar norm or directive, but if they are very successful the content of their new standard may ultimately become a social norm or a directive. Once that has happened the standard loses its importance, and the standardizers can concentrate on constructing new standards. But the initial standard has certainly shown its power. Using a fork to eat with was an important standard in sixteenth-century etiquette books (Elias 1939, ch. 2), but it is now such a powerful social norm in most of Europe that it no longer calls for specific mention in such books. Management by objectives, which was a popular standard for organizations some time ago, has now been incorporated as a directive into Swedish national legislation about local government, and quality standards have been incorporated into the legislation about health care. Management consultants selling models based on these ideas can now refer to the mandatory directives, rather than to the weaker standards that preceded them.

Finally the characteristics of a directive, a norm, or a standard can vary in practice: directives vary in their imperative force, norms in how thoroughly they have been internalized, and standards in how voluntary they are.

For all these reasons we prefer to leave our exact definition of standards fairly open, regarding some of the main characteristics of both standards and standardizers as variables rather than constants. Standards can vary in many respects. Even though standardizers cannot compel people to follow their standards, other parties may do this for them. The extent to which standards agree with established norms and present-day practice can also vary considerably. The standardizers vary in the resources available to them for spreading their message, and in the extent to which people accept them as standardizers. In Chapter 4 of the book we discuss some aspects of the boundary between standards and directives, and in Chapter 11 we provide some examples of the boundary between standards and norms.

Related meanings of standard

There are other meanings of the terms standard and standardization than the ones we use. The terms evoke the idea of similarity and uniformity: what is standardized is supposed to be similar. This connotation of standardization has its origin in the rule aspect of standards: following a rule implies doing similar things on similar occasions, thus producing uniformity across time. When rules apply to many actors, as standards do, these actors will tend to behave in a similar way, producing uniformity across space. Items that are uniform due to standards are described as 'standardized', but one does not use the term standardized to describe the natural world, as this is not supposed to be under human rules: screws and behaviour are said to be standardized, but not flowers and mountains, however similar these may be.

Rules also specify what is proper behaviour, and ideas of appropriateness thus become associated with standardization; the standard way of doing things is often understood not only as the most usual way, but also as the generally accepted, normal, and even best way.

In this book we define standards as specific kinds of rules and standardization as the production of such rules, but we will also examine the two other connotations of standards and standardization described above: more specifically, we will question the notion that standardization always leads to uniformity and that standards are, or should be, accepted as defining appropriate behaviour.

Finally, it is worth noting that there are also standards for what a standard is. The following is ISO's standard for what a standard is:

A document, established by consensus and approved by a recognized body, that provides, for common and repeated use, rules, guidelines or characteristics for activities or their results, aimed at the achievement of the optimum degree of order in a given context (SS—EN 45020 1999).

Fortunately, since this definition is a standard, its acceptance is voluntary. But we agree that it succeeds in capturing a number of the essential characteristics of standards. We have just one objection to it, however: we must emphasize that there are a great many more bodies issuing standards besides those that are 'recognized'.

Controversial standards

Whether we like it or not, standardization has had a dramatic influence on the way our modern society functions. Although some individual standards have little impact, the enormous and ever-growing total number of all standards certainly does. Thus a proper understanding of standardization is a prerequisite for understanding the way modern society functions.

Of course it could be said that some standards tend to reflect common norms and practices, and are not therefore of any great importance. But in the case of many standards, this is at most only partly true: a strong element of innovation may also be involved. Besides, the fact that a norm or a practice is formulated as a standard is not without its implications. For instance, a standard can be expected to spread more easily than a norm or a practice. Norms spread by socialization processes that often take a long time and require very special conditions to occur at all, and practice among other people or in other organizations is often difficult to observe. Successful standards can also have an inhibiting effect on innovation, perhaps diminishing the effect of subsequent standards. A particularly successful standard may freeze developments into a fixed form that is difficult to change, even with the help of new standards.

That standards are important does not mean that they are beneficial or that standardization is a desirable form of regulation. On the one hand, standardizers tend to argue that standards facilitate co-ordination and communication. Standards are also said to make a complex world simpler and to provide optimal or at least good solutions, policies or products and so on. On the other hand, critics may point out that all these goals can often be achieved more effectively in other ways, for instance by market processes, or that market processes give more power to individual consumers. How can we be sure that standardizers find the best solutions for everyone? Critics may also reject any form of regulation—including standardization—in certain areas, as a threat to the individual actor's freedom and right to be different and to innovate. Other critics may point out that the co-ordination, communication, and simplification benefits of standardization are examples of benefits provided by rules in general. So why prefer standardization as the form of regulation? Standardization may be seen as an undemocratic form, as compared with state legislation, for instance. Whatever our own conclusions, these controversies demonstrate that the production and adoption of standards in various areas is by no means a matter for indifference.

Structure of the book

What we discuss in this book is not primarily whether standardization is a good or a bad thing. Instead we examine a number of questions connected with possible ways of describing and explaining standardization and its effects. In this chapter we have described standardization as an essential element of the regulatory system in a society. This discussion is further developed in Part I of the book. In Chapter 2 we compare standardization with three other basic social forms that are similar in their effect, namely, the formal organization, the market, and the normative community. We analyse similarities and differences between the various social forms and the way they relate to and influence each other in society. We argue that the present development towards increasing individualization and globalization tends to support standardization as a social form and to add to its importance.

Standardization is closely related to expertise, and is usually justified on the grounds that there are some people who know best. The character of such expertise and its implications for democracy are discussed in Chapter 3, where we address, among other questions, the risk that expert groups may emerge claiming to 'know what is best' but remaining responsible to no one.

In Chapter 4 we discuss what can be regarded as the boundary between standardization and formal organization. Those who want to standardize may create not only standards but also an organization to the members of which the standards apply. This may affect how the standards are spread, who follows them, to what extent they are followed, whether they are changed along the way, and, if so, how.

In Part II of the book we look at a number of empirical studies in order to examine the supply side of standards, in other words, their production and distribution. We focus on administrative standards, seeking to answer such questions as the following: Who become standardizers and why? How do standardizers organize themselves and how do they acquire legitimacy? What determines the content of the standards created? How can the various standardizers agree on the standards that are to apply? How do standardizers persuade people to follow their standards?

In Part III we discuss the demand side of standards, and will look at questions such as the following: What motivates actors to follow standards? What does it mean to follow standards? How do adopters interpret standards and how do standards affect the behaviour of those who adopt them? The acceptance of standards is also discussed here on a more aggregated level. Under what conditions and to what extent do standards make actors more alike—what is the relation between standardization and uniformity? And how should we as followers of standards appraise them—what are the pros and cons of standards?

Although we address a great many different questions regarding the supply of standards and the demand for them, we see this as a small selection only of the interesting questions that can be studied in connection with standardization. We regard this book as a beginning and not as an end, as belonging to the first chapter on the subject rather than the last. Standardization is a matter of central importance, although our knowledge of the subject is still limited. We see this situation as a challenge to further research and hope that many others will think likewise.

PART I

Regulating by Standards

2

Organizations, Markets, and Standardization

Nils Brunsson

In modern society much of human action is highly co-ordinated, often over great distances. We can co-operate, interact, and communicate, even when we are far apart. Hierarchies, or formal organizations, and markets are usually cited as the principal forms of social co-ordination; they prescribe procedures for human interaction. In a formal organization, such as a company, an association or a nation-state, an authoritative centre can issue rules or orders that co-ordinate people's actions. In markets buyers and sellers co-ordinate their activities by exchanging goods, services, and money. And what sellers offer and what buyers demand is co-ordinated, at least in the long run and to a certain extent.

However, the concepts of organization and market do not cover all forms of co-ordination. Standardization is a third, and different, form. Standardization is just as fundamental as organization and market. Without standardization the world would look quite different, and co-ordination would be much more difficult. Standards facilitate contact, co-operation, and trade over large areas and even throughout the world.

All three forms of co-ordination—organizations, markets, and standardization—may also be viewed as forms of control, as ways of guiding the behaviour of various actors. In organizations the leaders control or influence what members such as employees or citizens do or may do. In markets buyers and sellers influence each other. Standards, too, affect what people do. As with organizations and sometimes with markets, standardization can also be used expressly for control. Standardization may be a way to influence individuals, organizations, or nation-states to do their work in a certain manner, accomplish a certain result, report in a certain way, etc.

Organizations, markets, and standardization may also be considered forms that affect actors' choices; they may be used to explain why actors behave in a certain way. In organizations, much of people's behaviour can be explained by the fact that they work in an organization with certain tasks and traditions, and with a certain management. In markets, actors' behaviour may be partly explained by their adaptation to supply and demand. And sometimes what actors do is explainable by the fact that they follow standards.

Organizations, markets, and standardization may also be described as fundamental societal institutions, or rather a kind of meta-institution. Like other institutions, they include defined, and different, patterns of action, rules, and beliefs (Berger and Luckman 1966).

In the first part of this chapter we discuss some basic similarities and differences between organizations, markets and standardization. We also compare them to another form of co-ordination in society, namely, via shared norms in what we term normative communities.

Theoretically it is not difficult to distinguish between the four forms. In practice, however, they tend to appear together, sometimes supporting each other, sometimes competing. In the second part of the chapter we provide some examples of mixed forms, to be found in practice. In the third section we focus on the competition aspect. We argue that the absence of one form opens the way for another; the extent and range of standardization thus partly depends on the prevalence and strength of the other institutions. Finally, we argue that standardization is favoured by two major contemporary trends, individualization and globalization.

Comparing organization, market, and standardization

Formal organization, market, and standardization, as institutions share some basic characteristics. The patterns of action are well known and legitimate. If we claim that we are acting in a way that is consistent with one of the institutions, most people will understand what we mean. It is also completely legitimate to do so in fact, in the right situation. All three include specific systems of beliefs, with arguments as to why the institutions are justified, beliefs as to who the actors are and what they want and do, and intentions that can be used when rationalizing actions within the institutions.

Organizations, markets, and standardization are highly rationalized; they are usually defended by reference to their allegedly desirable consequences, rather than by reference to tradition and long-established custom. Organizations, markets, and standardization provide co-ordination and control on the basis of agreed procedures, and in the case of standardization on the basis of agreed names, product designs, etc. as well. Co-ordination and control do not arise from agreement on values and norms. Actors do not need to share common norms to interact in markets or organizations, or to follow the same standard. In this respect they differ from normative communities, which we discuss later.

Like all institutions, organization, market, and standardization may be partly inconsistent: our general beliefs may be somewhat at odds with actual patterns of action and written rules may sometimes be inconsistent with one or the other (Hernes 1978; Brunsson 1996). It is therefore important to distinguish between these phenomena. We begin by discussing similarities and differences among the three institutions as belief and rule systems, and then compare these to patterns of action.

Legitimacy

Markets are generally perceived as systems in which parties choose to interact with others by exchanging goods, services, and money. A fundamental feature of formal organizations is that their leaders can issue orders or interdictions, or mandatory rules, that is, directives. Standardizers, however, can resort to standards: they can offer advice of a general nature to many others.

Standardization, like markets but unlike organizations, seems to leave the individual actor free, at least in a formal sense. In principle we are not required to enter into a particular market relationship and thus to accommodate to another party; nor are we required, in principle, to observe a particular standard. We consider ourselves free to buy and to attempt to sell what we like, and we should be free to follow whatever standards we want. We are equally free to issue standards. Organizations are different. In most organizations membership is voluntary. But once we are members, we are obliged to follow orders and directives. And only certain people are empowered to issue orders and directives. These aspects of institutional beliefs and rules have important implications for how the institutions are given legitimacy, for how particular actions are legitimated, and for how responsibility is allocated among actors.

All forms of co-ordination and control require strong arguments in their favour if they are to be accepted as legitimate in a world of many actors—that is, individuals who believe in their independence and set great store by it (Brunsson 1996). Organizations customarily claim legitimacy on the somewhat shaky ground that their leaders are selected in a manner that entitles them to tell others what to do. The claim may be based on the right of ownership, or on democratic principles, with the governed having the opportunity to influence the selection of their rulers and also to debate and protest. Legitimacy is claimed for markets and standardization on the ground that in principle these forms are voluntary. Defenders of markets usually maintain that all market actors may influence their terms of exchange and that no actor is master of another. And the voluntary nature of standards is one of the principal arguments in favour of standardization.

Usually it is also claimed that standards are in the direct or indirect interests of the people who are going to observe them, or that they fit with their values and ambitions, just as products are said to serve their potential purchasers. This argument is needed since compliance with standards and the purchase of goods are voluntary acts. Furthermore, the argument makes standardization and markets appealing. Other common arguments for standardization are that standards generally reflect what is best or at least desirable, or that they are objectively appropriate (Guillet de Monthoux 1981, ch. 7).

Thus the general arguments for the three institutions differ. And so do the arguments in favour of particular measures or items for the institutions—for a particular directive, merchandise, or standard. Here, too, compulsion and voluntary acceptance lead to different strategies for claiming legitimacy, making these strategies different in organizations than in markets or for standardization. When people are supposed to obey leaders in organizations, there is less need to demonstrate the benefit their compliance will bring. Instead the leaders themselves must enjoy a high degree of legitimacy. If orders or directives are to be accepted, the issuer must be considered to have the right to give these orders and directives.

If a voluntary course of action is proposed, more persuasive arguments are required to support the proposal itself than to give authority to the person advancing it. Those offering something voluntary are more readily accepted than whatever they are offering. When one moves beyond organizations, virtually anyone is entitled to propose anything, but persuasive arguments are usually required to win acceptance; compulsion cannot be used. This point becomes particularly clear in situations in which many take advantage of the opportunity to offer something, since 'competition' often arises. In open societies many are free to offer their views to the mass media, though they will have to argue quite convincingly to get anyone to agree with them. Products sold in a market usually require much more advertising than the producer. The same is true of standards; the standardizer does not need the same legitimacy as the legislator, for example. But standardizers who really want their standards accepted must argue that the standards are morally right, beneficial for the users, and the like.

All this tends to generate numerous standardizers and standards, but does not guarantee that the demand for the standards will be equally strong. This is similar to a problem common in markets, namely, lack of demand, but it is different from the common tendency in more organized, socialist economies, where, instead, there tends to be a notable lack of supply (Tarschys 1988).

Allocation of responsibility

The three institutions allocate responsibility differently. In Western culture responsibility is given to the one who is considered influential, who has by his own free will caused something to occur (Aristotle, 3. 1). In formal organizations it is assumed that leaders are powerful; leaders therefore bear most of the responsibility. When organizational leaders issue directives or orders, their responsibility is demonstrated very clearly, but leaders can also become responsible when they have not acted in this way. In states and companies, governments or boards of directors may even be held responsible for events of which they knew nothing.

In markets, and with standardization, responsibility is allocated differently. Anyone who purchases a good or follows a standard assumes a large portion of the responsibility. Buying goods and observing standards are supposed to be voluntary acts, so it is the adopter who is supposed to make the choice, and thus bear the responsibility. In markets, however, sellers in some cases become partly responsible. For example, sellers may be held legally liable for products which prove dangerous after purchase: the customer's free will is presumed not to have been reflected in the choice of product since she or he lacked the necessary information. It is difficult to hold standardizers responsible, even if we would like to do so, for they provide general advice for certain types of actors in certain situations, normally without direct contact with the adopter. It is easy to claim that an individual adopter has misunderstood who he or she was or the nature of the situation.

When standards govern procedures and functions rather than the specific design of a product or process, the standardizer's responsibility is even more limited. The standardizer does not specify exactly what must be done, or what the result is to be, but leaves these to those following the standard.

Even though standardization places most of the responsibility on the one choosing to follow the standard, that responsibility may have its limits. Our responsibility may be less if we observe a popular standard than if we go our own way. A company that follows 'generally accepted accounting principles' is less likely to be liable for misleading financial statements than if it had devised its own accounting principles. There appears to be a similar 'safety in numbers' in relation to markets— if everyone sells toxic goods, the responsibility of the individual seller is probably less than if there were only the one.

Complaints

The differences between these institutions in the allocation of responsibility are also reflected in the extent to which they generate complaints, as well as in who complains and where the complaints are directed. Markets and standardization generate fewer complaints than organizations. In organizations most people can blame someone else, whereas market actors or those who follow standards have themselves to blame. Organizations tend to generate systems to collect, support, and handle complaints. The systems may include legal procedures, labour unions, or protest movements.

Complaints are particularly frequent in organizations where membership is compulsory, such as nation-states, since dissatisfied members lack the option of resigning. Complaints also become important in other organizations when it is difficult or awkward to exit, such as may be the case with the organizations where we are employed. In non-monopolistic markets and with standardization, the exit option is normally more realistic; it is often easier for a dissatisfied party to stop buying the product or observing the standard than to complain. A combination of strong inertia when it comes to changing employers and fairly competitive markets tends to reinforce trade unions and leave consumer organizations weak. And we rarely hear about resistance movements against poor standards.

In monopolistic markets complaints are more likely, and in markets that do not become more competitive, for instance because of high entry barriers for new sellers, complaints will continue. When it comes to standardizaton, however, 'entry' is generally easy; so rather than complain, those who are dissatisfied with a certain standard are more likely to suggest a new one. Dissatisfaction in the standardization field may well lead to more standards.

When fewer complaints arise, less information emerges about what is wrong. In markets sellers can see that they are losing customers, but they often find it hard to know why. Sellers run the risk of having only satisfied customers—the dissatisfied ones do not come back. Sellers are therefore less likely to receive complaints, and will then miss out on information that could have helped them to attract more customers (March 1981). Standardizers face a similar risk, that they will not learn very much about what is wrong with their standards or how to improve those standards and others in the future.

Support in legislation

Both formal organizations and markets are regulated by extensive legislation, which for the most part facilitates their functioning. Various legal forms of organization, and the rights and obligations of their leadership, are established by law. The rights and duties of buyers and sellers are regulated in laws applicable to purchases, contracts, etc.

There are no laws regulating standardization in itself; anyone may issue standards. There is no legislation which holds standardizers responsible for having given bad advice. Only if the standardizers also occupy another role—such as that of professionals, of organizational leadership, or of market actors—can the legality of their standards be tested and complaints have legal consequences: a physician who publishes advice on how to commit suicide or murder may run into trouble. A salesperson whose instructions for a product lead to an accident may face legal action. The management of an organization whose recommendations endanger the health and safety of its employees also risks prosecution, or complaints at the very least.

General and distanced

Standards also differ from organizations and markets in another respect: there is co-ordination and control only at a general level—many people are to act in the same way in many situations. For standards are rules for the general case; standardization is not a method for deciding a particular case on its own merits. Even if large organizations and markets may also treat a great number of similar cases alike, at least in theory it is always possible to fit the solution to the situation, to act on a case-by-case basis. In an organization orders may apply to a particular individual and a particular situation. In markets, products and prices may differ depending on the occasion and the customer. Market transactions normally take place as direct interactions between specific buyers and sellers.

By comparison with organizations and markets, standardization is a more indirect form of co-ordination and control, exercised through large, impersonal systems rather than direct interaction. Standardization is done at a distance in time and space from both the people and the situations concerned.

Foundation in science

Finally, organizations, markets, and standardization also differ in the extent to which they are related to science. Most modern institutions are reflected, studied, and partly constructed by modern science. Different academic disciplines concern different institutions: for example, psychology relates to the individual, economics to markets, political science to the nation-state, and organization theory to organizations. These disciplines help to legitimize their respective institutions, to create and spread knowledge about them, perhaps even to call them in question, but they also help to develop them further, to increase their complexity.

Standardization as an institution is much less rooted in science, despite its considerable practical importance. This fact seems to be reflected in how standardization is treated in the mass media: we would maintain that standardization is given less attention and is discussed in a much less complex way than markets and organizations.

On the other hand, it is often argued that particular standards are based on scientific evidence. Individual organizational directives and market transactions generally need much less reference to a foundation in science. But a standard is supposed to incorporate what is generally best, and often that question is ultimately decided by the weight of scholarly authority. However, actual academic support for a standard may be tenuous. As will be demonstrated in Chapter 5, many contemporary administrative standards reflect administrative theory from the turn of the last century rather than the current state of the discipline.

Principle and practice

Formal organizations, markets, and standardization are thus distinctly different forms of co-ordination, control, and choice; each has its own particular features. These fundamental differences are usually cited when the institutions are discussed, questioned, and defended. The different features belong to our institutionalized belief systems, and they are often incorporated into the rules in each institution. It is less certain that they are part of our institutionalized patterns of action. For instance, in many formal organizations control by the top may be limited; in fact, top-down control may be only nominal, with actual control being exercised from the bottom up or from outside (Scott 1998, ch. 12; Evans 1995). In these cases organizations concentrate responsibility to a greater extent than power: the perceived power is greater than the actual. In addition, organizational leaders may not in fact be appointed according to the principles, democratic or otherwise, cited to legitimize their power. As for markets, there are situations where market power is so highly concentrated that any notion of voluntary participation by certain actors is an illusion (Persson 1992). Nevertheless, institutionalized beliefs describe many actors as powerful; responsibility in markets tends to be diluted and to be held even by those with little actual power (Brunsson 1996).

Similarly, standardization in practice may differ from standardization in principle. The voluntary element in the adoption of a standard may prove meagre in practice, as we describe in more detail in Chapter 9. A third party may make it difficult for actors to avoid a standard. Buyers may prefer products that comply with certain standards. Interaction with other products may be so important and so difficult to achieve otherwise that standards cannot be ignored. Certain standards may be generally considered so obviously superior that even someone who doubts their value is virtually forced to adopt them. All these situations make it more likely that standards will be adopted, and consequently that their co-ordinative effects will be realized. So it is precisely when standards are in fact not voluntary that they are most effective in co-ordinating.

Also, when the following of standards is largely involuntary, the influence of standardizers and standards on others is considerable. Even if standardizers bear little responsibility, they may thus have great power. As with monopolistic markets, standardization sometimes concentrates power but dilutes responsibility. This phenomenon is discussed in further detail in the next chapter.

There may be further differences between belief and practice in relation to standardization. It is argued that standards facilitate co-ordination, but there is no guarantee that this actually occurs. For instance, if only a minority observes a particular standard, differences may be accentuated, thus making co-ordination more difficult. And whatever the standardizers say, the process of standardization may produce a standard which is clearly suboptimal.

Normative communities

As has been mentioned, organizations, markets, and standardization can provide co-ordination and control even when the actors do not agree on the same values. But co-ordination, control, and choice may also be achieved through shared values and norms, in a normative community; this form has sometimes been termed the clan (Ouchi 1980). Like other rules, such as directives and standards, norms may control actors and their choice of actions. Norms also co-ordinate; if a number of individuals share the same norms, they find it easier to work together to attain common goals. In societies or situations where many observe the same norms, it should be possible to achieve co-operation and co-ordination with less resort to the more procedurally oriented forms, formal organizations, markets, or standardization. There is less need for markets, organizations, or standardization in a family community which is based on well-entrenched shared norms than in a multicultural city.

To a greater or lesser degree, a locality—be it a village, a province, or a nation—may show characteristics of a normative community. A normative community may also consist of groups of blood relatives, such as nuclear or extended families. Professions are examples of normative communities that are particularly important in contemporary society.

For outsiders, some normative communities do not possess the same unquestionable legitimacy, as controlling and co-ordinating forms, as organizations, markets, and standardization do. The normative community of a village, a nation, or a family is difficult to justify rationally; legitimacy is based rather on factors like tradition, which have little convincing power in modern times. This does not apply to professions, which in this respect constitute more modern normative communities. Today's professions also have strong ties to science and the academic world. To a large extent, contemporary professional norms are created and instilled at universities (Abbott 1988).

Normative communities differ from the other forms in additional ways. It is easy for leaders of organizations to issue directives, and for standardizers to promulgate standards. Whether anyone accepts or follows them, or is even aware of them, is another matter. Establishing norms is generally much more difficult. By definition a norm must be not only accepted but also internalized. Most norms are created by prolonged processes such as upbringing, training, or, perhaps, a close long-term affiliation with others. In addition, norms usually have a certain stability and are difficult to change; they do not easily lend themselves to manipulation, not even from an otherwise powerful leadership.

Mixed forms

So far we have described formal organizations, markets, standardization, and normative communities as distinct and different forms for exercising co-ordination, control, and choice. They are easier to distinguish in theory than in practice, for in practice they usually appear together and influence each other. Organizations may include some market solutions, and what we call markets may in practice include some organizational aspects. And standardization is often an ingredient in existing organizatons and markets. Moreover, all three forms may influence jointly held norms, and be influenced by them. Sometimes the various forms are complementary and mutually reinforcing; sometimes they conflict.

Organization and standardization

Organizations often use standards for co-ordination, control, and choice. By following highly legitimate standards imposed from outside, they can avoid making their own decisions. The task of governing becomes more limited in scope. It may also become easier to get orders and directives accepted and implemented, when management can refer to standards, rather than just exert its own authority; for instance, members of organizations may more readily accept management by objectives during periods when this is a popular standard than when it is not.

Some standards become incorporated in directives. The management of industrial companies may decide that certain product standards should be followed by the company's designers and production managers. As described in Chapter 1, some standards may be turned into national law.

Standards may also be based to a varying degree on directives; the two may be intermingled to some extent. For example, standards should be adapted to existing law (Stuurman 1995). When the EU initiates standardization, as described in the preceding chapter, it may be said to require standardization by directive. When seeking to legitimize their standards, international standards organizations use the same kinds of argument as other organizations; for example, they claim that the standards have been issued by a body that has been established through a fair and representative procedure (see Chapter 6).

Markets and standardization

Standards are important in most markets. Standards may facilitate market transactions by making it easier to obtain information on the goods exchanged or on the opposite party, thus reducing transaction costs. If the same standard applies in many countries, more companies are in a position to compete. Moreover, there are greater opportunities for mass production. This is the kind of reasoning that the EU is using to justify its efforts to establish and support common standards for the entire European market.

The absence of common standards may even prevent markets from arising. For example, national markets may be tightly closed if products have to be especially adapted because of national legislation, particular local market conditions, or national standards. This poses an obstacle to a common international market. Such conditions made the EU decide to use common European standards to promote the common market.

In addition, many standards are connected to markets in an even more concrete way: there are markets for standards. For example, a standard may be purchased from a standards organization, and if help is needed in interpreting and introducing standards, or certifying that they have been adopted, such services may be obtained, at a price, from organizations or individuals.

Normative communities and standardization

Norms, too, are present with markets, organizations, and standardization. For example, market transactions are facilitated if the actors share and respect the norm that condemns cheating. Nation-states and other organizations, the members of which share certain fundamental norms, are easier to manage or govern. Professions may sometimes create standards for others. For example, physicians may publish books on self-care.

Standards are usually based in part on norms: standards which differ too greatly from norms are not readily accepted. Administrative standards are based largely on shared ideas and norms for how organizations should function (Furusten 1999). Standards may help to establish and maintain norms. For instance, budgeting was introduced as a standard for companies in the Anglo-Saxon world in the 1930s (Miller 1999); now it is a strong norm, something most administrators take for granted (Wallander 1994).

Standardization as a problem

That the different forms are found together does not necessarily mean that they complement each other in a harmonious way. They sometimes conflict, with one form having negative effects on another.

Standardization may undermine organizations. If some standards become very popular or some standardizers are highly credible, the leadership may find it difficult to go against them. For example, in periods when decentralization is a popular standard promoted by respected experts, managers who want to centralize their organization will have an uphill battle on their hands.

Similarly, standardization may undermine markets. If market solutions to environmental problems, for example, are inferior to proposed standards, legislators and others may reject markets as a form of control in this sphere. Also, in markets standards tend to favour some actors to the disadvantage of others. A particular standard is likely to be better adapted to the hardware, know-how, and traditions of one manufacturer than those of others. Once a standard has become established and accepted, it is very difficult for new and better ways to win market approval. Thus, standardization may not only promote but also inhibit competition and innovation.

Standards may undermine normative communities like professions by offering solutions contrary to the values of the profession, though attractive to outsiders. Examples include administrative standards which go against doctors' professional norms but which are nevertheless introduced into health care by administrators. Such standards may substantially complicate professional health care.

Standardization as an alternative

So even if formal organizations, markets, and normative communities sometimes complement and support each other, they may also clash. Often they are alternatives, with one form weak or non-existent where another is already established. The frequency of one form is then inversely correlated with the frequency of the others: both the need to use a form and the possibility of doing so diminish if one or more of the other forms are already present.

Which form will predominate in a particular context depends on the special characteristics of each form and how well it fits the situation. The use of standardization is at least partly explainable by the need for it: if other instruments of control and co-ordination are not available, standards will be in demand. But a need is not sufficient; it must also be possible to create and follow standards. We now look at situations in which we are likely to find standardization rather than organizations, markets, or normative communities.

Standardization instead of organizations

If formal organization and standards are alternatives, standardization is more likely if there is no organization. National standards organizations have usually been founded with the backing of the state and large companies; however, their mission was to develop standards for aspects of industrial activity which were not and should not be subsumed under a formal organization, be it the state and its legislation or individual companies. As will be argued below, the growing importance of global standardization in recent decades may be due to a vast need for global co-ordination in the absence of a strong supreme global organization or world state.

The absence of a formal organization creates not only a need, but also an opportunity, to standardize, since there will be little competition from directives. Where there is an organization, the scope for standardization is much more limited. If there were a strong state that issued administrative directives for all other organizations in a society, there would be substantially less scope for a vast array of administrative standards. In many countries laws stipulating the basic requirements for a joint stock company prevent standards from emerging in this area. Also, the scope for generating standards is more limited within individual companies than outside them. Therefore the scope for generating standards is greater when we have many small organizations instead of a few large ones (see also Chapter 10).

Standardization is also favoured when organizations are weak. When states or other organizations cannot resort to directives or orders, the need and opportunities for standardization increase. The leadership may lack the authority, legitimacy, or power to exercise control through directives and orders; subordinate units may consider themselves so independent that they need not comply. Organizations with few common norms or with conflicting norms—examples include many political bodies—may also find it difficult to exercise control through directives and orders, and easier to use standards. If there is conflict among the leaders, they may find it harder to agree on mandatory directives than on voluntary standards. Directives and orders also entail greater responsibility than standards; unwillingness or inability to accept responsibility may be yet another reason for choosing standards rather than directives and orders. While not totally preventing organizations from issuing directives and orders, these factors may restrict their capacity to do so in all areas and situations.

The EU appears to be illustrative in these respects. The EU has limited authority, since its members are nation-states, which by tradition guard their independence. The EU rules for reaching decisions make it difficult to reach a consensus, and the systems of accountability are poorly developed (the so-called democratic deficit). It is understandable that standardization is important in the EU and in similar organizations.

There are cases where standards play an increasingly important role in nation-states. So-called deregulation of activities in the public sector has limited the scope of central directives. Instead, standards have become more common. In Sweden a number of authorities have found their role has become one of advising rather than controlling. One example is school administration, where the national board of education, with a predilection for directives, was replaced by an office of education, with largely an advisory role and issuing a great number of standards; in several instances the office has explicitly refused to issue directives (Jacobsson and Sahlin-Andersson 1995). Such advisory bodies derive their authority from their expertise, rather than as an arm of official power. This development is concurrent with a new self-image of schools and other public services as independent actors rather than part of the larger government hierarchy, and with their ensuing unwillingness to take orders from above.

As we have previously mentioned, standards need not in fact be completely voluntary; indeed, they may be fairly binding. And directives and orders may entail little control (Brunsson and Jönsson 1978; Jacobsson 1984 and 1989). In effect, the degree of control and co-ordination may not always be reduced if directives and orders are replaced by standards. Standardization may be a means of maintaining extensive control when orders and directives are unavailable. Thus, the EU may be able to achieve a high degree of control and co-ordination in certain areas without being transformed into a strong organization, with a strong management.

Sometimes standards have an even higher degree of control than directives. Those who follow standards have themselves decided to do so; therefore, they may be more loyal to standards than to directives decided and imposed by others. At least in certain situations, people tend to be sceptical toward directives issued by organizational management, to take them not too seriously, perhaps to make light of them, or even to violate them. People may find it more difficult to maintain the same distance toward standards, which they have freely adopted, thus establishing a commitment which they would rarely feel to directives.

Standardization instead of markets

Good solutions and co-ordination are sometimes achieved through markets, in which case there is less need for standardization. But markets frequently lead to poor solutions or poor co-ordination, or both. It may be difficult for better solutions to take hold; for example new companies with new products may find it hard to enter the market. As described in the preceding chapter, the need for co-ordination and compatibility with previous products may lead to lock-in effects, preventing new and better solutions from being adopted. Or new and worse solutions are adopted by some, forcing others to follow. An example sadly familiar to us writers is the fact that we have been forced to use word-processing programs which are declining in quality while requiring ever more powerful computers.

In other situations market mechanisms lead to multiple solutions, with no possibility of co-ordination. For example, there is a global market for electrical products, but we do not have identical plug-and-socket connections throughout the world, and this incompatibility is a problem for travellers the world over.

In such situations there is a need for standardization. Unfortunately, it is precisely here that standardization is often especially difficult to achieve. For instance, differences in plug-and-socket connections have not been eliminated, despite years of effort to establish common global standards. When major market actors have made substantial investments in a particular solution, they have little interest in abandoning it. While companies in that situation may participate in the process of standardization, they may wish to retain the undesirable standards, or perhaps to dispense with standards altogether. It may be somewhat easier to agree on standards in new areas where neither sellers nor buyers have made substantial investments.

By contrast, there are fewer obstacles to market solutions in relation to administrative practices in organizations. Here there is little need for co-ordination among different organizations; the only challenge is to introduce appropriate solutions. The sums that organizations must invest to change their administrative systems are normally quite modest. Market mechanisms should help obviate the need for standards; competition should force organizations to adopt the best solution.

Yet many standards are created in precisely this area. Markets do not produce one winning solution; instead there is room for standards. The reason is probably uncertainty as to which solution is economically most advantageous. While the problem with achieving product standardization which we described above was that too many actors knew what was best (for them), what prevents markets from selecting the best administrative solution is that we know too little.

Standardization instead of normative communities

Where many actors share the same norms, there is less need for standardization. If, for example, everyone agrees that organizations should have objectives, there is little point in establishing a standard to that effect. If such a standard is nevertheless introduced, it does not always reinforce the norm. Instead, at least in some cases it conveys the message that a norm is now voluntary because it has become a standard. The case of directives, such as laws, which also express shared norms, is different. They are by nature involuntary; they lend authority to certain norms and specify the sanctions for non-compliance.

However, although administrative standards often correspond in large measure to established norms in administration, they are still created in abundance, and there is obviously a demand for them. Such standards may be created because standardizers to a substantial degree share prevailing norms, or because they adapt their standards to prevailing norms in order to get them accepted. It is more difficult to explain why there is a demand for standards that agree with prevailing norms. One reason may be that they not only express norms but develop them further: they indicate in greater detail and with more technical specificity where the norms may lead. There may also be a need for written confirmation of this kind of norm by an outside party; approval by outside expertise may add to the legitimacy of the norm. Nevertheless, we are again left with the impression that standardization is easy when there is little need for it.

On the other hand, there may be a need for standards when shared norms are absent. When we deal with unknown parties in foreign cultures, we would be well advised to use standard contracts, to use standard terminology, and to know that the opposite party observes certain accounting standards, so that we may feel confident about his financial position. As previously mentioned, when there are few common norms, it is also easier to issue voluntary standards than directives that all must obey. However, it does not follow that standardization is without problems: differences in norms may make it difficult to agree on standards, too.

Areas dominated by strongly established professions, such as health care and the legal system, tend to show relatively little standardization. Within professions and their sphere of activity, co-ordination and control may be exercised largely through shared norms. In any case, there is not much room for following standards imposed from outside. In this respect, strong professions resemble strong organizations. Professions also reduce the need for standardization by offering an alternative form of co-ordination and control. A patient may be treated by several different doctors who have little contact with each other, since each can be confident that the others will follow professional norms and procedures. Doctors throughout the world can easily communicate with one another, thanks to their system of common norms.

Supply and demand

Thus, the extent of standardization in a particular situation may be expected to depend on the availability of alternatives—organizations, markets, and shared norms. The alternatives may reduce the supply of standards as well as the demand for them. But the opposite may also be true: we have previously shown how the different forms are sometimes complementary rather than mutually exclusive. To determine when we may expect standardization to occur and standards to be accepted is no easy task.

Supply and demand in regard to standardization are sometimes interdependent. Supply may affect demand; a standard may become popular once it exists, even though no one asked for it previously. And demand may also affect supply, so that standards which are expected to be in demand are created. But harmony between supply and demand with respect to standards, or between the capacity and the need for standardization, is far from guaranteed, for several reasons.

It is easy to issue standards as long as it does not matter whether they are accepted. Perhaps this is why academics and clergymen are so generous with advice. If standardizers want to have their standards applied in practice, their task becomes considerably harder, sometimes even impossible. If they really care whether their standards are observed, as opposed to merely believing that they should be observed, the supply of standards may decrease.

Sometimes supply and demand are closely interlinked. The effect may be to reduce the supply. If those to whom a standard will apply are involved in developing and approving it prior to introduction, it may be difficult to arrive at any standard at all. The average time required to develop a standard at ISO has been seven years. On the other hand, such a standard is sometimes readily accepted once it has come into existence.

When supply and demand are separately determined, and those for whom the standard is intended are not involved in developing it, the process may be more expeditious and successful. Administrative standards are formulated in rapid succession by consultants, pundits in management, and others. The difficulty lies in getting others to follow them.

Naturally, it is easier to gain acceptance for standards which bring substantial improvements to many people. But it may be hard to find such standards: good solutions may have already been implemented, leaving little demand for standards.

Greater uncertainty as to the best solution may result in more standards; as mentioned above, this may be one reason why it is so easy to create and sell administrative standards. Since it is hard to know or to learn what will turn out to be a good administrative solution, both standardizers and potential users are prepared to try something new.

Standards may be more or less controversial, and the least controversial may be the easiest to formulate and propagate. This may be the case with standards that do not deviate substantially from current practices (or practices planned for the future), or which are not expected to produce any dramatic negative effects.

Thus, the most easily created and accepted standards may be those of minor importance to users and their activities, with uncertain benefits, and of little practical significance. Standards with a clear and substantial impact are harder to create and establish. Often, though, the difficulty is not insurmountable, and standards are still a very significant phenomenon for society as a whole. Nevertheless, we may note once again that standardization is an area where needs and opportunities do not always match, and where supply may exceed demand and vice versa.

Individualization, globalization, and standardization

Two current trends should tend to make standardization even more important as a form of co-ordination and control. One is towards individualization, a growing number of stronger actors. The other is towards globalization.

Individualization

Individualization means that people increasingly see themselves and are seen by others as highly independent individuals, with clear boundaries and their own norms, interests, and goals, and that they want to or have to express their individuality in their social relations (Thomas *et al.* 1987). Such individuals do not readily submit to organizational hierarchies. Normative communities, even professions, are not particularly compatible with strong individualism. Markets should suit individuals better, since the market is an institution which in principle presupposes genuine individuals with distinct preferences, clear economic boundaries, and the capability to make their own independent choices.

For individuals, standardization is also preferable to organizations and normative communities. If people see themselves as free and independent, it will be hard to control them, either by directive or by orders, and they will be suspicious towards common norms. They can be expected to be more receptive to standards, which they are free to follow, and which are also said to be in their own interests; to follow standards, an actor does not have to give up his freedom of choice or sacrifice his or her interests. Standards are a form of advice, and advice is a form of attempted influence that even strong individuals have relatively little problem accepting. Advice is becoming a more common commodity, within organizations as well as outside them. Not only are standards appropriate; so also is advice in the form of a recommendation to an individual person in a specific situation. A modern school tends to send a troublesome pupil to a psychologist for counselling rather than try to correct his behaviour by reprimanding him. And parents have access to an enormous literature offering standards on how to raise children (which by the way tends to contain advice on how to turn them into true individuals).

It is not only individuals who have difficulty with directives. A formal organization is expected to have a substantial degree of autonomy, clear boundaries, and its own interests. None of these fits very well with the acceptance of directives from outside. Following standards is more consistent with the image of an integral organization. So, the more organizations there are, the more standards can be expected. And the number of distinct formal organizations does seem to be increasing, just as the number of real individuals is.

At least in Europe, in both public and private sectors, large hierarchies are splitting up into small, separate organizations, each with its own goals and clear boundaries. Government agencies and corporate departments are less popular now than autonomous entities or companies that deal with others on market terms. Concepts in favour in recent years are concentration on the core business, back to basics, outsourcing, and privatization (Brunsson and Sahlin-Andersson, forthcoming).

The more autonomous organizations that emerge from the processes to which these concepts give rise can no longer be controlled by directives from their former headquarters. But they may well be receptive to standards. For instance, a former department that has now become a subcontractor can no longer be ordered to install certain management principles, but the buyer can expect it to follow an ISO 9000 standard. Public services which traditionally followed centrally decided directives will now be both able and willing to listen to advice.

Interaction may make the interacting parties into stronger actors. It has been argued that by co-operating in the EU, European nation-states have become stronger actors, more conscious than before of their own interests in many other fields than the traditional domain of foreign policy (Jacobsson 1997). This should pose a dilemma for the EU as an organization: it will have contributed to the emergence of actors which are easier to co-ordinate with standards than with directives, and which are better adapted to looser forms of intergovernmental co-operation with other states than to a more hierarchical and more strongly organized federation.

Globalization

Standardization is also influenced by globalization. Globalization manifests itself in many ways (Robertson 1992). First, there is more interaction between actors which are far apart geographically; global markets provide one example. Secondly, we find there are more international or transnational organizations, such as Shell, the EU, or the International Federation of Football Associations (FIFA). Thirdly, globalization means that it is easier to communicate over vast distances. Finally, we are caught up in a kind of mental globalization: we feel more familiar with people and with life in faraway places; more of us find them relevant; more of us compare them with ourselves and our own situation. We find that more things are basically alike, belonging to the same category, or at least related. Such fundamental similarities make differences truly interesting and measurable.

Fundamental similarities among many actors permits the widespread adoption of standards: when many define themselves as belonging to the same category or being in a certain type of situation, many will also be receptive to the same standard. For instance, individualization is a global phenomenon, and individuals consider themselves basically alike, compare themselves with each other, and become receptive to the same standards.

The need for standardization increases with globalization, because of the absence of a strong formal organization at the global level, and because, in the multitude of cultures encompassed, there are often no common norms. There are also many obstacles to truly transnational, global markets; many so-called world markets consist essentially of numerous separate national markets, each with its own special traditions, conditions, and rules. Global standardization can be an important instrument for creating truly transnational markets.

Thus, globalization in its present phase appears to augment the need for standardization. Until more normative communities have been created and markets have become less national, many may contend that standardization will be necessary. Standardization is also a form of regulation which is possible to implement in situations where organization is weak and a common culture is largely absent.

Standardization is also appropriate in other ways for the emerging global structure. Most standardizers are in the private sector—as befits a structure without a (world) government. There is no lack of standardizers; plenty of individuals and organizations are willing to create standards which they would like to apply globally, in view of the fundamental similarities that they find among actors and conditions in different parts of the world. For the same reason, many people throughout the world are ready to listen even to standardizers far away. A final factor favouring global standards is that most standards are defended by referring to expertise, which generally knows no boundaries. Experts in most areas consistently hold that their expertise is independent of geography or culture, they communicate and interact with each other on a global scale, and they often refer to modern science, a global phenomenon of primary importance.

At the same time, there are certain tendencies towards globalization of social forms other than standardization; consequently, global standardization may become less important than if it had been the only form of co-ordination at the global level. The market for many products is becoming more global. There is some tendency towards greater globalization of normative communities, often canalized through professions and normatively oriented organizations. Many professions are becoming more global; their values are largely the same the world over. In addition, a number of global organizations founded on shared values are being created; examples include Amnesty International and the Worldwide Fund for Nature.

Furthermore, as we have argued above, a need for standards does not guarantee that it is possible to create standards and to gain acceptance for them. At the global level the standards that it is easiest to generate are those that do not have important co-ordinative effects; efforts to establish more co-ordinative standards sometimes fail. For instance, there are many administrative standards that have adherents world-wide, whereas we still have to struggle with differing national standards for many technical systems. Both Swedish and Malaysian companies follow ISO 9001, but they use different electrical plug-and-socket connections. Railway authorities throughout Europe try to be up to date with the latest trends in administration, but differences in their technical systems still make it difficult or impossible to roll a locomotive across a national boundary. And Great Britain is introducing the metric system inch by inch, as the saying goes. We may have to put up with monotony where we would have appreciated variety, while having to live with costly and irritating technical incompatibility where we would have appreciated uniformity.

3

Standardization and Expert Knowledge

BENGT JACOBSSON

Standardization is closely linked to expertise and is usually motivated by the view that there are some persons who know best. Self-appointed experts or organizations working for a good cause try to convince others that they—or even all—would be better off if they only followed some specific rules about what to do. Reference to expert knowledge is often used to give standardization legitimacy. Experts do indeed play an important part in standardization. In this chapter, we discuss the relationship between standardization and expert knowledge.

From studies of organizations, we know that information gathered and prepared with the greatest care by experts may not be used at all in making decisions. It may serve primarily as a signal or symbol (Feldman and March 1981). Nevertheless, there may be a strong demand for what experts have to say. And there is ample indication that this demand may be increasing. Every day we see evidence of the demand for expert knowledge in society. This kind of knowledge is viewed as a scarce commodity when important issues are being considered. Wrong decisions are explained by the absence of expert knowledge, or by failure to listen to the experts that were available.

For example, it has been considered a problem that nation-states ignore the common knowledge that has been developed within so-called epistemic communities (Haas 1990). In discussing the rules for European Monetary Union (EMU), a Swedish professor of economics added that decisions in other important areas (economic policy, traffic, health care, housing, etc.) should also be left to experts. When new environmental legislation was being debated, a municipal official contended that major environmental issues should be decided by a 'competent superior environmental court on the basis of law'. He reasoned that politicians almost never give the environment as much priority as competent experts do.

Modern societies place great faith in abstract systems, particularly the work of experts (Giddens 1990). Toulmin (1990) maintains that our modern way of life dates from the seventeenth century and is based on our trust in what is general, written, universal, and timeless rather than what is specific, spoken, concrete, and conditioned by its time. Since that time, Western thought has been dominated by Descartes rather than Montaigne and Shakespeare. It is easy to see that standardization is well adapted to a Cartesian world. Standards are abstract, written rules which apply to many cases; the facts of each case are considered less important.

In pre-modern times, according to Giddens (1990), individuals both in principle and in practice could 'ignore the pronouncements of priests, sages, and sorcerers, and get on with the routines of daily activity. But this is not the case in the modern world, in respect of expert knowledge.' (Giddens 1990, p. 84). Just doing things has become increasingly complicated. We need more and more rational justification and documentation for what we plan to do and what we have done. Expert knowledge is all around us and hard to avoid. Experts play a major role in organizations and societies.

Admittedly, arguments along these lines do not go unchallenged. In a humorous vein, it has been said that an expert is someone who makes all of his mistakes in a limited area and according to precise rules. We also find warnings about the dangers of expert dominance: the allegedly technical and objective knowledge of experts is said to eclipse, partly or totally, other ways of thinking and acting. It is considered acceptable to allow expert opinion to govern, but only if the area is highly complex and policy is undisputed. Otherwise, for example if there is disagreement on policy or between different groups of experts, there will be difficulties. Thus, experts have been viewed as both a solution and a problem. Nevertheless, in our opinion, the growing importance of standardization is linked to a high degree of legitimacy for those who are presumed to know more than the rest of us.

In this chapter we begin by discussing what kind of expert knowledge is said to be embodied in standards. We emphasize that standards are expert knowledge stored in the form of rules. We then point to the danger that groups of experts will set their own agenda, often claiming a scientific basis for their knowledge. This basis in science is the foundation of their legitimacy, although in reality the scientific connection may be quite tenuous. We then discuss how it is possible that standardizers may sometimes be very influential but usually need not answer to anyone.

In the discussion that follows, we relate standardization to the role of experts in modern societies. The expert knowledge stored in standards has tended to become increasingly important and, at least in the social sciences, that expertise has not been rightfully recognized. But not all experts are standardizers; some are not involved in standardization at all. And it is debatable whether all standardizers should be considered experts. Some of those that we call standardizers have often been criticized precisely for their lack of expert knowledge.

Rules as a store of expert knowledge

Standards are created by groups of people who develop solutions which they regard as good for all concerned. While people are involved in this process, they are not of primary importance. A significant feature of standards and standardization is that expert knowledge is stored in *rules* and in technical solutions. Knowledge is transformed into rules that are abstract, general, and recorded in writing. Standards are de-contextualized in space and time. However, some kinds of knowledge are not easily stored in this manner. We seldom find in standards what we call knowledge through familiarity, or 'tacit knowledge', and knowledge of individual cases.

Standards are by no means the only way to store expert knowledge. For example, knowledge can be stored in *other rules* besides standards. Binding rules may be considered a product of gradually distilled human experience. When it comes to directives, expert knowledge is related primarily to how these rules should be interpreted. The experts in this domain are not only prosecutors, judges, and defence attorneys; they are also legal counsellors in the broadest sense. Norms that we follow without question are often considered to embody a kind of evolved knowledge possessed by everyone. But we do not usually associate experts with norms. Norms are rules that need no interpreters.

Some expert knowledge is stored in *machines*. Using a computer may not require any technical knowledge whatever. In such cases it is essential that those with the know-how—the experts—agree on what is to be stored in the machines and on the way in which it is to be stored. Co-ordination and technical compatibility require standardization that provides a certain degree of homogeneity. There may be competing systems for computers, video recorders, and the like, but preferably not too many. Much of what we refer to as technical standardization is related to this issue.

We normally think of expert knowledge as being stored in *human beings*, not in rules or machines. Most people will realize that they are dealing with an expert when they talk with someone who has mastered a body of abstract knowledge, such as a physician, a therapist, or an accountant. Sometimes this knowledge has been developed within a profession. Professional groups exercise their profession on the basis of knowledge acquired through years of professional education. Their competence is considered so advanced and special that it cannot be evaluated or controlled by persons without the same education and the same access to research. The exercise of the profession is governed by the professional's own definition of the problem and manner of reaching conclusions, and it should be characterized by autonomy and responsibility (Abbott 1988).

Science and academic disciplines are customarily considered to be the principal form of storing expert knowledge in modern societies. Professional groups are also linked to higher learning; they are surrounded with an aura of knowledge, and what they say is considered extremely credible. Commissions, investigations, televised debates, etc. often go to great lengths to involve scientific or academic expertise that will give them an aura of legitimacy. Science now exercises a dominating influence on a growing number of spheres in our lives; today we have scientific expert knowledge—and by extension, standards—in everything from how to clean toilets, how to feel better, how to shield ourselves from noise, to how to manage companies.

Still another repository for expert knowledge is *organizations*. Society has become increasingly organized. Organizations develop directives for their internal functioning, and special procedures that are routinely followed; some even maintain that organizations create their own cultures. It is not easy to distinguish the knowledge stored in organizations from the knowledge stored in its people and machines, yet in modern society some of the conflicts that people experience may well be between their own (professional or scientific) knowledge and that of the organization. For as we have noted, the exercise of a profession is governed neither by organizational culture nor by the particular rules of an organization.

In discussing different types of expert groups, Reed (1996) distinguishes between experts in independent/liberal professions, such as physicians, architects, and lawyers, and those in so-called organizational professions like managers, administrators, and technicians. These two distinct types of expert group are assumed to differ as to their knowledge base, their power strategy, and their form of organization. The classic independent professions are based on abstract, codified, cosmopolitan, and rational knowledge acquired substantially from academic disciplines and through academic education. These professions follow a strategy of monopolization, and their form of organization is based on collegiality.

As for the organizational professions, their expert knowledge relates to the development of the organization. According to Reed, it is founded on technical, tacit, local, and political knowledge, its strategy is not one of monopolization but of credentialism (the importance of academic degrees, positions of authority, etc.), and its form of organization is bureaucracy. In our opinion, Reed probably underestimates the degree of general and abstract knowledge also present in areas which are more specific to organizations. Abbott (1988) has described this kind of knowledge as more craftsmanlike. Despite its rather fragmented character, we will show that management and organizations are becoming increasingly subject to standardization.

The third group of experts identified by Reed is what he terms 'knowledge workers'. By these he means financial and business consultants, IT experts, and others who possess a kind of specialized expertise based on a much less clearly defined knowledge base. In their work they use a combination of theoretical knowledge, analytical tools, and knowledge of a more esoteric nature. They are entrepreneurs who carve out their own space in markets and act through networks. We would definitely call some of these experts standardizers, but to a greater extent than Reed we emphasize the similarities rather than the differences between the three groups of experts.

The scientific bases of standards

In practice, these different ways of storing expert knowledge are thus interwoven. For example, standardization is strongly based on academic disciplines, is linked to professions, and is often directed at organizations. Standardization of the physical world (encompassing flora, fauna, minerals, planets, stars, clouds, etc.) was preceded by rapid progress towards standardization in the natural sciences. There was a similar development, though later and more gradual, in the social sciences (Meyer 1997). The twentieth century has witnessed the emergence and proliferation of general models relating to human beings, societies, and organizations. In Meyer's view, science seems to have a pre-eminent role in explaining the expansion and diffusion of standardization. More and more fields of society are being treated as sciences and then subjected to standardization.

According to Meyer, the strong position of the sciences may explain the voluntary character of standardization: 'The participants are, in their voluntary activity, simply doing reasonable social action given the prior and taken-for-granted scientized context' (Meyer 1997, p. 11). He emphasizes the importance of distinguishing between academic knowledge, on the one hand, and the 'development industry' of professional, international, and national organizations, on the other, which often follow in the wake of academic knowledge. The activities of the latter group require the existence of science and academic disciplines, but need not be particularly consistent with them. Science gives actions legitimacy. Turning an area into a science creates a basis for its standardization.

We examine this 'development industry' in some of the later chapters of this book, for example in the discussion on standards for the management, control, and quality assurance of organizations. We treat academic knowledge, especially in the area of management, as a standardizer distinct from a number of others. In disciplines such as management, economics, and political science, the boundary between academics and standardizers does not seem very clear. It is shown in Chapter 5 that the relationship between standards for management and those for research on business has long been quite tenuous. Here, too, the movement for standardization seems to be based on knowledge that apparently lacks a solid scientific foundation, although it may claim such a foundation as a ground for legitimacy (Giddens 1990).

In this way we can see that storing expert knowledge in the form of standards is not unrelated to other ways of developing expert knowledge. Admittedly, the expert knowledge generated by professional groups may be incorporated to a large extent in standards, but it often includes elements which are not easily written down. If standardization is carried too far, as with systems of medical expertise, it may even be viewed as a threat to professional expert knowledge. The claims to special knowledge by professional groups have a kind of 'sacred quality' that is hard to reconcile with requiring that everything be put in writing. It may be added that professionals as a category are experts who apply their knowledge in practice, unlike many standardizers who work more at a distance.

Standards as technical expert knowledge

People who regard themselves as producers of standards refer to their work as 'technical standardization'. What do we mean when we say that expert knowledge is technical? We certainly do not mean that it is easy to agree on the optimal solution. The development of standards may also involve substantial conflict, for example between companies with different interests, or between standardizers seeking acceptance for different quality systems. While such disputes may matter little to users, standardization may have major consequences for the competitive position of the standardizers. In spite of the aura of objectivity surrounding standardization, and behind the façade of technical expert knowledge, there may be considerable disagreement in practice.

Knowledge of management and quality previously resided to a substantial extent in individuals and has been transmitted through professions and scholarship. Now that it is being subjected to standardization, partly through the growth of academic knowledge, it will be increasingly embodied in rules. Once traditional standardizing organizations involve themselves in regulating quality and management systems, these matters are treated as technical. Here we may find an explanation for why form and procedures are considered more important than content and purpose. As an illustration, quality in medical care today may sometimes be related more to whether objectives, procedures, and documentation conform to some standard, than to whether good medical care is being provided.

Technical standards are being introduced in more and more areas. One of these areas is quality, as we show in Part 2 of this book. A partial explanation is the need for control and supervision, which follows from a reliance on decentralized systems. Delegation calls for control, which in turn necessitates supervision; the latter is simplified when interpersonal contact is not required. Naturally, it is easier for a labour inspectorate (responsible for supervising work safety) to review documentation on a workplace than to examine the workplace physically. An on-site inspector must travel and put up with all kinds of problems, whereas so-called systems supervision can be done at a desk.

It appears as if much of the control in society is concerned with whether organizational units have the right procedures and produce the right documents, rather than whether they are actually doing something differently. For example, organizations in Sweden with more than ten employees must have a plan for equal treatment of men and women, even though most people would probably hold that such a plan is no guarantee of equal treatment. Documentation of this kind, which is often based on standards, is easy to review. The need for review thus leads to the production of documents that can be reviewed (Power 1997). Perhaps decentralization and the creation of autonomous units are giving rise to a demand for standards which would permit the examination of them as autonomous units.

There must be a way to exercise control over units that are defined as separate and autonomous. Standards make organizations visible and possible to control and audit. When standards are assumed to embody what the experts have found to be best—that is, treated as technical in nature—it may be held that this control is objective and non-controversial. This does not mean that there is no need for people. A whole new industry has emerged in the service sector, populated by armies of consultants, accountants, certifiers, accreditors, etc. who are charged with applying and interpreting standards.

Even greater are the problems of describing standardization in the European Union (EU) as merely a codification of expert knowledge. In the EU, private standardizing organizations have been given a major role in 'filling out' very generally worded directives in areas such as health, safety, and environmental protection (Bundgard-Pedersen 1997). Some kinds of rules that were previously considered politically important are now set by the European standardizing organizations, and thus by experts who might be representatives of companies, interest groups, or public agencies. By being linked to directives, these standards became, in some cases, virtually mandatory.

Greater reliance on standards may involve a danger that so-called technical expert knowledge will become a substitute for ethical and political discourse. This subject becomes increasingly relevant as the domain of standardization expands. There will be a growing focus on how things are done—a focus on form rather than content. Another reason why standardization has increasingly concerned procedure rather than substance is the combination of the growing importance of standardization and the prevailing ethic of self-interest. Organizations are increasingly doing what is in their own best interests.

Thus, while attempts are made to justify standardization with arguments relating to technique, rationality, and optimality, and with the assertion that experts develop solutions that benefit everyone, a much more complex view of the technical sphere is emerging. In this book we seek to show why it is important to study the standardizers, and thereby to understand what is meant by expert knowledge. There is also another interesting aspect of standardization besides its allegedly technical nature: namely, the power of standards to create order without responsibility.

Expert knowledge, the voluntary nature of standards, and responsibility

In professions and in the sciences it is easy to link responsibility to certain individuals, to the professional or to the researcher who is personally responsible for developing the expert knowledge. But the impersonal and voluntary character of standards complicates the issue of responsibility. The impersonal aspect is manifest in the references to written texts rather than to the ethical values of a particular individual or to professional or political considerations. The voluntary aspect—no one is forced to follow a standard—makes it relatively easy for those who draft standards to disclaim responsibility.

One reason why the voluntary character of standards fosters a kind of irresponsibility among standardizers has to do with the mechanisms for feedback. Since standards are voluntary, the mechanism for feedback is ineffective. In other words, anyone who is dissatisfied will tend to 'exit' from the standard and choose another one next time, rather than 'voice' a complaint about the standard causing the dissatisfaction (compare Hirschman 1972). There is little incentive to complain, and little incentive to try to change the rule. The case of directives is different; these often include very explicit rules for appealing against decisions.

This is a special feature of the expert knowledge embodied in standards, which distinguishes it from other forms of expert knowledge. In the sciences there are well-developed systems for expressing criticism; in professions there are often quite specific procedures for filing complaints and for determining whether there has been unprofessional conduct. In the case of standards, however, not only is there often little incentive to complain; there may not be any established procedure for doing so, either. These two factors are of course related.

Standardizers seem to grow noticeably apprehensive as soon as standards (as in the EU) are linked to directives; an example would be the provision of the EU directive that manufacturers of machinery are to follow the ISO 9000 standard. Suddenly there is no longer any choice as to the manner of complying with the directive. Anyone dissatisfied with the standard now has a powerful incentive to complain to those who have developed the standard or are in the process of revising it. And the standardizers will find it difficult to disclaim responsibility now that the formerly voluntary standard has become a mandatory directive.

In spite of such tendencies, standardizers appear essentially disinclined to assume responsibility. Expert knowledge is 'stored' in the standard and not in any person. No one need follow the standard against his or her will. Standardizers are seldom held to account for what they do. Thus, one may say that standardization is a system in which responsibility is both fragmented and diluted. Not surprisingly, people who like markets also seem to like standardization. Regulation is considered more adapted to the needs of the market, if done by standardizers than by centres of power with more legal authority.

The growing importance of standardization in the EU is related to the creation of a free market. Many decisions in the EU develop through transnational networks involving several different levels and actors in both the public and the private sector. The EU Commission relies frequently on the expert knowledge found in companies, interest groups, the civil service of member countries, etc. There is an extensive interchange of information and views among companies, interest groups, and civil servants—and less among politicians. The explanation for this is partly that efforts to promote integration in the EU have focused primarily on the economy and the creation of an internal market.

The legitimacy of EU decision making to a large extent derives from the idea of a free market. Decisions are limited to areas where they are essential for guaranteeing a market. Its legitimacy is also based on the utility of markets. It is authorized because it is performed by experts who make good decisions in their respective fields, much as classic technical standardization is justified on the ground that it is good for everyone. The legitimacy of these decisions is based on the assumption that the sector networks in which they emerge are best at solving the problems that may arise. It is less important to know who is speaking on behalf of whom than who possesses the necessary knowledge.

It is interesting in this connection that in the EU matters pertaining to health, safety, and the environment have been largely delegated to European standardizing organizations—that is, to private organizations with thousands of standardizing groups at different levels that include actors from both the public and private sectors. The stated goal is to find the best solution, the one that is good for all concerned. Decisions are legitimated by expert knowledge, but it is always difficult to regard expert knowledge as neutral. In practice standards are used by companies as a major competitive instrument.

Politicians in the member countries of the EU assume responsibility for the entire system of rules which has been designed to make the internal EU market a reality. Constant changes in this system of rules are made largely by committees and standardizing groups far removed from politics. In Sweden, to take one example, the determination of what occupational safety actually meant was previously delegated to employer associations and trade unions, although in principle politicians could always intervene. Now decisions in this area have largely been turned over to transnational groups of experts; it is difficult to ascertain who belongs to these groups and how they function. The politicians remain responsible, but the scope of their influence has been reduced.

We are thus moving away from a situation where elected officials even in principle could assume responsibility on particular issues. Formerly, when there was a danger that decisions would lack legitimacy, the usual response was political intervention, but now that possibility has been curtailed. The critical question is whether, and how, decision making in these transnational processes can be given legitimacy. One way of course would be to create a European state with the same authority that its constituent members previously possessed as nation-states. In the absence of a European state, standardization would still appear to help provide coordination.

Standardization may be regarded as a way of regulating in a situation where there is no legal centre of authority. We will have a kind of symbolic and secularized society based on the premise that people voluntarily conform to the decisions of authorized expert knowledge. But while order is being established, responsibility may be vanishing.

Standardization, expert knowledge, and the Cartesian heritage

The emergence of groups—transnational and even global—with authorized expert knowledge has its dangers. Experts form their own groups that set their own agendas and often claim a scientific basis for their knowledge. They derive their legitimacy from being associated with academia, even though the relationship in practice may be quite tenuous. In our opinion, it is important to cast the spotlight on this group of standardizers; at least sometimes they are in a position to exert substantial influence, while generally not having to answer to anyone.

In the literature on international organizations, these groups have been called 'epistemic communities'; defined by Haas (1990) as groups 'composed of professionals . . . who share a commitment to a common causal model and a common set of political values. They are united by a belief in the truth of their model and by a commitment to translate this truth into public policy, in the conviction that human welfare will be enhanced as a result' (p. 41). Their claim to knowledge extends both to procedures and to content. The link with the sciences is strongly emphasized. The importance of these expert groups is contrasted with habit-driven action, which in our frame of reference would probably be termed action regulated by norms.

Researchers in this area are mostly concerned with explaining why organizations and nation-states often find it so difficult to accept the advice and ideas developed by these experts. It appears that the knowledge developed by so-called epistemic communities has not been given nearly enough influence in a political process characterized largely by inertia and habit-driven action. Experts are sometimes called in, but usually when politicians find that it serves their own purposes, in time of crisis, or when there are obviously better solutions elsewhere that can be imported.

Part of the solution, according to Haas, is to be found in science; the language of science can function as a 'transideological and transcultural signification system' (p. 46). We find it somewhat naïve to view the role of science and of experts in this way. Instead, we have called attention to a number of major problems related to standardization, which stem from reliance on experts: depoliticization, technicalization, and the emergence of regulation without responsibility. Standardization is important as a form of co-ordination and control in modern societies. Growing standardization will probably be accompanied by a greater role for experts in regulating society.

In this chapter we have called attention to the importance of expert knowledge in standardization, and to the kind of knowledge expressed in standards. We have emphasized the link between science and standardization, as well as the relationship between standardization, its voluntary character, and the absence of responsibility for it. We may conclude that the road that we travel takes us from Descartes to the ISO 9000 procedures (which is our focus in Chapter 5). All the same, it is worth asking, with Toulmin, whether there might not have been another road, narrower and probably more winding, but an alternative nevertheless—a road that would have led us from Shakespeare to stories and tales with a more specific, local character, and more in tune with what gradually emerges over time.

4

Standardizing through Organization

Göran Ahrne, Nils Brunsson, and Christina Garsten

I don't want to belong to any club that will accept me as a member (Marx 1959).

Introduction

The task of standardizers is to influence others. Others should follow their standards, but how many will do so is uncertain. Standardizers have few means of influencing others; they have only their standards and arguments in favour of these.

Standardizers may be tempted to try other ways of exerting influence. They can address themselves to actors other than the would-be adopters; they may be able to persuade a third party with power or authority to try to convince others to follow the standards. For example, standardizers may try to convince large industrial buyers that they should require their suppliers to be certified according to some quality standard, or legislators could be persuaded to introduce a standard into national legislation. Another method is to try to achieve monopoly status within a certain area of standards. This is a clear ambition among standards organizations such as ISO or CEN, although they by no means always succeed.

A third method is to relate more closely to adopters. This strategy (for some examples of which see Chapter 8) involves giving those who follow standards symbolic rewards or helping them in implementing their standards. Standardizers may also establish certification organizations and initiate practices for monitoring individual cases of implementation of standards.

A further method whereby standardizers may increase the likelihood that their standards will be adopted is to create a formal organization, whose members must follow the standards. This method involves very close relations with adopters, and represents a border case between standardization and regulation by means of a formal organization. The organization is created with the purpose of supporting certain standards, but by choosing this method the standardizers have become organizational leaders rather than standardizers in the original sense. The standards previously directed to others in general have become directives for the members of this new organization. Compliance with these directives is voluntary since membership is voluntary, but, for membership, it is mandatory.

For example, the United Nations may be said to have been formed in order to make states follow rules of non-aggression and respect for human rights. The UN was created as an organization with these rules in its statutes and tried to enrol every state as a member. This strategy is clearly different from that used by Amnesty International, which tries to influence the global human rights situation mainly by issuing open standards, and by carrying out certain certifying procedures.

We term organizations, formed in the way described above, standard-based organizations. To become a member one has to follow certain rules, so membership is based on similarity. This is different from many other organizations which may prefer dissimilarity among their members: an industrial company needs organizational members with different areas of competence and experience in order to ensure that, jointly, they produce a good product. Some standard-based organizations organize individuals. Members of a national Bar Association must have a certain education and professional experience. Others organize other organizations. For instance, in trade organizations all the affiliated companies manufacture the same type of products, and the members of FIFA are national football leagues, which play football according to certain standards. Whether individuals or organizations, members of standard-based organizations tend to value a certain degree of autonomy; and standard-based organizations are normally able to influence only part of their members' activities.

There are two ways of viewing the formation of standard-based organizations, both of which make such organizations of interest to students of standardization. They can be seen as the end and opposite of standardization; as the point when standardization ends and formal organization begins. According to this view, those wanting to influence others can choose either standardization or organization. Some standardizers choose to become leaders of standard-based organizations. The crucial issues then become how we can understand the choice of one form rather than another, as discussed in Chapter 2, and how we can explain the transition from standardization to formal organization, an issue that is discussed later in this chapter.

Alternatively, the transition from traditional standardization to standard-based organization can be seen in a less dramatic way, as representing both discontinuity and continuity—as a way of standardizing but with other means. One reason for this perspective is the fact that many standard-based organizations not only turn to directives but continue to produce standards for their members, since these value their autonomy too highly to accept more than a limited set of directives. For instance, over the years the UN has produced a great many standards for modern states in fields such as education, labour, politics, and preservation of nature (Meyer 1987). In addition, a standard-based organization may well act as a traditional standardizer, producing standards for non-members.

Another, more fundamental reason for considering the creation of a standard-based organization as a continuity is that it can be seen as just another step in standardizers' attempts to organize their environment. In this case we let the concept of organization represent order and co-ordination rather than the institution of formal organization (as defined in Chapter 2). Organizing in this sense means to use various instruments of co-ordination (Brunsson and Olsen 1998). Such instruments include the power to include or exclude members, rule setting, common resources, and a centre with authority to issue directives and orders (Ahrne 1994). This view sees standardization as representing one way of organizing, although a fairly weak one, the only instrument being a set of non-binding rules that are not combined with an authoritative centre or with much concentration of resources. A formal organization, on the other hand, represents a much higher degree of organization. So when standardizers create a formal organization they try to use more and stronger means for organizing.

Standard-based organizations operate in organizational fields (DiMaggio and Powell 1983; see also Chapter 1). To understand how organizational fields function, it is necessary to understand processes of standardization in general and the creation and working of standard-based organizations in particular. Fields can be more or less organized. There are sets of common rules, for instance standards and laws, regulating exchange and interaction. Such rules can create high degrees of uniformity among organizations in the field. Fields often include a certain hierarchical structure, with some inspection bodies being able to use sanctions against those who do not comply with directives. Compliance with standards may be checked by certifying bodies. The formal organizations that organize individuals or organizations in the field may be few or many, strong or weak.

When standardizers create a standard-based organization they change the organization of the field as a whole. They try to acquire more control over the field. With their formal organization standardizers get access to more organizing instruments than they had when they only used standards, and their potential to influence and organize others is increased. Standardizers cannot normally enrol all actors in the field in their organization, however; there will be individuals and organizations outside those that are formally organized.

The control that a standard-based organization has over a field varies, but the existence of such an organization may be of great importance for field dynamics. In order to analyse the interaction, distribution of power, and degree of uniformity in organizational fields it is necessary to understand the structure and dynamics of standard-based organizations.

In discussing standardization through the formation of standard-based organizations we look at how, and to what extent, standardizers get their standards adopted and implemented by creating formal organizations. Many organizations can be seen as standard-based organizations, the creation of which could be interpreted as the choice of formal organization over traditional standardization or as a transition from standardization to formal organization. Such organizations include national professional organizations, trade associations, interest organizations, and a large number of international government and non-government organizations such as the UN, the OECD, the EU, the International Olympic Committee, and the World Union of Free Universities. To illustrate our discussion, we examine three fairly recently formed standard-based organizations, in three different fields. All are formal organizations of organizations, that is, their members are other organizations. A short description of each is given below. (Some names and other factual details have been changed, to ensure anonymity.)

Three standard-based organizations

The Association for European Schools of Technology (ASTE) is a co-operative organization, founded in 1988 and consisting of approximately ten leading universities of technology in Europe and 30 companies. ASTE has as its aim to train future company leaders, equipping them with the skills they need to work internationally, that is, to foster individuals who can understand and adapt to different cultures, who can work in several languages, and who are knowledgeable about European and international professional procedures. The aim is to develop and harmonize European technical training at the university level. The schools offer a joint degree, an ASTE Masters, which is based on four to five years of university-level studies. In order to take this type of degree a student must take certain courses available at all of the member schools, have certain linguistic abilities, and take one semester of courses at a member school other than the Alma Mater. Schools desiring to join the network are carefully evaluated with reference to their education standards and international profile. Only one school per country, the 'best', is approved for membership in ASTE, and the schools must comply with the basic rules regarding international emphasis and quality. ASTE evolved very quickly at the beginning, despite certain misgivings among outsiders regarding a joint degree, growing from four member schools to 12 within four years. ASTE determines what an ASTE Masters degree is, and regulates certain aspects of the education programme, such as what courses should be offered to students and how studies abroad are to be conducted. However, ASTE has no further rules for how the member schools are to be set up or how they are to conduct their teaching.

SPUR (Swedish Association of Temporary Work Businesses and Staffing Services) is a Swedish national trade association of companies specializing in providing temporary staff, and has the official purpose of 'working for high quality, ethical rules and a healthy personnel policy in the temporary employment business'. At the time of writing, 14 companies are affiliated with SPUR, and member organizations work actively to recruit new members. A few larger companies dominate the temporary employment business, and it was the head officers of a couple of these who set up SPUR. Every member pays an annual fee to the association, part of which pays for a consultant to help them in their contacts with other actors in the labour market. Meetings of members are held biannually at which information about new rules and events relevant to business operations are disseminated. SPUR offers training related to new employment constraints. Knowledge of the regulatory framework and of similar methods of working is considered important. On the member companies' initiative, SPUR has developed ethical rules to be used in-house, in relations between managers and associates, and externally in customer relations and marketing. SPUR has also set up an ethical council to monitor compliance with the rules, even by non-members. The council functions as a type of court, to which employees, customers, and member companies can report members who do not comply with the ethical rules. SPUR has its own emblem, which the member companies use, for instance in advertisements, as a guarantee that they are serious and as an assurance of providing quality.

SIBF is the Swedish Floor Ball Federation and was founded in 1982 as part of a move to get floor ball recognized as a top-level sport. The game has some similarities to so-called field hockey ('bandy' in Swedish), a game played on ice on skates, with sticks and a small ball. In floor ball a similar stick and ball are used, but the game is played indoors, not on ice. The literal translation of the Swedish word for floor ball is 'indoor bandy'. A student handball enthusiast introduced floor ball into Sweden at the end of the 1960s. Floor ball became popular among handball players, among students and at schools. By the end of the 1970s floor ball was an established form of exercise. Tournaments were used to popularize the sport. The first floor ball club, formed with the intention of making floor ball a serious, élite sport, played on a large court, was founded in the Swedish town of Sala in 1979. At the same time the hunt was on for other teams to play against. The Sala Club required that opposing teams play according to their rules. To begin with, considerable effort was put into finding opponents. An inner circle of six clubs was slowly formed which together continued the process of setting rules. They sought membership of the Swedish federation for bandy clubs but it would not accept floor ball clubs as a subdivision. Therefore they formed the Swedish Floor Ball Association. This association continued the work of regulating the sport and setting up championship tournaments. The association was replaced by the Swedish Floor Ball Federation in 1981. The association became affiliated with the Swedish Sports Confederation. New clubs were quickly created. There were 1,500 clubs in 1995. The number of players increased from 500 in the beginning of the 1980s to more than 60,000 in the mid-1990s (Liljeros, 1996).

The Swedish Sports Confederation requires that a sport represented in their organization be internationally recognized. The first international floor ball game between Sweden and Finland was played in 1985, and the International Floor Ball Association, consisting of three members, was founded in 1986. Ten years later there were 13 member countries and that same year the first world championship floor ball games were played.

Organizations such as ASTE, SPUR, and SIBF are important rule setters, and, unlike traditional standardizers, they are able to issue some directives for their members as well as standards for both members and non-members. In the following discussion we examine all these rules and the difference that the introduction of formal organization makes to rule setting and control, compared to traditional standardization. But first it is important to investigate why standard-based organizations are set up at all, and why they attract members.

The creation of standard-based organizations

The impact of standard-based organizations is many-sided. Standard-based organizations may give actors a certain status or they facilitate interaction, co-operation, and exchange between actors. A standard-based organization may also serve to advance the common interests of those who follow certain standards. All of these effects may be more likely to appear within a formal organization than when there are open standards only. Standardizers and others with an interest in such effects tend to support the creation and existence of standard-based organizations. Also, by forming an organization standardizers may expect to gain more control over those who follow their standards. How much control they actually achieve, however, is a different issue, to be discussed later.

Status

Standardization is generally expected to improve things: a standard is something good, and usually the best. The standards one has to follow in order to become a member of a standard-based organization may be distinctive and highly regarded. One reason for forming and joining a standard-based organization is that the organization gives its members a certain status and identity that differentiate them from other actors in the field. Certain standards have to be followed in order to qualify for membership, and by being accepted as a member in an organization that has certain standards, the members show that they meet these standards. Through membership in a professional organization one demonstrates that one is indeed a professional of a certain kind. Often at least some of the standards one has to follow in order to become a member are highly valued in society in general, thus giving the members a high status. The statement by Groucho Marx, quoted at the start of this chapter, can be interpreted as meaning that this gentleman only wanted to belong to élite, high-status organizations, clubs with such high standards that they would not accept Mr Marx as a member.

The organization's right to choose its members seems to provide a guarantee that members do indeed meet its standards. And the organization's formal right to control parts of members' activities seems to provide further guarantees. Standard-based organizations give credence to members' claim to status and legitimacy. The status that a standard-based organization can give to its members may have a greater impact than anything that individual members could possibly achieve on their own by claiming adherence to open standards. In this way standard-based organizations contribute to status differentiation within the field.

Membership in ASTE is a sign that a university of technology is the best in its country and that it has an international profile. One of the purposes of creating SIBF was to force the Swedish Sports Confederation to recognize floor ball. The founders of SIBF emphasized that they were dealing with élite floor ball as differentiated from unregulated, amateur floor ball. One important motive behind the creation of SPUR was to show that the members complied with state laws and common norms; thereby differentiating the serious member companies from the less serious companies in the temporary employment business.

Sometimes membership in standard-based organizations not only provides status and high credibility. It also may be constitutional, that is, membership becomes a prerequisite for being seen as a certain type of individual or organization. In some countries, it is only through membership of the national Bar Association that one can acquire all the rights necessary to practise as a barrister. Membership in SIBF is necessary for a club to be considered for élite floor ball tournaments. SPUR desired to play a role in the formation of a new type of company—the temporary employment agency—which has certain tasks and methods of operation. Through affiliation with SPUR a member company can describe itself as such a company. Membership thereby provides a signal to those who lack detailed knowledge of a specific member company and its operations. The standard-based organization provides members with a specific identity.

Interaction

Another important role that a standard-based organization can play is to facilitate interaction and exchange between members, and this role may be the main reason for forming the organization. Clubs that belong to the Swedish Floor Ball Federation can play with each other since they follow the same rules. The standardized ASTE courses make it possible for students to study similar courses abroad to those at their home universities. It makes it easier to combine courses taken at home with those taken abroad, and to count all the courses towards a degree. Student exchange is thereby facilitated.

A standard-based organization is often able to regulate interaction more closely than if interaction is regulated by open standards only. For instance, in situations of strong competition, firms may easily ignore open standards; while a trade association can be more efficacious in regulating competition between member companies. That which is subject to common rules cannot be subject to competition; that which is not subject to common rules is, therefore, left open to competition. The ethical rules in SPUR regulate the relationship between members and their customers and employees, and proper marketing conduct (cf. Boddewyn 1983). This is done to avoid competition through 'unethical' means. Competition is relegated to areas that are not the subject of common rules, for instance price setting and the exact design of the services offered by the various firms. In other trade associations accounting systems are made uniform among members, which may lead to common principles for price setting and little overall competition (Danielsson 1983).

Thus, standard-based organizations not only contribute to uniformity but also create free zones for diversity. The diversity allowed is also regulated, however. The organizations regulate where uniformity should hold and where variation may be allowed. To be allowed to play floor ball, one has to follow the rules of the game. But a clever player also knows how to stretch the limits of what is permissible in a creative way, to create unexpected situations. And some fundamental similarities are necessary to enable the teams to compete. Similarity is a prerequisite for judging dissimilarity, most importantly about who is best, that is, for the purpose of allocating status.

Like all forms of standardization, standard-based organizations may also make interaction more difficult, that is, interaction with those who are not members of the standard-based organization and do not follow its rules. When the floor ball players were required to follow some specific rules, those who did not accept these had to refrain from playing. The kind of football that was played at English public schools in the middle of the nineteenth century without any set rules was also beginning to be played in the United States at that time. After a few decades football came to be standardized differently in England and in the United States, leading to the emergence of two widely different types of football, Association or European Football and American football. These are regulated by different organizations and cannot be played on the same field at the same time (Markovits 1988).

Working on behalf of members

A third role of standard-based organizations is to promote common goals. By associating, the members can together become more powerful in their relations with other parties. One of SPUR's tasks is to defend its member companies' shared interests by working on behalf of its members in contacts with other actors in the labour market and influencing conditions for future developments in the temporary employment industry.

Standard-based organizations can also increase the common resources of their members. For example, through membership in SIBF individual clubs are entitled to receive funding from the Swedish Sports Confederation and access to municipal sports facilities.

Standard-based organizations can also save members from the imposition of other rules, such as government directives. It is very likely that states would be interested in regulating activities that now are regulated by some standard-based organizations. SPUR was formed as an active—and successful—attempt to avoid legislation regulating temporary employment agencies. To create a standard-based organization in such a case is a way of demonstrating that legislation is unnecessary, that the field of business is capable of self-regulation. It is more difficult to convince states of this if there are open standards only. Threats of state involvement in a field stimulate the creation of standard-based organizations. And such organizations make not only state involvement but also other forms of external involvement more difficult: if the EU wanted to set its own criteria for a European engineering degree ASTE and its standards would be an obstacle.

Organizing fields

Standard-based organizations do not organize their members alone. They also organize the fields of which they are a part. They create field actors; they increase status differentiation among actors; they affect what standards are set and accepted, they influence the number and kinds of laws that regulate the field; they concentrate resources to their advantage; and they reduce the influence of other organizations.

In all these ways, standard-based organizations also influence other characteristics of a field. They influence co-operation and competition, and the degree and kind of uniformity among actors in a field. Some standard-based organizations succeed in establishing a virtual monopoly, so that actors who desire certain benefits have to try to become members. In other fields, there may be substantial competition among several standard-based organizations trying to recruit the same members. And the degree of control within the organization may vary among various standard-based organizations, in different fields and over time.

A possible alternative to forming a standard-based organization of organizations in a field is for the potential member organizations to close down and then form one common organization instead, where the members are people instead of organizations— for example, to form one company instead of an associaton of companies. Similarly, in principle one could try to form for instance one consulting firm for a field rather than having independent consultants associated to a professional association. This alternative seems particularly feasible for standardizers who expect to achieve or who have achieved a monopoly for their standard-based organization. However, this option is not necessarily easy to realize. The actors involved may value their relative independence too greatly for that. There are also other reasons why it may be desirable to retain a standard-based organization.

If the prime motivation for the formation of a standard-based organization is the regulation of competition, as in the case of floor ball and SPUR, the element of contest means that the interaction demands a multitude of actors. In such a situation it would be inappropriate for the different individual organizations to cease to exist and merge into one. It would be better for them to agree on standards, and compete on equal terms.

In relation to status and legitimacy, the more exclusive the standards for entry to the organization, the higher the status for the member. Even so there are compelling arguments in favour of the formation of organizations with numerous members, rather than a single body. The status of an ASTE-certified university in Belgium could not be measured unless there were several other universities in other nations, of the same rank, to confirm its position.

When there is a need to make status distinctions, to interact, or to work for common goals, and these effects cannot be achieved by open standards, by state regulation, or in other ways, standard-based organizations are likely to appear and to survive. The formation of a specific standard-based organization is also dependent on the existence of empty, social space—that there is not a similar organization already in place. Both SPUR and SIBF are clear cases in point. It was in the initial stages of the development of their respective fields that there was space for such an organization. If a standard-based organization had already existed it would have been much more difficult for SPUR or SIBF to become established. The rules would already have been determined, and to designate different standards and to gain 'shares' of the organizational field would have been much more difficult.

Recruiting members

If a new standard-based organization and its rules are to gain strong influence in a field it must normally increase the number of members beyond the founders. If there are few members, the degree of organization of the field remains low, and is even lower than in fields with no standard-based organizations but with widespread standards. Since it is not normally possible to enforce enrolment in standard-based organizations, the number of members depends on how many perceive future value in that membership.

Becoming a member entails following certain rules and acknowledging similarity with others. It is common for individuals and organizations to value other ideals more highly than the conformity achieved through standardization (see Chapter 9). The possession of special, and maybe even unique, characteristics is valued more highly than standardized characteristics; being different is valued more highly than being similar. It is therefore far from obvious that standard-based organizations would have an easy time recruiting new members beyond the founders of the organization. What may induce others to become members?

The advantages to be gained from membership are similar to the purposes behind the formation of the standard-based organization. Belonging to a standard-based organization gives a member a certain status, facilitates interaction with important others, or provides resources or protection.

In certain cases membership is the only way to gain access to these advantages. It is difficult to run a floor ball association without the necessary financial backing provided by membership in SIBF, and membership is necessary if a club wants to play in a tournament. If SPUR's logo becomes the quality assurance label that customers want, it becomes almost impossible for non-member companies to gain clients or customers. In such circumstances it will be hard to resist membership. The standard-based organization has such strong control over the field that it is not possible to act in a certain role without being a member. The rules of the standard-based organization then become mandatory in practice.

So, even if the formation of a certain standard-based organization was not necessary it can, nevertheless, become next to impossible not to join it once it has been established. It is possible to conceive of SPUR, ASTE, or SIBF as not having been created, but once they were created they found it easy to recruit members. In such cases it is the formation of the organization that is the critical factor.

But it is not, of course, always necessary to become a member of a standard-based organization. Sometimes the advantages offered by the standard-based organization may not be valued highly, or the advantages can be found elsewhere. In such cases the disadvantages of membership can cause many to hesitate to join the organization.

Membership is facilitated, however, if compliance with the rules of the organization is not especially taxing, or if organizations already comply with them; in such a case they do not need to change their method of operating in order to become members. Or the requirements may be negligible. ASTE course requirements were deliberately set so that most European universities of technology could have joined ASTE without making any major changes to the courses they offered. Rules can also be so broad or so vaguely formulated that the operations of many potential members' already comply with them.

It may also be easy for members to adapt to rules if compliance is not costly or controversial, nor does it affect many of the member's operations. Rules may, for example, require a member organization to adopt certain ethical principles but monitoring compliance may not be effective in practice. Instituting such principles is cheap and non-controversial, and does not disrupt operations in the member organization. In the EU, to implement a rule is understood to mean to make it a law in the member state. If implementation also meant changes in practice, it would be more difficult to report compliance and members' life would be more difficult.

So it is relatively easy to recruit members when members are not affected much by the organization and its standards. This is meagre consolation for those who seek to influence others by forming a standard-based organization. When more extensive or more costly adaptations are necessary to become a member, and the advantages do not outweigh the costs, the organization will encounter severe problems in recruiting and keeping members. The organization may then have very little impact; its very existence may even be threatened.

So far we have discussed why standard-based organizations are set up and what makes individuals or organizations likely to join. In the next two sections we discuss how the creation of standard-based organizations affects the dissemination of standards as well as how it affects how these rules are applied, and how they are maintained or modified.

Dissemination of standards through formal organization

Traditional standardization leads to standards that can be followed by many. Anyone may attempt to comply with the standard. There may be some type of monitoring system to check that those who purport to comply with the standard actually do so, but apart from that, the standard is open to anyone. Standardization through formal organization can lead to a standard with a different compass than if other methods are used. Standardizing through organization offers a means for standardizers to control how many adopt a certain standard, to stimulate adoption of it, or to limit the number of adopters.

Stimulating the adoption of a standard

Standard-based organizations may propagate standards. They may also actively attempt to recruit new members and thereby increase the number of those complying with the rules. Many may want to become members for no other reason than that they want to be part of the organization, whatever its rules, but once members, they have to comply with the rules. The formation of the Swedish Floor

Ball Federation stimulated the use of its rules. The rules gained legitimacy through their designation by a body which itself has achieved legitimacy through affiliation with the Swedish Sports Confederation. And the formation of additional clubs, which use SIBF rules, is also stimulated, which finally has made World Championship games possible.

The rules laid down by the standard-based organization can also be spread outside the organization. The organization clarifies a rule, which, sometimes, receives credibility even outside the organization and becomes an accepted standard there. The ethical rules of one trade association for instance can be copied by another trade association. An organization such as the International Football Federation in practice defines what football is around the globe. It is definitely questionable whether those who do not abide by its rules can actually be said to be playing football. So, the fact that a standard-based organization is exclusive in its membership does not necessarily mean that its rules are not widely spread or that they do not have far-reaching effects.

Limiting the adoption of standards

Alternatively, the formation of a standard-based organization can be used for limiting the adoption of standards. An organization can be considerably more exclusive than an open standard. The organization can control who becomes a member and can strictly limit the number of members it accepts. The creation of an organization, based on certain rules, therefore often makes it possible to limit the number of individuals or organizations who follow these rules. Even if anyone who desires to do so can choose to follow the organization's rules, the value of doing so is limited if one is not at the same time accepted as a member of the organization. For example, even if you follow all the same rules as an authorized lawyer, unless you are a member of the national Bar Association you will still not be accepted as a 'real' lawyer. Even if a club complies with the standards set by SIBF for floor ball, it will find it difficult, if not impossible, to get a game if it is not affiliated with the Federation. And if one is not allowed to be a member of a trade association and to work for common interests with others, the incentive to comply with the organization's standards is reduced.

If standardization through organization is to limit the number of adopters of a standard, it is necessary for entrants to the standard-based organization to meet additional prerequisites; if everyone who follows the organization's rules is eligible for membership then the effects of the limitation are minimized. These additional prerequisites may include compliance with further rules: the organization's members comply with a combination of many rules instead of few constitutive ones. If a club aspires to membership in SIBF then it must comply with the rules applicable to all sports clubs in the Swedish Sports Confederation, as well as those pertaining specifically to floor ball.

Organizations may also limit entry by rules requiring members to be different— for example, many international organizations accept only one member organization per country, that is, all the members must be of different nationalities. This is the case with ASTE.

Also, a standard-based organization does not need to set general criteria (aside from its constitutive rules) for prospective members. Each membership application can be treated on its own terms. Organizations are generally regarded as having sovereign rights over who is allowed to join. For instance, no one can successfully claim membership in ASTE if the existing members do not accept that claim; it is not enough to claim to follow ASTE's rules. Finally, other conditions for membership can of course have a sufficiently limiting effect: organizations may have high fees or may make heavy demands on participation in activities, etc.

There may be several motives behind efforts to limit the number of actors complying with standards. If the purpose of the standard is to facilitate interaction perhaps one does not want to facilitate interaction with everyone. It may be important to regulate competition with a few large, important competitors while it would be troublesome to regulate interaction with a large number of minor competitors. If the purpose is to co-operate, to serve mutual interests, one would not necessarily wish to co-operate with all who share these interests. The more numerous the members are the more difficult it is to co-operate, and the more widely shared must be any resources the standard-based organization creates.

If the purpose of the standard is to give actors a certain status or prestige this provides an additional reason for limiting the number of members of the organization. If membership has a certain status the members can increase their own prestige by letting only a few others be members. The standard becomes more like a patent— a rule which only some specified few are allowed to follow—than a standard open to anyone. Only members can gain status from following the rule. A rule which is tied to an exclusive organization in this way resembles a trade mark rather than an open standard. An ASTE degree has become a trade mark of ASTE and ASTE schools, and it is hard to duplicate. Even if other schools could set the same rules for their degree, they cannot call it an 'ASTE' degree. Even if the trade mark 'ASTE' does not have legal protection, such a claim would have dubious credibility at best.

When standard-based organizations succeed in delimiting the use of their rules to their members and restrict the number of members, they contribute to an increased differentiation of the organizational field.

Application and modification of standards

Standardization of practice

Traditional standardizers have little control over the adoption and implementation of their standards. Formulating and spreading a standard is one thing; applying it in practice is another. In theory, a formal organization represents a higher degree of organization than traditional standardization. So the creation of a standard-based organization should increase standardizers' opportunities for control. But, as a long tradition in organization studies tells us, there is a considerable difference between the theoretical and the actual degree of organization that a formal organization can achieve. So how much organization is actually achieved by creating a formal organization varies. As we have already seen, standardizers cannot be certain that their new organization will attract members. Also, generating resources for the organization may be difficult. To gain and keep control can be equally difficult. The members may prove to be quite unwilling to accept rules, at least in all areas, and they may be even more unwilling to follow them in their own practice. Besides, the members are likely to demand some influence on what directives and standards are issued; in situations of conflict such demands tend to hinder the production of rules. In the worst case standardizers may achieve less by creating a formal organization than by standardizing in traditional ways.

Incentives to actually apply the rules can be expected to vary, depending on whether the main aim is to use those rules as part of one's status or to facilitate interaction between members. In the latter case the incentive is strong; the application of the rules may be required for interaction to take place. In many sports there is a full-fledged system for monitoring compliance with the rules, namely the system of using referees. The training of referees was one of the first measures instituted by the newly formed SIBF, and the lack of trained referees delayed the start of tournament play in Sweden.

If rules are primarily developed as a status enhancer, it is not always as important for the standard-based organization and its members to ensure that the rules are applied. Monitoring need not be so strict. There is no continuous monitoring to ensure that SPUR's ethical principles are followed. It was proposed that schools should be checked for compliance with ASTE's rules on the students' linguistic performance. A few language teachers proposed that joint tests be used for language testing. This became a controversial issue, which was discussed thoroughly for a long time in ASTE. In the end the opponents to such a system of joint tests won and the proposal was rejected.

One indication that a standard-based organization is serious about compliance with its rules is the imposition of sanctions for non-compliance. If such sanctions exist, errors and deviations can be managed relatively easily. When one has paid the fine or penalty imposed, one is back in business. After the requisite time in the penalty box one is allowed back on the floor ball court. An organization which does not have such sanctions is more likely to suffer a credibility crisis, or to be forced to expel the erring members, when non-compliance is detected. Both circumstances may even threaten an organization's survival. Such an organization could therefore have greater inducements to avoid monitoring or to hide non-compliance.

It is not necessarily easy to determine whether rules are complied with or not. Rules can be expressed in such broad or vague terms that it becomes unclear exactly who is complying with the standard and who is not. ASTE made its descriptions of required courses very general and non-specific. The course descriptions, therefore, allowed for great differences in content, which made it easy for the organization and its members to claim compliance. SPUR's ethical principles are similar. Standards which are meant to facilitate interaction, however, are often different. SIBF rules for floor ball are detailed and clear.

Paradoxically, standard-based organizations sometimes function as obstacles to the application of the rules they espouse, in that they are able to protect their members from external monitoring. Outsiders see membership of the standard-based organization as a guarantee of compliance with the rules, whereas the organization may only have relatively weak instruments for monitoring compliance. Members are protected from excessive demands for compliance, whether from internal or external sources: the standard-based organization becomes a buffer between its members and the outside world. For example, there are open standards for universities. It is only possible for a university to claim adherence to these standards if it has undergone external inspection and certification. Such inspection and certification is not required for membership in ASTE. The very existence of the ethical council and ethical rules in SPUR may actually serve as a buffer against the outside world, allowing members to be less ethical than if SPUR and its ethical rules did not exist. Regulation of oneself may prevent regulation by others even if the self-regulation is more in the mind than a reality.

For the same reason outsiders are sometimes forced to comply with an organization's standards more closely than a member. A non-member has to demonstrate much more clearly than members that it is following a standard; members are expected to follow them and are therefore not checked on very carefully. In the case of the EU, for example, such mechanisms may make states which have chosen to remain outside it, like Norway and Switzerland, follow some EU rules more closely than most EU members.

The weaker are the demands for the application of a rule, the more rules an organization can have. Since compliance is not monitored, the outward acceptance of many rules is possible. If strict compliance is demanded, if conformity is the goal, then the rules cannot be too many or too difficult to comply with.

Maintenance and modification of rules

In the cases we have studied, the standard-based organizations and their rules were created by a small number of people, representing a small number of organizations. The organizations represented were the first members. After the constitutive rules were determined, new members were recruited, members who for the most part had to accept the rules created by the founders.

When élite floor ball was created, it was essentially done by a single club. Their rules became standard through their inviting other clubs to come and play on their terms. An inner circle of six clubs participated in setting the rules for the matches and larger tournaments in the first few years. When the Swedish Floor Ball Federation was created the standardization process was in essence complete. ASTE's constitutive rules were decided through informal consultation between two university rectors from two countries, who knew each other well. It was not until after the rules had been set that other universities were recruited. A few businessmen in the temporary employment business, who were already co-operating in another association created SPUR. SPUR offered a forum for businessmen, in a new and expanding business sector, where future strategies and challenges could be discussed. SPUR membership later began to be recognized as a quality trade mark, and the recruitment process largely assumed its own momentum.

In time, and as new members are added, there may be demands for revision of the rules which were the impetus for the formation of the organization. But there may also be strong opposing forces, forces that work to retain the original rules. A desire to retain the rules derives from the larger number of members and the fact that it is difficult to agree on new standards. Also, many, maybe most, members joined because they agreed with the original rules. The most severe critics may have chosen to remain outside the organization. In some cases it is possible for those who prefer alternative rules to transfer to another standard-based organization or to create a new organization. This makes them less inclined to fight for revision of the rules within the original organization. For instance, when the floor ball—'indoor bandy'—players were rejected for membership of the old Bandy Federation they created a new standard-based organization and the new subfield of floor ball.

Also, the external environment may wish the existing rules to be retained. The standard-based organization and its members have a certain position in the field— a position that is based on its rules. New rules might mean a new position and a new position for other actors too, which these other actors may not readily accept. For instance, it is not certain that new rules will give the members the same status in the eyes of the rest of the world as the old ones, at least not without time-consuming rhetoric and expensive marketing on the part of the standard-based organization.

For these reasons, changing rules is particularly difficult when the rules give legitimacy to the members themselves or their activities. Once temporary employment agencies that follow SPUR's guidelines are accepted as the only serious and legitimate agencies, it becomes difficult to change these guidelines. If the International Football Federation rules are the very definition of football, then they become difficult to change. To introduce radically new rules would be seen as introducing a completely new game, requiring a new standard-based organization. The Bandy Federation's negative position on floor ball can be explained by the fact that the floor ball clubs were in fact not engaged in bandy according to the federation's rules.

Of course this does not mean that basic rules never change. For instance, ASTE modified its rules somewhat to accommodate the practice of some of its new members. We assume though that it is more common for standard-based organizations to expand and add rules than to change them.

Standard-based organizations in a globalized world

In our three case studies we noted that there is an international or global dimension to efforts at standardization through organizing. Many standard-based organizations have, like ASTE, members from several nations. And national standard-based organizations are often members of international standard-based organizations. For example, SPUR is a member of CITT (Confédération International du Travail Temporaire). The Swedish Floor Ball Federation, SIBF, contributed actively to the creation of an international floor ball federation, which aims to introduce the game into yet other countries.

The lack of an equivalent of the nation-state at the global level makes this level comparatively less organized than the national scene. The space for standard-based organizations is therefore great at the global level, where they do not have to compete with state rules and state agencies. The great number of international standard-based organizations can be seen as a partial substitute for a non-existent world state.

International standard-based organizations have a complex relationship with nation-states. Most of them are private organizations, not public. To some extent, they and their members may be said to replace state governance within nations as well as providing global order. At the same time, however, it is surprisingly common for standard-based organizations to be organized with the nation-state as the guiding principle, even when the members are not nation-states. The organizations are international, not transnational. Even in an organization like ASTE, where it is very hard to see why the nationality of the member schools should be important, the nation-state was the organizing principle: only one school per state could be a member. The nation-state contributes to the organizational structure, even if it does not influence the content of the organization's activities.

On the global scene

In earlier sections of this chapter, we identified several reasons why standard-based organizations are set up and why they are able to attract members. The same reasons apply in relation to international organizations. The establishment of international standard-based organizations can facilitate interaction and co-ordination among members all over the world. And common interests are advanced more strongly at both the global level and within individual nations. For instance, many international standard-based organizations act as powerful lobbyists both internationally and within nations.

International standard-based organizations provide members with an identity that can be understood abroad and they may increase members' legitimacy abroad as well as at home. Individual members find it easier to explain who they are and what they do, and to achieve acceptance, when they can refer to membership of a standard-based organization which in turn is part of a recognized international parent organization. For example, SPUR's membership of CITT makes it easier for Swedish temporary employment agencies to explain to people in other countries what type of company they represent and its primary type of activity. The membership tells others what kind of actor they are dealing with and what actions they can expect.

The need for this type of identity and status is often greater in a transnational environment than in one's own country, or local environment, where it is easy to recognize 'the usual actors'. The need to create similarity is greater, the more different and varied the environment is. The creation of standard-based organizations is a means of establishing a new type of affinity, or family name, to counteract anonymity when acting outside one's home arena. The same categories of floor ball players, Masters students, and temporary employment agencies are found across the world. Standard-based organizations for these categories of people create order and reduce complexity at the global level.

International standard-based organizations may also reinforce the status of their members. For instance, some organizations select world champions. Restrictions on membership of a standard-based organization renders this an even more exclusive status if the members are to be found throughout the world.

A globalizing process

The forming of international standard-based organizations is not merely a response to increasing globalization, but a globalizing process in itself. International standard-based organizations influence global organizational fields as well as national fields.

Sometimes international standard-based organizations are created by national standard-based organizations. But the reverse process is perhaps more common. The existence of an international standard-based organization facilitates the creation of national organizations. Those wanting to set up a national standard-based organization see themselves as part of an established, international order, and they may affiliate themselves at an early stage to the international organization. Their organizing efforts are thus given a higher degree of legitimacy than if there were no such organization to refer to in the first place. Once the national organization is established, membership in an international organization may also confer on the national organization greater authority at home. It becomes easier to refer to established international practice and a common set of rules. The international achieves significance for the national.

International standard-based organizations contribute to global order. They define a certain category of organization, such as temporary employment agencies, that share common characteristics across the world. They initiate the founding of national organizations, and they have a say in deciding what actors and what kind of activity are considered legitimate. Just as standard-based organizations create actors and activities in the national organizational arena, they likewise play a role in the constitution of organizations at a global level.

International standard-based organizations also influence the activities of their members and their members' members by setting directives and standards. They contribute to the spread of these rules world-wide. The companies that are members of SPUR and similar national organizations are often established in other countries besides their country of origin. They support their national organization as well as the global organization CITT, since these organizations help standards that the member companies comply with to achieve wider distribution and increased global penetration. For example, CITT regularly arranges international conferences at which standards are described and discussed among representatives from a number of countries. Many of the standards concerning the organization of a flexible labour market in Sweden stem from contacts and discussions between senior managers of temporary agencies of different national origins at CITT meetings. The influence of American know-how and perspectives on how best to organize temporary staff can to some extent be traced through links between members of the respective standard-based organizations.

The globalization of standards should be understood as a delicate balance between similarity and difference. In large, international standard-based organizations it can be especially difficult to ensure that rules are followed. Member organizations in different countries are often given leeway to run their operations much as they please, without interference from or monitoring by the international standard-based organization. Such flexibility may be a precondition for the operation to be able to function within a local, national institutional framework. The joint rules then function as a point of reference, or as generally formulated standards, rather than as detailed directives. ASTE members should follow some common rules, but there is still much space within which to adjust education to comply with established national practice. While CITT has set common standards for how a temporary staffing agency should operate in both Europe and the USA, state and federal laws differ. Hence, their structure and ways of operating vary considerably.

These examples illustrate the important point that while the rules about how a certain activity should be organized and conducted may easily achieve global spread through international standard-based organizations, the practices that develop within each nation still tend to vary to a considerable degree. In this way many organizations all over the world share some basic principles, even though they behave quite differently. International standard-based organizations provide an important, but restricted, degree of order and control over global organizational fields.

PART II

Producing and Distributing Standards

5

The Knowledge Base of Standards

STAFFAN FURUSTEN

In this second part of the book we examine the supply side of standardization, and the production and distribution of standards, on the basis of a number of empirical studies. We discuss questions about who become standardizers and why, how standardizers organize themselves, what determines the content of their standards, and what strategies they use to convince people to follow their standards. We focus on administrative standards—standards for how to design and manage organizations.

The present chapter discusses how the content of standards is formed and on what kind of knowledge standards are based. Chapter 6 describes how an international standards organization is organized and how one can create agreement about standards and legitimacy for the organization and its standards. Standards are sometimes created by organizations other than those which have standardization as their official purpose. Chapter 7 describes how an international organization set up as a forum for the discussion of public administration issues ended up being an active standardizer. Finally, Chapter 8 uses three case studies of standardizers within the quality area as the basis for a discussion of how standardizers try to persuade others to follow their standards.

In this chapter we use ISO's 9000 series of 'quality' standards as our empirical example for discussing the knowledge base of standards. The ISO 9000 standards are widely known, and they have influenced many other standards relating to quality and to the management of organizations. We begin by describing the standard in more detail and summarizing the assumptions about organizations from which the standard was developed. We then compare the standard, first with scholarly thinking on how organizations function, then with the popular management culture.

What is ISO 9000 and what does it provide?

ISO 9000 was developed by the International Standardization Organization (ISO), in recent years ISO 9000 becoming one of ISO's principal fields of activity (Tamm Hallström 1996a). ISO 9000 consists of 'internationally agreed principles and requirements for managing an enterprise so as to earn the confidence of customers and markets' (SIS 1994, p. 2).

In somewhat loosely referring to ISO 9000, we are not really talking about *one* single standard. The concept of ISO 9000 designates what is usually known as 'a family of standards'. Thus, ISO 9000 is a generic term for a set of partial standards. These make up different elements of a system for assuring quality in production processes and are supposed to apply to different kinds of businesses, such as services and manufacturing. It follows that organizations cannot be certified for general compliance with ISO 9000, but only for complying with the requirements of any one of the partial standards, contained in ISO 9001 to ISO 9004.

There is no single text that includes all of ISO 9000. We must look to several texts. In most texts the standards are divided into two categories: ten partial standards, which are recommendations, and four which are 'mandatory' (if one wants to be certified as a ISO 9000 user) (SIS 1994, p. 9). The recommendations are on the whole more general, whereas the 'mandatory' standards are more specific. A recommended standard will usually refer to provisions of a 'mandatory' standard.

It is not easy to read the text of a standard and understand exactly what it says. Possibly for this reason, many national standards organizations sell not only the standard itself but also a number of different publications which are supposed to tell us what ISO 9000 really means. Our analysis of ISO 9000 is based both on the text of the standards and on the written information provided by SIS.

Quality

ISO 9000 is often referred to as a standard of quality, the critical word being 'quality'. The words 'improving quality' are key words. Improving quality is defined more precisely as enhancing the value of a product or service for the customer. Improving the quality of an organizational process means enhancing the value for the customer in a commercial exchange with an organization that sells its products or services. All processes in the selling organization are to be aimed exclusively at providing such quality for the customer.

This reasoning is used as an argument for quality assurance of the operations of organizations selling products or services. For example, it is considered important that 'the business be managed efficiently, with a customer focus, and by competent staff' (SIS 1994, p. 2). If an organization is successful in this regard, it will supposedly thrive and be profitable in the long run. The standard EN ISO 9004-1: 1994, entitled 'Quality management and the elements of quality systems—Part 1, General Guidelines', provides that every organization should give the quality of its products the highest priority. Quality leads to success, and the products of a successful organization should serve 'a well defined need, area of use, or purpose' (op. cit., p. 3). Further, products should 'satisfy customer expectations' and conform not only to 'applicable standards and specifications', but also to 'the demands of society'. They should also meet 'environmental demands', be 'obtainable at competitive prices', and be 'delivered economically'.

Product quality and quality systems

In providing for quality in the processes of a given organization, we must distinguish between product quality and what is called the quality system. In seeking to specify what is meant by product quality, the standard defines four different aspects of the term:

Quality due to definitions of needs for the product: quality due to defining and updating the product to meet marketplace requirements and opportunities.

Quality due to product design: quality due to designing into the product the characteristics that enable it to meet marketplace requirements and opportunities, and to provide value to customers and other stakeholders.

Quality due to conformance to product design: quality due to maintaining day-to-day consistency in conforming to product design and in providing the designed characteristics and values for customers and other stakeholders.

Quality due to product support: quality due to furnishing support throughout the product life cycle, as needed, to provide the designed characteristics and values for customers and other stakeholders (EN ISO 9004-1: 1994, pp. 5–6).

In other words, product quality, according to ISO, can be described as guaranteed reliability in terms of the properties of the product. The customer is guaranteed that the product will be continually updated so that market demands are met at all times. The customer must be assured that the product is what it purports to be and that it meets customer needs.

The second form of quality, the quality system, does not relate directly to the product itself but to the system of processes by which the product is manufactured and distributed to customers. Product quality is only one component of the quality system. The standard which describes the quality system states that the system is based on

the understanding that all work is accomplished by a process . . . Every process has inputs. The outputs are the results of the process. The outputs are products, tangible or intangible. The process itself is (or should be) a transformation that adds value. Every process involves people and/or other resources in some way . . . There are opportunities to make measurements on the inputs, at various places in the process as well as on the outputs (op. cit., p. 6).

The concept of quality systems thus refers to processes which are already in operation before product quality is achieved. The system includes all processes relating to the manufacture of the product, its delivery, and its use in the customer's organization. The standard covers 'organizational structure, responsibility, procedures, processes, and resources for managing and controlling the business in regard to quality' (SIS 1994, p. 24). Determining whether the organization's processes are of the requisite quality requires that they be clearly defined, as must the inputs needed to perform them. When this step has been completed, measurements can be made at all stages: input, process, and output.

While the concepts of quality and quality systems may be key words in the standard, it is not easy to determine what they mean. Quality is defined as 'all properties, taken together, of a good or service which render it capable of satisfying explicit or implicit needs of customers and the market' (op. cit., p. 24). This statement is simple enough to express as a principle, but putting it into practice is a different matter. For instance, the principle assumes that customers always know their own needs and can also communicate them to the seller. But how can customers know and communicate their 'implicit needs'? Neither the standard itself nor various information brochures mention the possible problems and limitations of the standard. Instead, these materials tell organizations what to do to implement the requirements of the standard.

Quality assurance

Another key concept in ISO 9000 is quality assurance: that is, principles for assuring the quality of the quality system, or, in other words, for guaranteeing utility and value to customers. These principles of quality in an organization must be universal; they must tell every organization aspiring to quality what to do. Thus, they must be general enough for use at a steel mill in the United States and at a public dental clinic in a small Swedish town. The following excerpt expresses the scope of the standard:

The principles of ISO 9000 are universal. If it is appropriate to use the concept of 'customer' when speaking of the operation, then it is covered by ISO 9000. It makes no real difference whether a business is exposed to competition or not. Optimal use of resources and satisfaction of customer needs are desirable in all businesses (SIS 1994, p. 3).

Even though the standard is universal in regard to principles of organization, it does not claim to indicate *how* these principles are to be implemented (EN ISO 9001: 1994, p. 3). It is always clear that procedures for implementation are regarded as dependent on local conditions which vary from case to case. For example, it is stressed that 'principles and requirements are what is standardized'. Implementation, on the other hand, 'is unique to each situation; to have an enduring effect, it must be clearly and directly related to earnings and to the requirement of profitability' (SIS 1994, p. 3). This idea is reflected in the following excerpts:

Must all companies have the same quality system? By no means . . . Standards are tools which provide opportunities and flexibility, not obstacles (op. cit., p. 12).

'The ISO 9000 series gives no answers to the question 'How?', but it does answer the question 'What?' . . . There is basically no difference between business development at a manufacturing company and at a services company. All activities which affect quality must be organized and managed so as to achieve established objectives (op. cit., p. 17).

Thus, ISO 9000 is not intended as a detailed prescription for *how* quality is to be achieved, but as a tool adaptable to the particular local conditions of each user. Thus, ISO 9000 somewhat paradoxically tells every organization to follow the rule while at the same time leaving it free to do so in its own way! Despite this paradox, it is assumed that ISO 9000 will have considerable impact, as is indicated in the following excerpt from the SIS information brochure:

Development in the field of quality today focuses on improvement, on constant prepared-ness and anticipation, on continually reassessing, analysing, following up, and deciding on changes and improvements. Improvements provide stability; they make the business sound in the long run and more competitive. The quality system based on ISO 9000 is intended as a framework for value-creating improvements of this nature, which benefit customers, sup-pliers, society at large, owners and employees (op. cit., p. 4).

Assumptions about organization: An interpretation of ISO 9000

We have just taken a first look at ISO 9000, as conceived by the standardizer. As we see it, the standard is based on certain assumptions about what makes a good organization. These are embodied in six principles for achieving quality: customer orientation, clearly defined processes, a view of organizations as manageable units, the use of measurable objectives, management that exercises control, and ongoing documentation of each process. We shall now discuss these assumptions, while also familiarizing ourselves more thoroughly with the provisions of the standard.

A fundamental first principle is that all organizational processes, both social and technical, should be designed to satisfy customer needs (SIS 1994, pp. 3–4, EN ISO 9000-1: 1994). While the term *customer orientation* is not mentioned, this concept is central to the standard.

Organizations should be seen as a network of processes, and these processes shall focus on satisfying customer needs (SIS 1994, p. 24). The same idea is described and illustrated in the standard itself in this way:

An organization needs to identify, organize and manage its network of processes and inter-faces. The organization creates, improves and provides consistent quality in its offerings through the network of processes . . . To clarify interfaces, responsibility, and authority, a process should have an owner as the person responsible. The quality of executive manage-ment's own processes, such as strategic planning, is especially important (EN ISO 9000-1: 1994, p. 7).

A second principle is that what the organization does should be differentiated into various *clearly defined processes*. At the same, these should be integrated, inter-acting to fulfil specified customer needs. However, process ownership is an impor-tant aspect here. If each process has an owner, interfaces can be defined between organizations, as well as between organizational processes within an organization. The idea of process ownership is that the owner also controls what happens in the process and is responsible for it.

A third principle is that *organizations* are assumed to be *manageable*. They are seen as separate from their environment, other than in relation to their customers, of course. Organizations and organizational processes are assumed to operate as closed systems, except in defined interfaces between different processes. Moreover, the only needs to be met in these interfaces are those of customers. Other factors in the environment of an organization are assumed to be irrelevant.

While the needs to be satisfied are those of customers, ISO 9000 is also regarded as a tool which organizations can use to achieve their own purposes and goals.

Under the heading 'Organizational goals', the standard EN ISO 9000-1: 1994 discusses what is required for success:

> In order to meet its objectives, an organization should ensure that the technical, administrative and human factors affecting the quality of its products will be under control, whether hardware, software, processed materials or services. All such control should be oriented towards the reduction, elimination and, most importantly, prevention of quality nonconformities (EN ISO 9000-1: 1994, p. 3).

ISO 9000 is thus said to be an instrument for co-ordinating technical, administrative, and human factors to enhance utility to the customer. The organization is considered a tool which can be reshaped to conform to the standard. People are regarded as interchangeable components of the system. Management controls people, technology, and administration so that goals are achieved. The organization is seen as machinery which receives an input of customer needs as 'perceived' by management.

A fourth principle, expressed in the standard EN ISO 9000-1: 1994 (pp. 5–6) and elsewhere, relates to goals. Organizations are presumed to be capable of setting *measurable objectives* and monitoring progress towards goal achievement. This principle requires that customer needs can be defined and that measurable goals can be set accordingly. It is assumed that it is possible (1) to define customer needs clearly; (2) to offer an output (product, etc.) which meets them; (3) to organize processes aimed solely at producing that output; (4) to direct, manage, and control processes so that they are continually improved from the customer's viewpoint; and (5) through continual auditing, both internal and external, to ensure that all of the preceding is in fact accomplished.

These principles are combined in an argument for clarity and order in the organization. The organization is subdivided into a number of distinct processes, each with clear boundaries. Integration of the various processes is assumed to take place at these boundaries. Co-ordination is provided through the management's quality system. It should be possible to see clearly what is being done in each unit and in each process within the unit, how this activity is linked to the overall strategy of the organization, and how value to the customer is ultimately increased. At each step it should be possible to measure whether established goals are being met.

ISO 9000 is based on the belief that all operations will be made more efficient by thinking first, then by establishing a structure and determining what is to be done and how, and finally by carrying it out. The purpose and goal of each activity are to be documented so that later it will be possible to measure whether the goal has been achieved. The role of measurement is emphasized in the standard for 'Quality management and the elements of quality systems—Part 1: General Guidelines':

> It is important that the effectiveness of a quality system be measured in financial terms . . . Such measurement and reporting can provide a means for identifying ineffective activities, and initiating internal improvement activities. By reporting quality systems activities and effectiveness in financial terms, management will receive the results in a common business language from all departments (EN ISO 9000-1: 1994, p. 9).

As soon as any variances are observed, they are to be explained and corrected in relation to the goals which have been set for each process. It is the duty of management to perform the necessary measurements and to keep operations moving ahead in a common direction. The organization is quite clearly regarded as separate from its environment, rationally functioning, and manageable and controllable. Quality assurance is assumed to guarantee that an organization which has been certified as conforming to ISO 9000 will meet these criteria.

The fifth principle is that management, after defining the boundaries of the organization, both can and must *manage it, and control it*. Management is also given the vital responsibility of designing the quality system, of monitoring it to see that it functions efficiently, and of continually upgrading it so that quality will be enhanced. The standard 'Quality systems—Part 2: General Guidelines', designated SS-ISO 9004-2 (p. 6), provides, for example, as follows:

Management is responsible for establishing a policy for service quality and customer satisfaction. Successful implementation of this policy is dependent upon management commitment to the development and effective operation of a quality system.

Management exercises control so that the business will achieve its established goals. It is up to management to define what the text of the standard terms the 'interfaces' between different processes. Management is also responsible for designing the structure of the quality system and for furnishing the necessary manpower and resources. Further, management is to establish the policy of the business on quality (in other words, what is referred to as its reputation for quality, goals for quality, and methods for achieving these goals) and to see that this policy is 'known, understood, implemented, and upheld' (op. cit.). In addition, management must set goals for quality, allocate responsibility and authority in regard to quality, and motivate, train, and develop employees accordingly (op. cit., pp. 7–11). Thus, the management of quality is critical to the effectiveness of the quality system.

EN ISO 9000-1: 1994 (p. 6) defines the concept of quality management as follows:

Quality management is accomplished by managing the processes in the organization. It is necessary to manage a process in two senses:
—the structure and operation of the process itself within which the product or information flows; and
—the quality of the product or information flowing within the structure.

According to this definition, managing a process involves establishing an organizational structure and controlling the quality system (various organizational processes), as well as product quality. Management and control are treated as synonymous. If quality management is effective, the organization will be managed so that utility to the customer is maximized. This thinking is expressed in the following statement:

A well structured quality system is a valuable management resource in the optimization and control of quality in relation to benefit, cost, and risk considerations (EN ISO 9004-1: 1994, p. 4).

In brief, quality management is about management's setting goals for the business. Once goals have been set, responsibility and authority are to be allocated so that it is clear who does what, without duplication of work. In other words,

The quality system of a company reflects the aims, goals, and methods of its management . . . These aspects of management are crucial to the business and to an effective quality system (SIS 1994, pp. 17–18).

It is up to management to control the overall aspects of the business, and it seems virtually taken for granted that management is in a position to exercise this control. In other words, it is assumed that management will be able to keep the business on a particular course and to see that the system is receptive to influence by customers.

Guaranteeing processes is the object of the sixth principle for achieving quality. Processes are to be guaranteed by *documentation* of the methods of quality management and by the design of the entire quality system. All processes of the organization are to be documented. While each organization is to develop its own specially designed model, the steps and procedures required by the standard must always be included.

In addition to the requirement that goals, responsibility, and authority are to be clearly documented, more detailed operating plans are required for achieving documented goals. These plans must also be documented systematically, as must the strategies for carrying out the plans. The plans and strategies are to be implemented so that the goals are achieved, and implementation, too, must be documented. After implementation, the results can be reviewed and evaluated in a procedure known as a quality audit, in which documented results are compared with documented goals, plans, and strategies. There is a special series of standards related to the 9000 family, ISO 10000, for use by quality auditors. If the audit shows that these special standards have generally been met, it will be assumed that efficiency, and thus quality, are high. Otherwise it will be necessary to improve procedures, change goals, revise plans, and/or improve implementation:

Efficient, understandable documentation of the business, its processes and its procedures is a useful aid to all employees . . . Documentation should not be more extensive than required by the business. All documents should be up to date, relevant, approved, and available to those concerned (SIS 1994, p. 20).

It is believed that documentation of every subprocess in an organization will permit timely detection and correction of 'errors' in processes. If this requirement is met, the standard is considered to have a built-in 'improvement ideology' which ensures that 'errors' will be corrected more or less automatically. The purpose of documenting procedures is to guarantee that products are designed as intended.

Limited academic influence

The provisions of ISO 9000 have been summarized above. But why is the standard designed as it is? What kind of knowledge has been codified in the standard? As we proceed in this chapter, we shall ask where the ideas originated, on which the standard is based. We start by looking at the provisions of ISO 9000 in the light of what academics say about organizations. We then compare ISO 9000 with the mainstream of what we call popular management culture.

Research has shown that organizations do not function as rational instruments for managements seeking to achieve their goals. In other words, it is questionable whether success is a function of predetermined strategies, optimal decisions, and actions implementing these strategies and decisions. Studies emphasize that business executives spend only a small portion of their time on planning for the future and are often compelled to react to what has already occurred (see, for example, Carlson 1951/1991; Mintzberg 1973). Moreover, it has also been pointed out that management does not have access to perfect information and does not consider all alternatives before finally determining and implementing the best course of action (e.g. March and Simon 1958; Cohen, March, and Olsen 1972; Brunsson 1985).

Consequently, academic research has shown that the notion that success and failure depend totally on what management does is not very realistic. Nor is it clear that organizations function as rational social machines that can be designed in the same way regardless of the special circumstances of particular situations. It is even uncertain whether it is always possible to establish goals and to develop plans and strategies to be followed (e.g. Mintzberg 1978; Rombach 1991). It is also debatable whether efficiency and success can be measured in terms of congruence between outcomes and goals (Rombach and Sahlin-Andersson 1996). Lindblom (1958), for example, maintained that organizational development should be viewed primarily as an effect of incremental rather than instrumental efforts; in other words, development generally occurs in steps and not from achieving large, predetermined goals. It may follow that goals are often formulated after the fact; in other words, organizational management attempts to validate the outcome by presenting it as if it had been intended and planned (March 1981).

Contemporary research customarily portrays organizations as complex social systems governed by the interplay of various societal forces, management action being only one of a number of factors. What happens in the environment of an organization, in its exchanges with other organizations, and through interaction of the people who work within it, may often largely determine its range of choice and even the best choice. Thus, customers are not the only significant factors in the organization's environment. For example, a number of studies show that organizations live in long-term relationships with each other, where it is often unclear who controls whom and what (Hägg and Johanson 1982; Håkansson 1982; Johanson and Associates 1994). Studies have shown, for example, that it is in these relationships that technological development often occurs (Håkansson 1987).

It is also claimed that the specific technical arrangements used by a particular organization, or in co-operation involving several organizations, are dependent on the general technological development of society (e. g., Latour 1987; Law 1994). Similar reasoning is applied to cultural aspects of society: norms, values, ideas, knowledge, and ideologies which assume how organizational control is supposed to work. These are seldom unique to a particular organization. It is more likely that what people believe in one organization will also be believed in others (cf. DiMaggio and Powell 1983). Nor may knowledge be regarded as generated exclusively within the boundaries of an organization. We return to these ideas later, since they may help to explain why the standard is designed as it is.

The sort of thinking outlined above seems to a very small extent to have found its way into the ISO 9000 standard. The standard is said to provide principles; thus, it does not address the problems connected with putting principles into practice. How can this be explained? Why do these specific principles become standards? That they should do so is all the more remarkable in view of the growing criticism in academia, over the last two or three decades, of this kind of reasoning. The thrust of this criticism, which is based on empirical studies of how organizations function and what leaders do, is that organizations do not serve as instruments for leaders to achieve their goals. If goals are retrospective constructions, just what do measurements of consistency between goals and results actually tell us?

Thus, it is readily apparent that contemporary research on organizations has had virtually no influence on the ISO 9000 standard. Researchers in the field have been highly critical of what this standard holds out as the hallmarks of quality in organizations. Later in this chapter we try to explain why standardizers have ignored the findings of scholarly research. First, however, we discuss what seems to have been preferred as the basis for the standard.

The strong influence of popular management culture

Let us now compare ISO 9000 with what we call global popular management culture (Furusten 1999). We are referring here to discussion in popular books and articles in the business press, at management development seminars, and between consultants and clients. This discussion is not open to the kind of thinking that is so prevalent in contemporary research on organizations.

The ISO 9000 standards are based on the idea that organizations should focus on the customer, clearly allocate responsibility, be viewed as separate from their environment, and have measurable goals. These are not new ideas, presented for the first time in ISO 9000. Nor is it new that organizations are assumed to be controlled by management, and should specify who does what. It comes as no surprise, either, to be told that organizational goals should be broken down into more specific objectives for different groups and processes. Let us go back in time and see where these ideas belong.

Scientific management can be seen as the first wave of managerial thinking to achieve considerable popularity (Barley and Kunda 1992). The concept held that every task must be analysed in minute detail; on the basis of this analysis, specific techniques for performing the work would be developed and formalized. Once this step was complete, employees could be trained with special manuals telling them how to carry out their tasks. Production processes would then be as efficient as possible, it was believed. Optimal efficiency and maximum profit for the owners were watchwords. The perspective was decidedly top-down; it was most important to enable the owners of the company and their appointed managers to control the business.

There are a number of differences between this approach and ISO 9000, but there are similarities as well. The latter relate to the degree of detail and formalization of each task. Every process is to be documented and monitored continually. While putting less emphasis on direct supervisory control, ISO 9000 stresses that each process must have an 'owner' in charge. It may seem somewhat far-fetched to compare the documentation referred to in ISO 9000 with Taylor's formalized work manuals, but since the documentation is to be followed, the end result is similar. The principal difference is that in ISO 9000 most of the documentation is to be done by the employees themselves, who thus formalize their own duties. In *scientific management* employees were not considered qualified for this task, which was entrusted to time-and-motion specialists who worked hand in hand with management. Another major difference is that ISO 9000 is intended to optimize efficiency for the benefit of the customer, whereas *scientific management* is aimed primarily at maximizing the return to the owners on their investment.

Hence, what is embodied in an ISO standard is not *scientific management* in its original form, despite certain basic similarities: a call for clarity and order, and for formalizing the system of processes. The difference boils down to the more humanitarian tone of ISO 9000, based largely on the ideas of management by objectives and customer orientation. Both of the latter have their own history; neither made its first appearance in ISO 9000. In some respects their roots even go back to Taylor.

Taylor's ideas were developed further and popularized by others, including Gulick and Urwick (1937), both Americans. Their version of Taylorism is summarized in the acronym POSDCORB (which stands for Planning, Organizing, Staffing, Directing Co-Ordinating, Reporting, and Budgeting). Here organizational management is supposed to plan first, then lead, co-ordinate, monitor, and control so that the plans are implemented. Essentially, organizations are to be designed as tools for achieving their own goals and those of management.

These ideas were subsequently developed further by Peter Drucker, who has been presented as the grand old man of the management gurus. Sometimes Drucker is also regarded as the father of management by objectives, although Rombach (1991) prefers to consider him as one of several pioneers. In any case, Drucker's *The Practice of Management*, published in 1954, is a milestone in the spread of the concept of management by objectives. To this day, management by objectives is a dominating theme of many publications on management. For example, it was central to the discussions in the 1980s on how to improve the efficiency of the public sector in Sweden (Rombach 1991). It has also been claimed that most writing in the field of practical oriented management literature is based on POSD-CORB (Mintzberg 1991), at least as far as the most widely read studies are concerned (Furusten 1999). Consequently, since the standardizers primarily consist of practitioners and consultants it is hardly surprising that these ideas have had an influence on them.

The human relations side of the subject is not virgin territory, either. For example, in recent popular literature on management and control of organizations, we often find that POSDCORB has been taken a step further in that its human relations and psychosocial aspects (for example, in the discussion on what is commonly known as human resource management) have been considered. This thinking stems from the so-called *human relations* movement, which like so many other ideas on management and control originated in the United States. Two leading representatives of this school are Chester Barnard and Donald McGregor.

In *The Functions of the Executive*, published in 1938, Barnard held that organizations should be viewed as social systems for co-operation among individuals. The latter must communicate with each other in order to agree on where, when, and how to perform their tasks. What Barnard meant was that informal organizations develop spontaneously among employees. If the goals of the formal organization are to be achieved, these informal organizations must not be allowed to grow too strong; management must get them to share the views of the formal organization. For this purpose management has written and oral communication at its disposal. In Barnard's opinion, management can manipulate the group and teach them what to do by formulating policies and objectives and distributing documents explaining why and how they are to be pursued. At the same time, employees can learn why and how certain tasks are to be performed. Barnard added that management is responsible for decisions affecting the business as a whole and for keeping employee motivation at a peak. Only then, according to Barnard, can the formal organization be efficient.

Reasoning along similar lines, McGregor (1960) criticized ideas that go back to Taylor and others. McGregor, too, suggested motivation as an alternative, but he placed greater emphasis than Barnard on the personal conduct of the manager. According to McGregor, a manager should be a kind of guide or counsellor who uses indirect means to see that his employees achieve the right goals. While not measuring whether and how individuals meet their personal goals, the manager should encourage them to evaluate their own work. To assist employees in their self-evaluation, he should be available for discussions with them.

These ideas expressed by Barnard and McGregor, as well as other writers, have been developed further in more recent management literature. They are the very core of the best seller in this entire field, *In Search of Excellence*, by Tom Peters and Robert Waterman (1982). Roughly one million copies were sold in the first year after publication; six years later, the figure had passed ten million (Thomas, 1989). The authors hold that good organizations are dynamic, customer oriented, nonbureaucratic, and led by individuals who can motivate employees and influence the value system and culture of the organization so that employees are encouraged to be creative entrepreneurs. For this purpose communication has to function well within the organization; it is essential to spread fundamental values throughout the organization so that they guide all operations.

Peters and Waterman also emphasized the need for firm principles of quality, service, innovation, and experimentation, but to help the company grow rather than limit what it can do. Going beyond Barnard and McGregor, Peters and Waterman added a number of features typical of a good organization. In addition to being customer oriented and non-bureaucratic, as mentioned above, organizations should be infused with an entrepreneurial spirit; in other words, organizations need to be creative and to experiment continually in their search for new products and new fields of business. Similar reasoning can be found in subsequent literature on management. Interesting examples are Osborne and Gaebler (1993) and Osborne and Plastrik (1997), who discussed the importance of non-bureaucratic but entrepreneurial and customer-oriented thinking for government agencies.

There are a number of similarities between the standard ultimately formulated in ISO 9000 and dominant ideas in the global popular discourse about management and leadership of organizations. Moreover, the standard appears to be based on the most basic ideas in popular thinking; in other words, ISO 9000 has codified the layman's conception of a successful organization. Thus, the present standard may be said to offer the tenets of an ideology on organizations. This ideology holds that organizations are manageable and controllable units which can be used by management as instruments for fulfilling predetermined goals, strategies, and visions.

Why research has not influenced the standard

Standards always have some foundation in knowledge. We have compared ISO 9000 with academic thinking and with the conventional wisdom of popular management culture. The latter appear to have become the standard. Our analysis indicates that certain kinds of knowledge, rather than others, more readily find their way into a standard. The knowledge underlying standards does not necessarily reflect an empirical reality: it is highly questionable whether the ISO 9000 standard really codifies the existing practices of successful organizations. We shall conclude by speculating on why the findings of scholarly research have apparently been ignored.

One reason may be that the standardizers do not consider the research findings indicative of the practices of successful organizations. Peters and Waterman (1982), for example, maintained that existing research was based on studies of unsuccessful organizations. Could the findings of that research, they asked, show anything other than shortcomings in comparison with successful organizations? Yet Peters and Waterman claimed to have studied only successful organizations, there being nothing to learn from the failures. Other consultants, who also seem intent on taking an academic approach (e.g. Rhenman 1969; Normann 1975), have gone even further; they claimed that it would be morally wrong to consider unsuccessful examples in trying to determine the best form of organization. Need we mention that the scholars, to whom Peters and Waterman referred, have never admitted that their studies were limited to instances of failure only. And they would be likely to claim that we have at least as much to learn from failures as from success.

There is another reason why the debate in academic circles has not influenced the standard: not only have scholars found fault with rational models for control and management of organizations; they have cast doubt on the whole conception of being modern. Thus, indirectly they have also questioned the very foundation of modern society: that is, the notions of progress and growth, and the belief that these can be realized through rational action, every event being an effect with an identifiable cause (cf. von Wright 1993). These ideals are so highly institutionalized in modern society that people generally find it difficult to break from their grip. Explanations inconsistent with conventional wisdom are not readily welcomed.

People repeatedly exposed to the same image of the successful organization, in their education, in the mass media, and in what they read, are constantly reminded of an ideal world. They may well find it depressing to contrast the ideal with the complexity and chaos of their own everyday lives. Perhaps not surprisingly, many people in these circumstances yearn for rules that would reduce the complexity, perhaps even re-create the ideal situation; finding ways to understand the complexity is something they would rather not talk about. People want order and structure; they would like to believe that there is a relationship between success, growth, and a certain kind of management on a practical level. That is what they would like to hear. They need no reminding that everyday life in organizations can be difficult and demanding.

Customers, suppliers, partners, financiers, owners, employees, politicians, and others often expect individual organizations to be presented in a way that inspires confidence. For this reason, it is probably important to provide a clear, seemingly logical presentation of what is seen as complex and chaotic. No wonder, then, that managements of organizations are not overly receptive to the findings of research. It is seldom appropriate for one's own organization to come across to others as uncontrollable and poorly co-ordinated.

We have asked why an ideal, rather than the findings of scholarly research, has been established as a standard, and why what laymen are currently saying, rather than what managers are actually doing, has been formally codified. Now we may have an answer to our questions.

We may simply be expecting the impossible if we believe that we can glean rules for what to do from contemporary research on organizations. As we know, researchers are seldom prepared to transform their own knowledge of what is into models for what should be. We also know that the purpose of a standard is to indicate what is best for all concerned: in other words, to tell us what general form of organization gives customers optimal quality. If such is our aim, it may be out of the question to take recommendations from actual practice, which is disparate and unpredictable. Order and clarity are not always typical of what really goes on in organizations. It is so much easier to relate to a discourse on general models which are supposed to reflect what is going on in successful organizations.

6

Organizing the Process of Standardization

Kristina Tamm Hallström

In the preceding chapter we discussed the knowledge base of standards, using the example of ISO 9000. In the present chapter we use the same example in order to discuss how standards are developed. We use a study of ISO's Technical Committee (TC) 176, which is responsible for the ISO 9000 standard, to analyse how international standards organizations create standards, and how problems and ways of solving them are identified and discussed within the organization. The study focuses on the organizational aspects of international standardization work.

ISO is a private association of national standards organizations. Membership dues provide 80 per cent of ISO's financing; the remaining 20 per cent comes from sales of standards and other publications. There are tensions in such an organization. For example, ISO must produce appropriate standards, and do this in an efficient way, but there are also demands for participation, openness, and representation. We discuss these tensions here.

TC 176 is one of a number of technical committees within ISO. The empirical material for our analysis consists of documents on strategy prepared by TC 176, mostly during the period 1987–98, and from interviews with the drafters of these documents. We also conducted in-depth interviews with other delegates to TC 176 of various nationalities (i.e., experts from the working groups), secretariat staff and others. We studied the ISO directives, which provide the formal framework for the process of developing the standard, and also directly observed the work of TC 176, both in the technical committee and its international working groups, and at preparatory national work sessions of the Swedish members of TC 176.

A standards organization at work: TC 176

Standardized quality systems were developed for the US defence industry in the 1950s (Jönsson 1994). During the 1960s and 1970s, the idea of using quality standards to guarantee quality in production processes spread to other industries: nuclear power, offshore oil drilling, and aerospace, for example (op. cit.). Several national standards organizations began to develop their own standards for quality systems, standards which were adapted to local needs. Referring to this growing interest, the National Standards Institute of Germany, DIN, submitted a proposal to ISO in 1977 for establishing an international technical committee for standards relating to quality (AQS-O No. 20-77).

After various discussions primarily involving the German, French, Canadian, and British standards organizations, an international technical committee—TC 176—was established at ISO in 1979. The purpose of the committee was to develop international standards for quality management and quality assurance (Brief notes—1 meeting, ISO/TC 176 QA). The first meeting of TC 176, held in Ottawa in 1980, was attended by 36 people; today the committee has over three hundred members and has become one of the largest of over two hundred technical committees reporting to ISO.

Organization and work procedures

Every technical committee at ISO has a formally assigned area of responsibility. In the case of TC 176, the committee's responsibility is to develop standards in the field of general quality management, which includes quality systems, quality assurance, and general supporting techniques to provide guidance in the selection and use of these standards. The development of standards for specific products and services is not part of the committee's responsibility. The work of TC 176 is allocated to various subcommittees; each of these is divided into a number of working groups charged with the drafting of standards. Each subcommittee has a chairman and a secretary, and a project manager is formally in charge of each working group. Other members of the working groups are experts in the group's area of competence.

When TC 176 was established in 1979, its operations were divided among three working groups. Today there are more than 20 working groups, each of which is responsible for developing or revising a specific standard. The number of places for experts in international working groups is limited. Experts are appointed by the national member organizations. Over fifty countries are represented on TC 176. In a typical group, work sessions are normally attended by 20 to 40 experts. The entire technical committee and all its subcommittees and working groups meet once a year. The working groups of SC2, the largest TC 176 subcommittee, hold an additional meeting for one week each year.

The standardization process at ISO must be structured according to ISO directives. These provide that a standards project must go through a number of specific phases. In the proposal phase an idea is formally presented as an ISO proposal, which includes a statement of what the standard is supposed to provide. The proposal is then submitted to the relevant technical committee for a vote. A proposal may be presented by a national standards organization, the secretariat of the technical committee or subcommittee, another technical committee or subcommittee of ISO, a co-operative organization, the technical board of ISO, or the managing director of ISO. A simple majority suffices for a project to be accepted and a working group appointed. In the preparatory phase the working group prepares a draft standard, a process which can take several years. The principle of consensus is considered important in this phase.

When completed by the working group, the draft standard is passed on to the technical committee and then referred to all members of the committee for comment. After revision it acquires the status of a DIS (Draft International Standard). The DIS is then referred to the entire membership of ISO for their comments and vote. If the DIS is supported by a two-thirds majority, it is accepted and given the status of an FDIS (Final Draft International Standard). There is still another vote in the approval phase, when the FDIS is submitted to the entire membership of ISO. Once an FDIS has been accepted in such a vote, no further changes may be made in the text apart from very minor editing adjustments. When this phase is complete, the draft may finally be published as an ISO standard. The technical committee is responsible for reviewing the standard at least once every five years and for making revisions if necessary.

Thus, a number of phases are involved in developing a draft standard; at several points it is referred for comment to non-experts, who may thus influence the subsequent work on it. Several votes are taken. The average length of time for an international standards project to develop from an idea into a definite standard was formerly seven years. Wishing to speed up the process of developing standards, ISO in 1995 revised its directives. Now working papers must be prepared and available when a new proposed standard is submitted to ISO. Time limits have become much more restrictive, and if they are not observed a decision may be made to discontinue the work (ISO/IEC Directives—Part 1: Procedures, 1992 and 1995).

Participants

'Expert' is ISO's designation for a participant in the standardization process of the working groups. A 1995 ISO directive contains the following statement about experts in working groups:

A working group comprises a restricted number of individually appointed experts brought together to deal with the specific task allocated to the working group. The experts act in a personal capacity and not as the official representatives of the P-member or A-liaison organization by which they have been appointed. However, it is recommended that they keep close contact with that P-member or organizations in order to inform them about the progress of the work and of the various opinions in the working group at the earliest possible stage (ISO Directives—Part 1: Procedures, 1995).

Three categories of experts have been observed: (1) users of ISO 9000 standards; participants in the work of TC 176 often represent major manufacturing companies which use the standards in their own operations; (2) participants from national standards organizations; and (3) those affiliated with organizations such as universities, consulting firms, and certification bodies.

The relative representation of the three categories varies from one standards project to another. In the area of quality, participants belong largely to the third category—outside experts. Typically these are intermediary actors who transmit the standards to users (Tamm Hallström 1996*b*). Examples of such intermediaries are consultants specializing in preparing organizations for certification or other activities relating to quality assurance, or certifiers who oversee and certify the quality systems of organizations (op. cit.). Quality managers of major manufacturing companies (often members of the organizational hierarchy) and representatives of standards organizations may also be regarded as intermediaries.

This classification of participants may be somewhat misleading. Participants in TC 176 quite often simultaneously belong to more than one category. For example, a consultant may also serve as a board member of a certification body. An independent consultant may have previously worked with quality at a large company before resigning to start his/her own practice. Consulting may involve advising organizations on how to implement a quality system such as ISO 9000. Consultants may also be retained by a certification organization to assist in ISO 9000 certification, or they may perform similar work for a standards organization.

While it may be difficult to assign participants in TC 176 to any one category, all of them are considered experts in the field of quality assurance and quality management. More generally, we may note that a profession of quality experts has begun to develop over the past twenty years or so (Mendel 1996, Tamm Hallström 1996). TC 176 has become a major international forum in which these experts can discuss issues relating to quality.

A catalogue of problems

Aside from the technical process of standardization in the working groups, activities take place in a number of special strategy groups where problems, solutions, plans, and similar matters are discussed. Such deliberations may be conducted by a permanent group such as the advisory group regularly summoned by the chairman of the technical committee (ISO/IEC Directives—Part 1: Procedures, 1992). Another way of responding to perceived problems is to create a temporary working group or task force, usually referred to as an *ad hoc* group (op. cit.), give it a specific assignment, and then disband it once it has proposed a solution.

Over the years, we have witnessed the appointment of various discussion groups and task forces to find solutions for certain strategic issues; normally some form of written proposal is produced. When interviewed, one expert referred to this as a 'jungle of discussion groups', adding that they sometimes competed with each other. We shall see below what kinds of problems have been taken up in this jungle.

Problems with numerous variations of a standard

The first problem has to do with variation. At TC 176 it soon became apparent that the initial version of the ISO 9000 series, published in 1987, was a success and was attracting a wide following, but clearly there were certain problems as well (Marquardt *et al.* 1991). At the end of 1990, a temporary task force called Vision

2000 was appointed to study how the work of TC 176 should be continued; its six members were active in various working groups. The purpose of this temporary group was to develop a strategic plan for the structure, numbering, and implementation of the ISO 9000 series. It had been observed that a growing number of variations on the original ISO 9000 series were being developed for different types of products, industries, and business sectors. This diversity was viewed as a problem; it was felt that the use and certification of *different* standards with inconsistent requirements would be an obstacle rather than an encouragement to international trade.

Among the conclusions in the Vision 2000 document were that there should be four general product categories embracing products of every kind, and that standards should be created only for these four categories. Also, efforts should be made to prevent the emergence of inconsistent standards and new variations of standards. The strategic plan that was presented aimed at tightening up all ISO 9000 standards and ironing out the differences between them; the plan offered a general set of concepts and common guidelines for future standardization.

In the spring of 1995 there was extensive discussion on the need to clarify the concepts of Quality Assurance (QA) and Quality Management (QM) and the relationship between them (ISO/TC176/SC2/SC2CG/N-30). For this purpose a temporary strategy group, which came to be known as the QA/QM Task Force, was appointed at the work group session that same spring. This step was prompted by an increasing concern both at TC 176 and generally among users of standards: as the number of working groups and projects grew, inconsistent standards had often developed, and many standards were considered lengthy, repetitive, and difficult to understand.

The ten-page report presented by the task force at the 1995 autumn session recommended a new 'architecture' for the ISO 9000 standards; it would simplify the ISO 9000 family, arrange it more rationally, and improve its internal consistency. In the report, problems perceived as related to the QA and QM concepts were discussed and illustrated with specific examples, but questions remained as to the difference and precise relationship between the two concepts.

The study of concepts had also been discussed outside the Vision 2000 group and the QA/QM Task Force. For example, written comments had been submitted by active members of TC 176. In addition, a report on problems related to QA/QM had been prepared by a special Terminology Task Force of Subcommittee One (SC1), which is responsible for the development of concepts at TC 176.

Problems due to lack of co-ordination

The second problem was a lack of co-ordination. The SPAG (Strategic Planning Advisory Group) was a temporary group charged with monitoring the progress of Vision 2000. SPAG was created at the 1993 autumn session. The group discussed problems connected with the increase in the number of ISO 9000 standards—from six of them in 1987 to 19 only seven years later. Other matters discussed were how the work of TC 176 should be organized and the relations of TC 176 with other standards organizations. As the report of the group repeatedly emphasized, what was happening in the area of quality was part of a larger trend towards international standardization of management systems, which also included systems for environmental and health-care management. It would be important to ensure that those using different standards simultaneously did not encounter problems, and also to see that the various systems met legal requirements in each area.

It would also be necessary to establish clear and effective contact between the activities of TC 176 and those of the other parties involved. Among the other organizations and units cited were ISO's central secretariat and other technical committees responsible for various areas of control, such as environmental-management systems, member organizations, industry organizations, and regional regulatory bodies (ISO/TC176/SPAG/N66, 1995).

Like the Vision 2000 document, the SPAG report included a discussion of the problems with this series of standards and the need to develop a series that was uniform and consistent. The report also recommended greater co-ordination with various technical committees and other important producers of standards and rules in the field of management.

Another step in the effort to improve co-ordination among the TC 176 working groups was the establishment in 1996 of a temporary Project Task Group. This group was charged with preparing a proposal for changing the structure of the organization; the new structure would improve the efficiency of the various working groups of the technical committee and make it possible to manage these groups more effectively:

A project team approach is proposed to manage the co-ordinated development of the new 9001 and 9004. The project team should consist of a strong project manager, a small project management group, and the managers of the subprojects of 9001 and 9004. Together with the subproject managers, the project manager would ensure throughout the development program that the individual standards meet the requirements of their respective specifications, and have consistent primary goals, scopes and contents as well as consistent structures (ISO/TC176/SC2/N298).

The discussion on strategy during the spring of 1996 was largely about creating this project group and who would be included in it. A group of 12 people from TC 176/SC2 was formally appointed in June 1996. The most urgent problem addressed by the group concerned structure and work methods—specifically, the lack of co-ordination among the various working groups of TC 176. The 1995 QA/QM report had already indicated that the new project group would propose a drastic reduction in the number of working groups (and experts) at Subcommittee Two as a means of improving the co-ordination. Thus, the structural changes proposed in this report were far-reaching.

Problems of standards unrelated to user needs

As we have noted above, many of the actors in the area of quality are so-called intermediaries; they pass the standards on to users but are not users themselves. In a number of discussions on strategy at TC 176, it has been said that users might not be satisfied with the standards produced. The third problem, then, is that the standards are not always what users want. The European Industry Expert Group (the Industry Group for short), is a discussion group of TC 176 which was started informally in 1993 (XB272-6593/RG); its work has subsequently become more formalized (ISO/TC176/SC2/N331).

Characteristic of the Industry Group is its emphasis on the interests of users, even though the members of the group are not necessarily users themselves. The users in focus are not just major manufacturing industries, but also smaller companies and service enterprises. The following suggestions are indicative of what has been discussed in this group: standards should not be overly specialized or abstruse; when a standard is revised, unnecessarily radical changes should be avoided, since these would make it more difficult to use the standard; new standards projects should be based on user needs rather than ideology.

The importance of satisfying user needs has been a recurring point of debate at TC 176. In addition to the strategy groups previously mentioned, there is a group called the Delegation Leaders Meeting (DLM), which was constituted and given formal status in the late 1990s. The DLM meets twice a year, at the same time as the working groups. The DLM has become an increasingly important forum as internal discussion on the need for reorganization at TC 176 has intensified; one indication is the growing interest in DLM meetings and attendance there.

A document prepared by the group, 'TC 176 Vision, Mission, and Key Strategies', was presented at a meeting in 1995. It laid out the following objectives for the organization:

- identify and understand user needs in the field of quality management;
- develop standards that respond effectively to user needs;
- support implementation of these standards; and
- facilitate meaningful evaluation of the resulting implementations using the ISO process to achieve international consensus, and compatibility with other ISO/IEC management standards (ISO/TC176/N242).

This excerpt illustrates the importance that TC 176 attaches to satisfying user needs but also the difficulty of maintaining the link to users in the process of standardization. Standards should satisfy user needs and be easy to follow. However, it has proven quite difficult to bring users into the international working groups; most people attracted to TC 176 are intermediaries. TC 176 seems to be dealing with this dilemma by continuing to discuss user interests, emphasizing the development of standards in response to user needs, and maintaining a dialogue with user groups.

Problems with self-generated interests

A problem that was not explicitly discussed in the documents studied, but raised during interviews, concerned the self-generated interests of both individual experts and working groups (cf. Tamm Hallström 1996). We have seen that the increase in number of ISO 9000 standards was perceived as a serious problem, and many efforts were made to improve the standards and the co-ordination between projects. To some extent the expansion of standardization projects has also been linked to problems with the organization itself, such as its strong survival spririt, combined with a lack of certain rules. As a Swedish interviewee put it:

'And there are no really good rules which are applied when a standard or a standardization field is to be qualified for a standardization project. There is just the voting (one vote for each country), so I think that it is a little bit too easy to start such projects. Once the work is going on, these working groups have an enormous survival spirit and it is impossible to stop them. In case the project is completely rejected or refused by the public opinion, the working group finds a new way of presenting the project and the work can go on.'

Another interviewee talked about the self-generated interests of experts and working groups:

'There is often a generating interest, once a standard is established and published, that you want to start something new. You review old standards, but there might also exist an idea about doing another standard within a certain field. And then it becomes a kind of autonomous process, I believe. I think this is the case with a lot of standards, and not only within this committee.'

Voting procedures have also been seen as unsatisfactory. One interviewee talked about the many unconsidered yes-votes:

'Every member country has a vote, regardless of the size of the country. Many countries are not that active, some fairly new members, not only industrial countries but also third world countries, or newly industrialized ones. Malaysia, Brazil and some African countries. When a new work item is proposed, there are many yes-votes because many of these countries that are not active, they always vote for yes. Yes, because they do not have a reason to vote no. If you vote no, this means that you need to study the problem and have a reason for your standpoint. If you don't do that—and I suspect that not many countries spend much time on this—then you vote yes and the proposal gets through. This is a problem, I think.'

Thus, not only the survival spirit of and the interests generated among experts and working groups have been regarded as problematic, but also the procedures directing the work of TC 176, for example when a new project is to be started, as indicated in one of the quotations above. As we saw earlier, some efforts have been made to change the procedures by revising the ISO directives. Among other things, there are now more stringent requirements on proposals for new work items.

We have briefly described the process of standardization in the working groups, and have noted that TC 176 at various times set up strategic forums for discussing various problems and solutions. We have identified a number of discussion themes: (1) the emergence of numerous variations of standards, each with somewhat different requirements; (2) lack of co-ordination both within the group and between TC 176 and other standardizers; (3) the chronic weakness of ties with users; and (4) the problem of self-generated interests among both individual experts and working groups.

Different principles of organization

We now examine how the description of TC 176—its organization and work procedures as well as the various discussion themes—can be analysed by means of a model that includes four different principles of organization. The principles concern the perceived mission of an international standardization body and the various ways in which the work of developing international standards is organized and managed. The model is presented in the figure below.

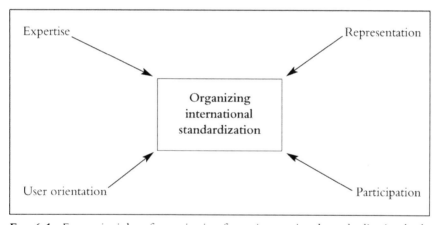

Fig. 6.1. Four principles of organization for an international standardization body

First we discuss each of these principles, then we focus on the tensions produced in the work of TC 176 by multiple and sometimes inconsistent requirements for organizing and regulating the work.

Expertise

The organization of TC 176 is heavily influenced by the principle of expertise. It is indicative that participants in the work of standardization are called experts, who engage in the technical work of drafting standards. These experts work in the tradition of rationalizing society and standards play a central role in this rationalization project. By virtue of their technical expertise, experts are implicitly considered best qualified to decide how a standard should be formulated. The majority of the participants in TC 176 are management consultants or quality managers in large companies; they may be viewed as a group of professional experts in the field of quality and business management. Their work is defined as technical, and is organized in the various technical committees and working groups where technical specifications are drafted.

In general, experts are understood to be neutral and independent; they contribute their technical expertise to the development of appropriate standards for many other parties (Sikka and Willmott 1995). The notion of expert and expertise also includes ideas of *how* experts work. By following professionally developed rules and concepts, experts can guarantee their independence and the production of high-quality standards (cf. Abbott 1988). According to Loya and Boli (1998) participants in the process of global standardization are typically motivated by a desire to strive for a common objective, and to improve efficiency and global welfare. These authors portray the work of standardization at the two standards organizations that they studied as free from political manipulation.

This description does not apply to TC 176. While people in TC 176 share a strong belief in scholarship and technical progress, and expertise is a central principle of organization, we have observed conflict between different groups of experts. In fact, the principle of expertise is not the only one observed in the work of TC 176.

Representation

Representation is a second principle of organization. The process of standardization is often described as being open to different interests and to all the parties concerned, as are governmental rule-setting processes. In governmental rule-setting processes there is an explicit mission related to the work: to serve and work in the public interest. Such a mission is not made explicit in the work of TC 176. However there are several organizational traits linked to the principle of openness and representation that usually can be linked to the mission of serving the public interest.

Steps have been taken to live up to this principle. Through provisions regulating voting procedures and the circulation of proposals for review, the ISO directives enable various interest groups to influence the work of standardization. Draft standards are submitted several times to members and to other interest groups. The rules for ISO membership also reflect a principle of representation: ISO is made up of representatives from different countries. Over the years TC 176 has also placed growing emphasis on its status as a truly international organization developing international standards. For example, appropriate geographic representation has been considered important in the appointment of various strategic working groups. For this purpose the world is divided into five major regions, all of which are supposed to be represented, as in the Chairman's Advisory Group (CAG). The emphasis on geographic representation is also apparent from the comments of different countries; the comments are channelled via the national member organizations, whose views are then considered. Work sessions are arranged at various locations throughout the world. Care is taken not to favour one continent over others. After the first TC 176 meeting in Ottawa, Canada, in 1980, plenary sessions of the Technical Committee have been held in Germany (1981), France (1982), Sweden (1983), Japan (1985), Italy (1986), the United States (1988), Portugal (1989), Switzerland (1990), Spain (1991), Australia (1992), Hungary (1993), Canada (1994), South Africa (1995), and Great Britain (1996).

User orientation

User orientation is a third principle of organization. One recurring problem at TC 176 has been that the standardization work is not linked to the interests of users. There have been various attempts to deal with this problem. The Industrial Group, in particular, has stressed that all new projects should be prompted by user needs rather than ideology.

Somewhat paradoxically, it has been difficult to bring users into the international working groups at TC 176. As mentioned previously, most of those interested in participating have been intermediaries. However, the formal procedure of referral for comment has given users and other potential interest groups a way to influence the process of standardization. On many occasions user interests have also been treated in various discussions on strategy. One of the explicit objectives of TC 176, as we saw in the earlier discussion of the document 'Vision, Mission, and Key Strategies' (ISO/TC 176/N242) is to serve the interests of the users.

There is also a question of efficiency in relation to meeting user needs. A number of changes to ISO's directives were made in 1995 to improve the efficiency of standardization procedures. The process of developing standards was considered too time consuming. ISO sought to speed up the circulation of proposals for review, while also taking other steps to become more efficient in meeting and fulfilling user needs. At the same time, the organization retained the formal rules governing the phases of developing standards, the circulation of proposals for review, and voting procedures. ISO's work on its strategy appears to reflect an ambition to be a self-critical organization that seeks to improve its operations and their efficiency.

TC 176 is systematically looking for ways to become more efficient. For several years the Working group 15 at TC 176 has been involved in a project termed 'Quality Management Principles'. The purpose of the project has been to identify the general principles of leadership and organization on which the ISO 9000 standards are based; one of these principles is the necessity for continuing improvement. From all the discussions on strategy and proposals for organizational change, we may conclude that TC 176 is seriously trying to improve its own efficiency as well, in order to better meet needs of the users and the market—in other words, to practise what it preaches.

Participation

A fourth principle of organization is linked to a more implicit mission of serving the principals. As mentioned above, international standardization bodies are private and there is no public budget financing their work. The financial structure of standardization work is close to an ideal of the market, with the participants paying most of the costs themselves. Thus, in this way strong private interests are able to influence what is standardized (and what is *not* standardized) as well as the shape of the standards.

It could be thought that the individual experts paying for this costly work, and not permitted to advance any personal interests, would complain about such an unfair financial structure, but the members of TC 176 have not made any particular complaints about this. However, TC 176 has perceived some problems with one-sided participation and financing. Many consultants and quality managers are attracted to the work of TC 176, contributing with expertise and resources to the drafting of ISO 9000 standards. Within TC 176 these experts are perceived as having great competence in, and knowledge of the field of quality, but there are also some problems of legitimacy in relation to intermediaries. The potential business gains linked to the work of private consultants working in this 'million-dollar industry', as one interviewee put it, is one source of legitimacy problems. We must point out that such legitimacy problems were not explicitly discussed in the documents studied, but were brought up during individual interviews.

Conflicts between different principles

TC 176 must consider several different factors in organizing its work. The emphasis varies over time and depends on who happens to be most active in the debate. To some extent, the four principles of organization are in conflict. Some tensions were noted above, for example those related to the financial structure and to the mix of private and public interests. We now turn to tensions that are produced by conflict between the principles of organization. We examine three areas of conflict in particular: conflict between expertise and user orientation, between expertise and representation, and between representation and user orientation.

Between expertise and user orientation

Participants in the work of TC 176 are referred to as experts. They are supposed to be neutral and independent, and to use their expertise to develop standards. But the process of developing standards to date shows that the neutrality of experts cannot always be taken for granted. Serving as an expert may be inconsistent with representing the users of a standard. As we have seen, the ISO definition of an expert reflects this contradiction. In a working group an expert not only provides specific, individual expertise unrelated to nationality, but also may be regarded as representing a particular interest.

Hypothetically, experts in a particular technical field might tend to be found in industries and companies which use that technique in their production processes. Where this hypothesis is borne out by the facts, (at least some) user interests will be considered, while at the same time the work of standardization will be done by experts in the field, since the experts and the users will be the same. In the area of quality, however, many experts are from the intermediary sector; they may be organizational consultants, for example. It is mostly intermediate actors like these who apply to join TC 176, people who possess the necessary competence, and who are prepared to spend time and money on participating in international work sessions. While consultants are generally appreciated as neutral experts in their field, they have been criticized for having a pecuniary interest as intermediaries. Motivated by self-interest, consultants might tend to draft overly complicated standards, thus creating a market for themselves, indeed a profitable one.

The lack of ties to the use of standards is often brought up as a problem in internal discussions at TC 176. Doubts are raised about experts who are neither users themselves nor connected with user interests, since there might be a conflict between the respective views of users and experts as to what should be standardized and what form the standards should take. Here the experts would be seeking to use standards to create a better world. It may be noted that the Industry Group mentioned above has warned against initiating projects for such ideological reasons, rather than developing standards which users want and need. Individual experts have also complained in interviews that there are too few participants from user industries and too many experts from the intermediary, non-user sector. The critics not only mentioned consultants, but also referred to non-user experts as 'professional standardizers' and 'standardization bureaucrats'. The disproportionate number of non-user experts has not only isolated the work of standardization from practical reality and user needs; it also appears to have raised the more fundamental question of legitimacy.

Between expertise and representation

Another aspect of the complicated role of the expert is the relationship between a participant in the work of TC 176 and his or her national delegation. The participants from the same nation make up a national delegation; one person is appointed leader of the delegation and casts that country's vote. The voting procedure is thus based on nationality. Each delegation also meets on a more informal basis during a work week, during breaks, and after the day's work to discuss what has happened in the various working groups or at strategy meetings.

The various national views play an important part in the process of standardization. They are submitted as written comments which are used at work group meetings. When the written comments are discussed, the views of a particular country will normally be presented orally by a representative of that country. Although presenting a national viewpoint, this participant must here, too, remain an objective individual expert.

Is a participant a neutral expert or the representative of a national viewpoint? The ambiguous role of participants was brought out in the interviews and has been readily apparent at the work group meetings of TC 176. How important are the written comments of various interest groups and countries compared to the opinions of the experts present? The process of standardization may be viewed as an open one which many interests can influence by submitting written comments; in that case the principle of representation would appear to have priority. The opposite would be to let the design of standards be determined primarily by the attending participants.

Still another example of the conflict between expertise and representation is the increasingly international character of the work of TC 176. Indicatively enough, there has been a change in the principle for appointing experts to the chairman's advisory group. Formerly the chairman of the technical committee personally selected a number of advisers for the group; nowadays it is important to see that all corners of the globe (the five regions) are represented. This new criterion for appointing advisers to the chairman has become a significant factor in the process of standardization.

Between representation and user orientation

There is also conflict between the principles of representation and user orientation, as is evident when the concept of a fair process according to rules is compared with the logic of action and effectively meeting market needs in the business world. To a considerable extent, discussions on strategy have been devoted to ways of speeding up the process of standardization and making it more efficient. The 1995 revision of the ISO directives was one result of this effort to improve efficiency. To this end, stricter time limits were set, while the substance of the process, with its voting procedure and circulation of proposals for review, was preserved. Although the ISO directives apply to all technical committees of ISO, the directives received special mention in the discussions on TC 176.

IT poses a particular problem for standards organizations, torn as they are between the search for efficiency and adherence to time-consuming procedures for the sake of fairness (Stuurman 1995). In view of the rapid technological development in IT, the dilemma is especially acute for standardizers in this area. As Stuurman notes: 'Bureaucratic restrictions, but also the effort to achieve consensus and the use of strict rules of procedure, make it impossible to keep up with the demands of governments (EU), suppliers, and users' (1995, p. 509).

We are familiar with this dilemma from what we know about TC 176. Even if the time required to develop a standard were successfully reduced (with the help of changes in ISO directives), there would still be a considerable cost in time, money, and effort. As one participant jokingly commented in an interview, instead of the massive effort spent on developing standards each year by more than three hundred experts at TC 176 and by referral organizations, the same results could probably be achieved in a few months by a much smaller group of hard-working consultants, and at much less cost to all concerned. But no matter how efficient this procedure, it would not satisfy the requirement of representation; the same participant added that no standard developed in this way could ever gain acceptance.

However, other work at TC 176 is less restricted by rules than the standardization process itself, and it also poses less of a conflict between representation and user orientation. Even though the ISO directives include certain rules governing the appointment and functioning of temporary task forces, these can operate more freely and informally than the regular working groups concerned with drafting standards. So, too, can advisory bodies charged with 'assisting the chairman and the secretariat with co-ordination, planning, and control of the work of the committee or with other specific duties of an advisory character' (ISO/IEC Directives—Part 1: Procedures, 1995). Since it is not specified who may participate in the advisory groups, they are even less formal than the task forces, which by directive must include experts from the committee. But as previously mentioned, it has also become more important in practice for these groups to represent a suitable geographic cross-section of participants.

Dealing with conflicting principles

In this chapter we have described and analysed the functioning and problems of an international standards organization as it develops standards. TC 176 has often considered how its work is organized. Here we have discussed four principles of organization: expertise, representation, user orientation, and participation. The use of different and sometimes contradictory principles of organization has been a source of conflict in developing ISO 9000 standards. We have discussed some of the conflicts of this nature at TC 176, and attempts by the standards organization to deal with them.

As we have shown, certain principles of organization may appear to be especially important in particular phases of the work, but none may be ignored at any time. The management of the technical committee must meet demands that are sometimes inconsistent. Despite the resulting strains, we have found TC 176 to be a successful organization. It has been able to develop and publish (via ISO) standards which command a wide following. In the next chapter we examine another international organization, where standards develop through processes that are different from the ones used in TC 176.

7

Arenas as Standardizers

Kerstin Sahlin-Andersson

In the previous chapter we described a standards organization, an organization with the explicit purpose of providing standards. But there are numerous other organizations that provide standards even if this is not their official or main purpose. Among them are many organizations whose task is to be arenas: they should produce and provide information and comparisons, report and propose initiatives for change, and generally facilitate exchange of experience, ideas, and ideals. Not least, many international organizations that have emerged during the last century have been intended to work as arenas, where people from different countries can share each other's ideas and experience. Even though these organizations have no explicit mandate to standardize, they still tend to provide recipes for others to follow. They represent cases of unplanned standardization.

In this chapter we describe one such organization, PUMA, and explain why it ended up producing standards although this was not its original purpose. PUMA is a committee of the Organization for Economic Co-operation and Development, OECD. PUMA serves as an arena where representatives of the OECD countries can learn and share their ideas and experience concerning the development of public management. In the chapter we show how PUMA emerged as an organization and explain how it developed into a standardizer, and we describe and explain the character of the standards it generated.

One line of explanation relates to the way in which PUMA collects, compares and disseminates information. In the form of standardization described here, representatives of different countries do not meet to negotiate a set of standards. Rather, standardization is a by-product of meetings held for other purposes; at these meetings various kinds of experience are presented, compared, and reformulated to achieve consistency in form and context. The process of gathering, handling, and disseminating such information is described below as a process of editing. We describe how such editing proceeds and how it leads to the formulation and dissemination of standards.

A second line of explanation lies in the origin and development of PUMA and the conditions which govern it. International organizations may hold themselves out as neutral arenas of interaction, but they are not, any more than other organizations are. International organizations not only co-ordinate and mediate interests and ideas. As is true for all organizations, international organizations influence and shape the activities that take place there (Finnemore 1996, Mörth 1996). How the organization conducts its operations is dependent on its environment and what it must do to be considered important and worth dealing with. The latter is relevant to the way in which the organization obtains legitimacy and resources. Producing standards seemed to be one way for PUMA to maintain its legitimacy as an independent and neutral arena and at the same time show results so that it would obtain resources and support from its environment.

The chapter is based on a study conducted in 1996, thus, the data refer to situations and operations as they appeared at that time. The study included an analysis of the documents produced by PUMA, interviews with PUMA officials and delegates, and observations from a two-day meeting with the PUMA committee (Lerdell and Sahlin-Andersson 1997).

We begin by describing PUMA and the standards it produced and disseminated. We then develop the two lines of explanation mentioned above for why this standardizer and its standards were designed as they were. First we describe how the standards were developed. Then we discuss the conditions governing the operations and continued existence of this arena. We conclude by noting that while the process of international co-operation may generate users of standards, it does not necessarily make states more receptive to the standards.

An arena serving as a standardizer

PUMA was formed in 1990 as one of OECD's committees. PUMA stands for both the Public Management Service and the Public Management Committee. The committee directs the work of PUMA and consists of representatives of the OECD member countries. The work programme is carried out by the Public Management Service in collaboration with appointed experts. The committee meets twice a year at the OECD, where decisions are taken on PUMA's focus of activity and programme. At its meetings the committee also discusses subjects and reports prepared by the secretariat and various working groups. Participants share their experience and information on what is happening in their own national administrations.

Aside from committee meetings, PUMA organizes groups of national representatives in a number of areas; each group arranges working meetings, symposia, seminars, etc. These are administered by the secretariat, who also prepare and follow up activities by producing documentation and publishing reports, as well as in other ways.

Work programme and reports

At the time of our study, PUMA conducted three principal work programmes. One programme was called 'Governance and Public Management'. Here strategies for strengthening central management and control of state administration were discussed and distributed. Reports also dealt with the issue of how to give central administration a more strategic orientation to enable it to avoid being limited to

day-to-day concerns. Methods for conducting studies on the future and for thinking strategically were emphasized. A second programme was called 'Performance
and the management of resources'. Reports were written and meetings held on
methods for performance evaluation, and on how to design effective systems for
audit, control, and budgeting—with special emphasis on cost cutting and introducing and using market mechanisms in the public sector. Other issues included
the separation of political control from management control, and how forms of
flexible pay and employment could be designed. A third programme was formed
around issues concerning 'Regulatory management and reform'. This programme
was designed to simplify legislation and reduce the number of state rules, and to
harmonize legislation internationally. The work included efforts to find examples
of greater self-regulation.

The clearest and most widely distributed results of PUMA's work were the written reports. Some reports were devoted to a single issue, while others were part of
a regular series. By the autumn of 1996, PUMA had published some sixty reports,
in addition to a number of less official documents. A typical PUMA report would
focus on some aspect of one of the areas mentioned above; the presentation would
be organized in the same way for all countries so as to permit comparison.
Promising attempts at reform would be described, and aspects that were relevant
for implementation would be highlighted. Often the reports would include a number of key indicators that summarized the reforms.

Issues of the kind dealt with in PUMA were widely discussed throughout the
Western world during the 1990s, and extensive reforms have been carried out
(Hood 1995; Olsen and Peters 1996; Olson et al. 1998). These issues have been
subsumed under the common heading 'New Public Management' (e.g. Pollitt
1993; Hood 1995; OECD 1995; Cheung 1996; Lerdell and Sahlin-Andersson
1997; Christensen and Lægreid 1998). Studies of the New Public Management
trend have shown that the ideas and reforms carried out exhibit a certain set of features. New Public Management ideas are universal in that they are applicable
everywhere, regardless of special circumstances in different countries. They are
general in that they state how organizations in general should be managed, controlled, and organized. They are apolitical in the sense that they are defended on
the basis of expertise rather than ideology, and presented as free from ideological
considerations (Hood and Jackson 1991; Boston et al. 1996).

New Public Management has sometimes been described as a school of ideology
that has emerged as different countries have tried to copy each other. However, as
more systematic reviews of the reforms undertaken in various countries have
shown, it is hard to identify any particular country that set the whole process in
motion. Those countries which were reformed along the lines of New Public
Management differed in regard to political orientation, the economy, and the size
of the public sector (Hood 1995). Admittedly, there was evidence of countries'
imitating and referring to each other, but by and large the reforms do not appear
to have been based on practices that were imitated and passed on from one country to the next. What emerges instead is a pattern of standardization.

And as we point out below, PUMA is an important source and mediator of New Public Management ideas. In fact several of the above-mentioned publications on the New Public Management trend were at least partly based on data from PUMA reports. This indicates that PUMA is an important collector, summarizer, and disseminator of information about New Public Management. In the next section we show that PUMA plays a more active role, as a mediator and editor of experience and ideas—ideas that have taken the form of a sets of standards that are distributed in the PUMA publications.

Standards

How can we say that PUMA's work resulted in standards, and what were the special features of these standards? In PUMA's publications and at its meetings, emphasis was repeatedly placed on the general features of the reforms and country presentations. Reports were not prepared on individual countries, but on specific subjects. National representatives summarized the material from different countries which served as the basic documentation for the reports. Some of the most widely distributed reports were based on questionnaires in which the OECD countries had been asked to indicate what reforms they were conducting or planning for management, control, and organization in the public sector. The results of national reform initiatives were neither requested nor studied to the same degree.

PUMA did not issue binding rules and had no authority to do so. PUMA provided general advice for improving the public sector. The proposed solutions were presented as a series of recommendations together with instructions on how to implement them. Thus general and universal models were formulated and disseminated for how the OECD countries should reform the public sector. These models were not related to any specific ideology but were argued for in terms of expertise. In other words, PUMA formulated and transmitted standards rather than providing examples or advice for particular countries. Adopting these standards was a choice which countries were advised to make, on the assumption that the public sectors in all countries were facing similar situations and similar problems.

Standardization by editing

In previous studies the OECD has been described as an information system (Sjöstedt 1973), a harmonizing agent (Harrison and Mungall 1990), an active disseminator of ideas and ideals (Egeberg 1978; Olsen and Peters 1996), and a driving force and creator of national ideas and ideals (Finnemore 1992, Mörth 1996). What PUMA did was to process information—collecting, editing, and distributing it. Our purpose in this section is to show how general standards emerge in the editing process involved in international co-operation. To illustrate, we analyse one of PUMA's principal reports in detail.

From reform initiatives to standards

One of the most widely distributed PUMA reports is entitled *Governance in Transition: Public Management Reforms in OECD Countries* (PUMA 1995). Described as a summary of PUMA's first five years, the report has been cited in numerous national debates on the management, control, and reforming of the public sector. The preface expressed the hope that the report would provide countries with a basis for comparison and evaluation of national reform initiatives and stated that it was intended to aid countries in their learning process. The report was divided into four parts. It began with the conclusions of the committee. Recent public management reforms in the member countries were presented in the following 13 chapters. These were followed by four chapters in which specific themes in which PUMA has been engaged were discussed more thoroughly. The report was prepared in close co-operation between the PUMA secretariat and national representatives. The data given by the countries themselves on their reform initiatives were presented in the report and provided the basis for comparisons and standards.

The design of the report is interesting from the perspective of standardization. From information on reform activities in each member country, it developed a collection of standards for management, control, and change in public administration.

The entire report emphasized reforms. Specific countries were identified as examples to follow. Direct references to the reform attempts in specific countries were made in the form of excerpts from statements by representatives of the member countries. It was emphasized repeatedly that even though public management reforms have been inspired by 'best practice' in the private sector, 'in the public sector they are, in many respects, journeys into unknown territory' (p. 27). It was also said that 'there is no single model of reform; there are no off-the-shelf solutions' (p. 25). Thus, it was seen as important continually to follow up and evaluate what had been accomplished.

The final, summarizing chapters, however, downplayed the differences and uncertainty; they presented a reform agenda which embodied the principal features of the national reforms. The agenda consisted of recommendations and normative pronouncements on how government should be reformed. Comparisons and summaries were presented as standards to be followed. Differences among countries were said to reflect differences in emphasis on particular standards, and in the rate of national reform, but the direction and the main content of the reforms were claimed to be similar from country to country and also to be the right (and only) way to go.

These reforms in the public sector of OECD countries were considered necessary because the countries were facing a number of similar new problems: the public sector had become much too costly and was facing insatiable needs and demands, and the importance of the public sector had grown. In addition, globalization was making the public sector more complex. To respond properly to all these increasingly challenging requirements, the public sector had to change, and radically, or as it was formulated in the report: 'Taken together the reforms represent a paradigm shift' (p. 25). Key concepts in the new paradigm were decentralization, management, result-orientation, autonomy, and flexibility. These key words were explained more specifically. For instance, it was emphasized that flexibility required delegation; an oft-repeated slogan was, 'Let managers manage'. Competition was advocated, and paragraphs were devoted to particular techniques for management in a competitive environment, such as citizen vouchers and contracting out. Also stressed was the power of example; a number of visible changes should be chosen as examples that would spark further change. In addition, top management had to 'maintain and develop strategic capacities' (p. 10) if reform of the public sector was to be successful.

The character of the standards

Even though the PUMA publication presented certain countries as examples, it repeatedly emphasized that the models and recommendations presented were not intended for any particular kind of country or related to any special situation or ideology, but were universal and general. There were numerous references to organizations in general. The organization of a government agency was repeatedly compared to that of other operations. The management and organization of private businesses was cited as a model with particular frequency. Government and its various parts were thus compared to organizations that operate in a market. Measuring the performance of units in the public sector was heavily emphasized, and the standards referred to a number of instruments for this purpose—accounting systems, contracts, and evaluation.

Recommended methods of management, control, and organization downplayed politics and ideology. For example, PUMA was careful to speak in terms of the right kind of regulation, rather than deregulation, in an attempt to keep ideology out of the discussion. Claims that problems, solutions, and techniques were unrelated to national differences reflected the view that questions of management and efficiency in public administration were apolitical. References to the right kind of regulation were also intended to emphasize that the standards were based on expertise rather than ideology.

The recommendations were not very specific; in their wording they were quite general and they were also referred to as such. Problems, solutions, and procedures were bundled together in a package, as is particularly evident in the reform agenda which summarized the report. The proposed procedures also indicated clearly that a central unit in each country should be given the primary responsibility for 'public management'. In the view of the international organization, individual countries could best manage this area by establishing units responsible for monitoring developments there and taking appropriate action. Perhaps the most fundamental of the standards generated by PUMA was one that packaged reforms of the management, control, and organization of public operations into a policy area which could be improved by the kind of reforms that were recommended in the PUMA publications.

While great emphasis was put on the need for a paradigm shift, the standards hardly broke new ground, since they were based on reform initiatives which member countries reportedly had already taken. The reason for basing the reports on initiatives taken in the countries was that PUMA intended to produce models that were useful in practice and directly relevant for the employees most actively involved. When PUMA was established, the reason given was the need to share experience and make comparisons between countries; thereafter, it was continually stressed that the work should be practically oriented and not overly academic. The preparation of the reports in close co-operation with national representatives reflected this ambition to be practically oriented and to publish reports that could be of direct practical relevance for officials in the member countries. While the standards by no means had to embody established practice in various countries, they did originate from what countries reported about their own plans and initiatives.

Another factor also tended to produce standards which were hardly novel, but only reflected the problems perceived, the solutions proposed, and the ideals prevailing in member countries: PUMA's publications were customarily reviewed for acceptability by the member countries prior to issuance.

The editing process

Reports on a number of reform initiatives were included in OECD's publications. Initiatives, discussions, and findings were presented, compared, and harmonized. The resulting collection provided a relatively consistent picture of the public sector—what it is, what it does, and how it could improve. PUMA edited data, collected from the countries in order to make it possible to compare, combine, and formulate these in terms of general models to follow. In this way standards were developed from the information that had been provided on organization, control, and management in different countries.

Not only does such editing reduce the complexity and specifics of country reports of reforms, but new meanings, new situations, and new ways of thinking are applied to these reforms as they are edited into a set of standards. Thus, the process of establishing standards involves more than just the reduction of complexity, and the context, meaning, content, specificity, of reforms etc. New meanings, contexts, specifications, and content may be added as well (cf. Westney 1987).

The manner in which this editing was done may help to explain why the standards were designed as they were. The editing process was shaped and restricted by the context: how data were reported, how the setting was organized, and the conditions under which the organization operated. Under the influence of these circumstances a set of conventions had evolved, and they would guide the editing. Such conventions are not explicitly formulated, but appear in the process and in the publications as 'rules that have been followed'. The term 'editing rule' is used to emphasize this aspect of the editing process (Sahlin-Andersson 1996).

In the next section we show which editing rules have guided and restricted PUMA's standardization process. The analysis covers three sets of editing rules: one set of rules for context, one for logic, and one for formulation.

In the process of editing, unique and country-specific aspects of the reforms were disregarded. The models were disembedded from their country-specific and time-specific contexts. They were distanced and disconnected from time and space and rendered generalizable (Giddens 1990; Czarniawska and Joerges 1996). In this way the models appear to be available for others to imitate or adopt (Greenwood et al. 1998; Røvik 1998).

We focused above on the editing evident in one of PUMA's major reports. One may assume, however, that this decontexualization of models from country-specific features is done in several steps. It may start early, as countries write their reports about their reforms. They may want to shape their presentation in a way that would make it interesting to others, disregarding those aspects of the reforms that seem unique and too time or country specific, and emphasizing those that seem to be general and generalizable. Compilations of data were focused on similarities and areas considered relevant to most countries.

While the background and context of public management reforms differed between countries and between reforms in individual countries (Hood 1995), they were put into a common framework as they were collected and presented in the same volume. They were generalized and assembled as a reform agenda or a policy package, and a common logic and common explanations were ascribed to the reforms. The reforms were justified as responses to a common set of problems facing all OECD countries. In this way the reforms were theorized. Strang and Meyer (1993) have shown that such theorized models tend to diffuse easily.

Connections were suggested between the reforms and certain problems and situations that the countries faced. Thus, the theorizing and categorizing of the reform models were accompanied by a parallel process of theorization and categorization relative to the countries that had been reformed as well as potential adopters of reforms: the situation, in both the countries that had been reformed and those that were advised to reform, was described and explained in similar terms, and in such a way the reforming countries were described as falling into the same category. In accordance with Strang and Meyer (1993), we may expect that as the reformers and potential reformers 'are seen as falling into the same category, diffusion should be rapid'. This editing of the logic of the reforms added a normative element to the models: they were seen as not only possible to adopt, but also appropriate to adopt (Greenwood et al. 1998).

As the context and logic of the models were edited, so were the formulations of these models. The labelling of reforms reflected the editing of logic as well as context. Ideological and structural differences between the OECD countries were downplayed as reported reforms were edited into a set of public management standards. Models were labelled in such a way that they were justified in terms of expertise rather than ideology. As mentioned, instead of talking and writing about 'deregulation'—which was seen as politically sensitive, at least potentially, in some member states—the Public Management Service talked about improving the quality of regulation. Higher quality was to be achieved through regulatory reforms and the label 'right regulation' was used in this context. Presentations were usually limited to what may be termed principles (cf. K. Brunsson 1995) and reform initiatives, rather than data on implementation and effects. One reason for this focus was that the latter were more complex and difficult to measure and present.

The reformulation of the models was also a way to reformulate collected data into models to follow. In this way the international organization not only served as an arena where country representatives could meet and share their experiences and ideas, but also could be much more active in disseminating ideals and ideas: it would teach countries what they should want to do, what they should do, and why (cf. Finnemore 1996).

In the next section we analyse the situation of PUMA, and show how and why PUMA was developed into an active teacher and standardizer in public management.

The organization and situation of the standardizer

The design of PUMA—the standardizer—and of the standards it produced is also explainable by the conditions under which it operated. In this section we describe how PUMA was formed and the requirements and interdependencies to which it was subject.

The establishment

PUMA was created in 1990 through the transformation of a pre-existing committee, TECO, which provided aid to European countries found in need of assistance in modernizing their societies. The programme covered everything from the art of growing potatoes to the administration of universities and the creation of social insurance systems. Since TECO was involved in providing financial aid, it had one of the largest budgets of any OECD committee. As the countries receiving aid were modernized and became members of the EEC (which also meant gaining access to another source of development assistance, the structural funds of the EEC and later the EU), TECO's continued operation was increasingly questioned. Its costly assistance programme also came under fire as the OECD gradually grew short of funds. TECO's technical and financial activities were cut back, and issues of management and control in public administration in general were given more emphasis. In addition, it was being stated increasingly often that all member countries could benefit from the knowledge of management and control in the public sector that was developing from co-operation in the OECD. The expression 'public management' was used to summarize what this new activity of OECD was about.

While PUMA retained a few of TECO's assistance programmes, its main responsibility was a new one: to analyse, report, and evaluate information relating to the development and reform of management and control of public agencies in the OECD countries. To smooth the way toward the best possible 'public management', PUMA was also supposed to facilitate contacts and the interchange of experience, particularly among senior officials in the public sector. In addition, PUMA was to develop tools for achieving objectives and to publish regular reports on the progress of the OECD countries.

PUMA's initial mandate was for five years; in 1995 that mandate was renewed for another five-year period. In the beginning the secretariat was anxious to get rid of its image as a source of financial assistance, and it launched into a process of transformation from a financial aid organization to an arena for discussion. The idea was to build up a special competence in 'public management' among the employees of the general office.

There was widespread scepticism about transforming TECO into PUMA. Representatives of some countries felt that the OECD, which was supposed to promote economic expansion and development, should concentrate on the private sector. One problem was that PUMA sought to organize its work in a different fashion to the rest of the OECD. PUMA would not just measure and compare structural models and results but would focus on processes; it would not rely too much on external experts, but would be an arena where the civil servants of member countries could compare notes on the transformation and reform of the public sector.

In our participant observations we found the PUMA meetings to be surprisingly informal for international gatherings; participants could present and discuss not only reform initiatives but also their effects and the conclusions to be drawn from the experience. The meetings thus had a much more reflective and critical tone than the reports. The informality of the meetings was an explicit aim, repeatedly emphasized by the chairman and the secretariat.

Gradually some of the sceptics became convinced that PUMA could probably fulfil an important function in the OECD. The argument for involving the OECD in matters of public administration was that efficient administration was critical to the economic development of entire nations. Another influential factor was that the USA, previously among the critics, had initiated its own comprehensive reform of its public sector—an undertaking quite consistent with PUMA's activities. It may also have mattered that TECO, which preceded PUMA, was such a large and significant part of the OECD, and that some of TECO's financial aid programmes were retained after that committee had been disbanded.

Thus, the reason given for co-operation was not that all countries should be equal, harmonized, or adapted to each other, but that all countries needed to exchange knowledge, ideas, ideals, and experience for the sake of their development. The fact that PUMA in the form of TECO had previously existed and accumulated valuable competence was used as a reason for continuing TECO's operations, although the nature and focus of these operations had to be changed. Thus, the formation of PUMA also illustrates how organizations may be radically reformed but are difficult to terminate entirely. Some scepticism lingered on, however, even after PUMA had been formed.

Attracting interest, involvement, and support

PUMA was financed by the OECD. The member countries of the OECD were free to choose how much attention to devote to each of its different committees. No committee could simply count on receiving from the OECD member countries the support it needed to conduct its operations. Funds were allocated within the OECD partly on the basis of evaluations of the different OECD committees by the member countries. There was competition on the global scene for the interest and resources of OECD members. In order to ensure its financing and continued existence, PUMA needed recognition by the rest of the OECD and by the member countries. It had to attract their attention and involvement and persuade them to participate in studies and at meetings.

Most member countries were always represented at meetings. However, the countries sent representatives of varying rank, who were not always active in presenting their own initiatives and sharing their experience. While some countries sent highly placed officials to the meetings, the participation of others was only nominal, effected through their permanent representatives at the OECD. Particularly since PUMA was supposed to encourage a candid interchange of experience, it was probably important for member-country representatives to supply the information desired and to attend scheduled meetings. The degree to which countries followed the standards offered by PUMA did not matter so much, and would, in any case, be hard to measure. For a country wishing to inform others about its reform initiatives, the greatest benefit would often be the favourable publicity gained from serving as an example of pioneering in reform. The country would be less interested in reports that critically examined the effects of its reforms, especially since such reforms often fail to accomplish what their advocates have promised (Brunsson and Olsen 1997). The countries that wanted to publicize their own reform initiatives and experience also appeared to be the most active participants in the work of PUMA.

Another way to attract the interest and support of different countries was to broaden the range of subjects discussed at the meetings. PUMA involved itself in a number of issues. When we sat in on a meeting, a variety of matters were brought up by participants and by the secretariat (Lerdell and Sahlin-Andersson 1997). No question was dismissed for lack of relevance to the subject at hand. Given what PUMA had to do to stay in existence, gain credibility, and obtain financing, it had no incentive to limit the scope of 'public management' or to be overly specific about what that term meant. On the contrary, its reviews of reports tended to be very general, and the field of 'public management' as well as PUMA itself became something of a general store.

But that role had its drawbacks. At meetings and in interviews with staff of the PUMA secretariat, a frequent complaint was that people from disparate parts of their countries' public sectors attended the meetings. And since the area of interest was not entirely clear, countries would send different people to different meetings. Some member countries also urged that more focused meetings be held for limited groups of countries with similar administrative structures. In opposition to these demands, it was argued that splitting up PUMA's work in this way would be wrong; what PUMA did should be useful for all members, and all members could benefit from better management and control in the public sector.

While published reports usually emphasize similarities, and while they tend to report successes and models to follow, they do not provide much help for people who want to learn about less successful initiatives or about unwanted effects of reforms. One could claim, however, that in order to learn one needs to learn both about what is working and about what is not working and why.

Country representatives who take part in the work of international organizations develop contacts with representatives from other countries. As such relations evolve, networks are formed. In such networks, country representatives can learn more about the conditions, initiatives, and experience of other countries. Even though the PUMA meetings were characterized by more reflective discussions on the reforms reported, the fact that the group of delegates was so diverse seemed to be a problem. Thus, published standards tended to be a major channel for the results of PUMA's activities.

PUMA also sought to attract interest, involvement, and participants in its meetings by developing closer ties to individual representatives of the respective countries. There is an integrative element in all co-operation. Among those who co-operated in the work of PUMA, it was natural to expect that views and definitions in the area of public management would gradually converge, particularly if the group developed to become fairly stable over time. We may also expect these individuals to support PUMA's continued activity.

International organizations may also cultivate close and lasting contacts in each country by encouraging the development of a similar official unit there. PUMA advocated that special national units be established in order to analyse and reform the management, control, and organization of the public sector; it also urged clearer definition of the field of activity covering issues in this area. Users of future standards could then emerge from the ongoing co-operation and exchange of information in this sphere.

Standardization: A way for the neutral arena to produce results

PUMA's secretariat, designated as the Public Management Service, was, like the rest of the OECD, located in Paris. The employees of the PUMA secretariat could be divided into two groups: those in temporary positions, who were usually on loan from the various member countries, and permanent employees. The temporary employees maintained close contact with their respective countries and actually functioned to some extent as national representatives. They served as channels of information between their respective countries and PUMA, and they were often assigned to projects considered important by their own countries. The permanent employees provided continuity and occupied the senior positions. Several of them had never worked for a government agency but had devoted their entire professional lives to careers with international organizations like the OECD. They were a part of the modern world society which has emerged largely since the Second World War and is continuing to evolve; in fact they have served as its intermediaries (Meyer 1987; Finnemore 1996).

The modern world society is built on and characterized by certain rules, norms, and beliefs that are based on a Weberian rational tradition, and these cultural rules of the world society thus have a major impact on what international organizations do, how they process information, and how they are evaluated and legitimized (Meyer 1987; Meyer *et al.* 1987; Finnemore 1992, 1996). Even though PUMA was formed partly in reaction to what the rest of the OECD and other international organizations were doing, the organization tended to face a situation similar to that of many other international organizations—the work of PUMA was infused with similar values, and the committee tended to be assessed by criteria similar to those applied to other international organizations, particularly the rest of the OECD. Hence, PUMA was tending to become more like the rest of the OECD. In PUMA a direct exchange of ideas on processes of reform was emphasized, but in order to get continuous support PUMA also needed to show more solid results. Such results took the form of the more or less formalized standards that were produced.

PUMA supporters emphasized that the committee—unlike its predecessor—was not intended as an organization for distributing financial aid. PUMA developed and offered standards rather than specific examples or advice for particular countries. Its legitimacy was based on the correctness of the information that it provided, and on its credibility in claiming to offer standards uninfluenced by self-interest or the adoption of a role as advocate for a particular party (cf. Meyer 1994, 1996).

In light of these factors, it was clearly important for PUMA to show that its operations did not serve political ends but were aimed at determining what was truly and objectively best. It follows that the standards formulated by PUMA should preferably be general and universal, and be based on expertise rather than ideology or political considerations. The justification for the existence of international meeting places is precisely that they are considered neutral. PUMA could not appear to serve the interests of some at the expense of others.

Standards created are not necessarily adopted

International organizations have sometimes had a major impact on how various areas of activity have been defined and on how countries have organized central units with responsibility for these areas. As Finnemore (1992, 1996) has shown, between 1955 and 1985 a large number of countries developed a national research policy and set up central bodies to be responsible for it. Finnemore differentiates between demand- and supply-based explanations for this trend. By demand based she means that special government units were created in response to a demand within the country. She found few such examples in the case of national research policy. Instead, countries were 'taught' by international bodies—the OECD and UNESCO—that all modern countries urgently and unquestionably needed to have a national research policy under the supervision of a central unit. These international organizations became important designers and disseminators of categories, meanings, principles, and general recommendations for others to follow. In the process of international co-operation, users of future standards emerged.

This was also the case with the standards that PUMA produced. After the standards were disseminated, people asked for new information and visited countries which had been identified by PUMA as examples. In some countries the standards inspired comprehensive reforms. Other countries were more reserved, and some even made clear that they wanted no part of the standards. In Sweden issues of control, organization, and management of the public sector were increasingly discussed as a distinct area of policy and reform. A public commission was appointed (SOU 1997: 57), and there were a number of reports in which problems and solutions were discussed and presented as issues of 'public management'.

However, the question of how standards are received is a complex one. One might assume that a country which followed the PUMA standard by setting up a special unit for management, control, and organization in the public sector would also be receptive to other PUMA standards relating to public administration. But this assumption does not necessarily hold true. Receptivity to different kinds of standards may vary. There is no sure way of predicting the behaviour of a unit designed according to a particular standard. Special units in charge of particular areas in a member country not only enhance the country's capacity to adopt standards and to initiate reforms. They also put the country in a better position to consider carefully what it is doing. When an area attracts attention, it also becomes exposed to discussion and criticism.

In this chapter we have described how standards were produced by an international organization that was intended to serve as an arena for the sharing of ideas and experience. The form of standardization produced by the international arena was partly a product of the editing process of gathering, collating, and disseminating information, and partly a product of the history, design, and situation of the organization. PUMA helped to convey a uniform perception of the problems and situation in the public sector, and to contribute to the spread of standards for its continued development. This perception, and the standards which emerged, were shaped in part by the presentations of the different countries, but also by PUMA's method of operation and the situation in which it found itself. To what extent will standards developed in this way be adopted by particular countries? The question is an empirical one and remains to be answered. To do so would require extensive comparative studies to determine how standards are perceived and applied in different local environments.

8

Selling Standards

ROGER HENNING

Developing standards is one thing. Getting people to use them is another. The latter is the subject of this chapter. We describe what standardizers do to persuade people to adopt their standards, taking as our example quality standards.

Standards for quality management have become an international trend. The most well known standards is probably ISO 9000, discussed in earlier chapters. These standards were developed in the 1980s, the first version being published in 1987. Many consulting firms have presented their own models for quality development, sometimes models of management by objectives. Total Quality System and Commitment Quality Management are other standards established by consulting firms. Quality awards have been established. The Malcolm Baldrige National Quality Award was formed in the United States in 1987. The European Quality Award was established in 1992 and many national awards have been organized as well.

We discuss three examples of standardizers and their standards, or rather 'families of standards', in the field of quality. All the examples are taken from the Swedish scene, which we do not expect to be very different from the situation in other Western European countries. The standardizers are the Swedish Institute for Quality and its Swedish Quality Award, the national standards organization Standardization in Sweden and the ISO 9000 family of standards, and a consulting firm with its model of management by objectives. The standards in question have much in common. None of the standards tells us what constitutes quality in the products or services offered. Instead, the standards are about methods for achieving quality; they are intended to guarantee that production has been organized according to a number of structural elements which reflect certain minimum requirements (Furusten and Tamm Hallström 1996).

These standardizers try to sell their standards to many, businesses as well as public services. We analyse the arguments advanced to convince public services that they should purchase and use the standards. But first we introduce the three standardizers and describe them in more detail.

Standardizers and standards

The Swedish Institute for Quality

At a forum for co-operation between business and government in 1984, there was a discussion on the need for quality development in Swedish business. One industrial organazation studied the matter and concluded that government action was called for. Certain actors, including the blue collar labour unions, urged that the discussion on quality be broadened to include the entire organization of Swedish society. With both the public and private sectors in focus, a committee was formed in 1986. This step was taken from the conviction that 'the competitive power of Sweden as a nation must be strengthened and the common welfare enhanced through a continual process of change so that work and production, goods and services satisfy the explicit or implicit desires and needs of customers' (SIQ 1996b).

In 1990 some twenty companies, state agencies, and other organizations joined forces in founding the 'Sponsoring Member Association'. The Association concluded an agreement with the government on the formation of the Swedish Institute for Quality (SIQ), which would continue the work of the committee. SIQ was formally established by government decision in 1990 with the following remit: to stimulate and contribute to the improvement of quality in all parts of Swedish society; to co-ordinate initiatives and resource creation in the national quality-development effort; and to promote effective participation by Sweden in international co-operation in this area. The Institute was placed under the authority of the government as represented by a state agency and the Sponsoring Member Association, whose members include both public and private organizations, labour unions, and business—major corporations as well as small businesses, industrial companies as well as service enterprises. Today the Association has some one hundred members; about thirty of them are public services (SIQ 1995).

SIQ has established the Swedish Quality Award, which is both a competition and an instrument to improve quality. Participation in the competition entails purchasing the standard, which is presented in an extensive manual of rules which supposedly assure quality in an organization. According to the Institute, the manual both can and should be used to improve quality in the operations of public bodies as well as the private sector. Participants in the competition are given the task of organizing their work in the area of quality so as to meet the standards of the Award. There are standards for management and control as well as for business information and analysis. Other standards cover methods of organizing work and the development of goals, strategies, and plans. Still others concern employee development, commitment, and participation. The standards specify how the processes of business development and improvement should be designed. Organizations which do not participate in the competition may still use the standard in its entirety. The competion rules have been published in a number of brochures, many of them intended for the public sector (SIQ 1996a).

Standardization in Sweden

Standardization in Sweden (SIS) is the Swedish national standards organization, founded in 1922. When ISO had formulated its 9000 series, SIS decided to help promulgate these standards in Sweden. It formed a special company for this purpose, a company with several tasks. It tries to persuade the public of the advantages of quality standards, it actively markets the ISO 9000 standards, and it sells advice and educational programmes on how to implement the standards.

As described in Chapter 5, the ISO 9000 'family of standards' is a structured quality system containing the elements of quality which allegedly should be present in the production process of an organization. The concept of production process covers more than just industrial production. Over time it has been extended to other kinds of processes and procedures, such as administrative routines and the production of services. The procedures of the production process should be identified, documented, and subsequently reviewed at regular intervals.

The standard may be purchased for some 50 Euro. To implement an ISO 9000 standard, the adopter will usually hire a consultant to help in interpreting what this extremely general standard means in the local context. After implementation, it is possible, though not necessary, to apply for certification—that is, for a formal certificate that the organization is in conformity with ISO 9000. Obtaining certification means that the organization is examined and then receives a written attestation by a certifying body that the requirements of the standard have been met. One of eight approved Swedish certifying bodies is another SIS subsidiary. SIS thus has a dual role; it is involved both in designing standards, marketing and selling them to customers, and in certifying that they are followed.

Professional Management

Both SIQ and SIS are supposed to create opinion in favour of the need for standards; this mission is official in character even though the two organizations are closely affiliated with units involved in 'consulting' on the standard. Professional Management (PM) is engaged solely in commercial consulting activities.

PM is one of several Swedish consulting firms that offer models for control and quality assurance systems based on management by objectives (MBO) to improve quality in the public sector. While there may seem to be many MBO models, they are very generally applicable and therefore quite similar. For instance, it is claimed that the models can improve the quality of politically mandated operations for the benefit of municipal inhabitants. One such standard is offered by this firm, which is one of the more active and well known in the field.

The managing director of the firm has many years of experience in the municipal sector, including service as director of child welfare. The firm's concept of business is to show how objectives, quality, quantity, and resources can be linked together in a quality assurance system. The model for MBO which is offered by PM teaches users how MBO works and how objectives should be formulated.

There are instructions for measuring results and for designing incentive systems. If the model is followed, there will be quality in operations, as intended. The standard is marketed as 'objective-oriented quality assurance'. Here, too, we are dealing with a family of standards based on the various elements of quality assurance, and in this case, of MBO.

The problem of persuasion

It cannot be assumed that persuading the public sector to adopt the quality standards described here will be easy. The reasons are numerous.

First, the standards will depart considerably from existing practice. While standards in general may represent various combinations of old and new, standards relating to quality are almost invariably intended to provide new solutions. For public services, the standards will to a large extent involve ideas, models, and concepts which are completely novel, thus making the task of persuasion harder. To date, the politicians responsible for the public sector have focused primarily on defining what good quality is, rather than on methods for achieving it. They have formulated their goals. For example, politicians have shown considerable interest in the number of traffic fatalities, the rate of unemployment, the level of knowledge of school children, and other indicators that measure results. The general processes by which the objectives are reached have also been of political interest. But the more detailed administrative procedures of the kind treated in quality standards have seldom been of political interest. In other words, the typical politician has focused on the actual quality of public products and services more than on the procedures for achieving good quality.

To be sure, quality awareness and standards relating to actual quality are nothing new in the public sector. Quality has normally been considered in the design of systems regulated by public law, such as the educational system, legislation, professional certification and authorization, supervisory boards of public agencies, and especially the supervisory responsibilities of civil service departments. State agencies with responsibilities in a particular sector have developed models for quality assurance. In the area of health care there is a state agency with the specific task of monitoring quality in actual services. As early as 1987 it published a report entitled 'Quality Assurance. On measuring, evaluating, and developing the quality of medical care'. The need for quality assurance in the Swedish public sector seems already to have been addressed by the time the standardizers entered the field. In addition, they seem to have a competitive disadvantage: unlike their competitors they have no supervisory responsibility for public sector activities.

Another reason why we should not expect people in the public sector to be particularly interested in the ISO 9000 or the Quality Award standards is that these standards have clearly been developed for use in private manufacturing industry. The language as well as the problems and solutions indicated in the standards are not easily immediately recognized as relevant for people in the public sector.

Thus, there are several reasons not to expect much spontaneous demand from politicians or managers in the public sector for the quality standards developed by the three standardizers. If the standards are to be adopted to any significant extent, they will probably have to be marketed actively. Last but not least: there is a wide variety of quality standards on the market, which is diverse and competitive. Even public service providers which are basically interested in quality standards from private providers must still be persuaded to purchase a particular standard from any given standardizer. For this reason standardizers devote a great deal of time and money into disseminating information, influencing public opinion, and marketing.

Arguments for standards

In this section we examine more closely the arguments advanced by these standardizers in favour of their standards. Since it cannot be taken for granted that potential users will be interested, standardizers attempt to attract their interest and turn it into a demand for the standards—in other words, they seek to create a 'market' for quality standards. Marketing and advertising are normally intended to build confidence in one's organization in general and in its products and services in particular—with the further motive of persuading potential buyers that these goods and services will benefit them. Arguments of this nature are used by the three standardizers under study. But the arguments can only be effective if there are people who are prepared to listen. As we shall see, the three standardizers try to convince public services that the standards are relevant for them.

Creating adopters: All are organizations and businesses

The standards discussed here are intended for organizations: in other words, highly autonomous, hierarchical units with clear boundaries (Brunsson and Sahlin-Andersson forthcoming). Business enterprises are often described as such organizations. An important assumption in the sales arguments of the standardizers is, therefore, that public services can and should be regarded as organizations or even as businesses. While seldom stated explicitly as an argument, it serves as a basis for other arguments, and is presented as an undisputed truth rather than as something that could be discussed. The standardizers simply refer to public authorities, state agencies, and county councils or municipalities, as organizations, thus assuming without question that the standards are appropriate for their use. Another central assumption is that these 'organizations' have customers. A corollary is that their mission is to satisfy the needs of customers.

But what are organizations, businesses, and customers? The answer is not a fact that can be objectively determined. It is far from obvious what sort of unit may be considered an organization. Public services normally lack certain properties of a complete organization—for example, they often have no clear boundaries and are governed from outside rather than by their own management (Brunsson and Sahlin-Andersson forthcoming). For most public services the concept of customer is problematic; to argue that they have customers is controversial at the very least. Customers exist where there are markets and typically relate to business firms. Who are the customers of a day-care centre, a school, or a state agency? Also, in the public sector, objectives are rarely clear, and there is seldom agreement on what they mean. And objectives frequently conflict. Therefore, disagreement on what should be considered good quality is easy. It is difficult to agree on 'the needs of the customer'.

The administrative procedures of the public sector differ from those of private enterprise. Administrative procedures for different kinds of cases handled by public services are more extensively governed by laws and ordinances. Public services are treated by the standardizers as autonomous decision makers who can 'buy' the standard. But public services seldom have the authority to make such decisions on their own. They are generally part of a larger legal entity, and adoption of a standard normally requires a decision on behalf of the entire entity. For example, it is reasonable to expect that a standard must be approved by the local government or the appropriate board before it can be used by a local roads department or a school.

The standardizers' arguments ignore all of these special characteristics of public services. The sales arguments for the Swedish Quality Award treat national defence, universities, and state agencies as organizations and enterprises with customers; and since they have customers, they should be involved in quality development. The standard is said to be based on 'principles of aggressive quality development, and the purpose of the analysis is to stimulate constant improvement so that there will be more satisfied customers' (SIQ 1996a). The objective is to make every kind of organization aware of the importance of quality issues: 'Through improvement of processes, quality is created'. The criteria and guidelines for the Swedish Quality Award are said to be 'tools of improvement for all organizations in Sweden' (SIQ 1996a). It is assumed that there are profit centres in the public sector which have an independent responsibility for their customers.

SIQ presents some appropriate examples from the private sector. A number of companies have established their own quality awards which are totally or partly based on the Swedish Quality Award. Among them are major enterprises like Telia, Ericsson, ABB, and Volvo. But the examples are equally applicable to public 'organizations'. The Institute notes that the use of the Swedish Quality Award as a tool is common in public bodies, including national defence, the national labour market administration, regional social insurance offices, schools, the system of higher education, and Statistics Sweden. Public bodies are supposed to adopt the general principles for the quality standard (SIQ 1995, 1996a, 1996b, 1996c. See also SIQ 1996–7).

SIS also treats public bodies as if they were businesses. It presents good examples from the public sector: nursing homes and homes for the elderly, and even public authorities, are considered organizations which have customers, and which should use the standard (SIS ForumCenter 1996). 'All businesses will benefit by using ISO 9000, including for example, manufacturers, service businesses, municipalities, county councils, government agencies, exporters as well as importers, and sole proprietorships as well as major corporations', claims SIS, which regards the standard as equally suited for the public and private sectors: 'The principles of ISO 9000 are generally applicable' (ibid.), since the concept of the customer may be used in the public sector. 'Whether an operation is exposed to competition is not a decisive factor. Making good use of resources and satisfying customer wants are desirable in all operations' (SIS KvalitetsForum 1995, p. 3).

If there is a relationship between customer and supplier and a need for them to work together, the standard can be used, for example in the procurement of services by a public organization. The standard is no less relevant if the operation is entirely within the public sector, as long as there are customers (SIS KvalitetsForum 1995; SIS Forum AB 1994–7).

Representatives of Professional Management (PM) also stress the potential use of the standard in both the private and the public sector; consequently, they also place public services in the same category as private businesses and indicate what is required for inclusion in this category. At the same time, they make an effort to show how extensively the standard is used by public services. PM states that nearly seventy municipalities and over thirty state agencies are among its customers for the standard. Day-care centres, nursing homes, police, regional social insurance offices, and local tax offices are presented as organizations with customers of their own.

The standardizers emphasize the similarities rather than the differences between businesses and public services; there will thus be more adopters of the standards—something the standardizers want. The standards are so general in nature that they may be used by all organizations and even by bodies with only limited resemblance to organizations. For example, they may be used by all of Sweden's 289 municipalities and by the national labour market administration as well as in schools. 'The importance of learning from others cannot be sufficiently emphasized! In the area of medical care, we have a lot to gain from looking at the experience of business. The similarities in methods of management and control, development, and improvement are greater than the differences.' These are the words of a physician quoted in one of the publications (SIQ 1996b).

Small organizations will benefit just as much as large ones from using ISO 9000 as a standard, claims SIS. Since quality development pays, it is an equally obvious investment for all operations regardless of their size and nature. With the logical structure of the standards, any and all can use them, we are told. The conceptual framework of the standard is generally applicable and thus relevant to service businesses as well as in public administration and in other organizations.

Only PM, which almost exclusively serves public-sector clients, emphasizes the special nature of public services. But here, too, we find that the service is supposed to be an organization with customers where the quality standard is applicable: 'The operation is there for the customer'. The object of quality development is said to be satisfied customers. It is also said that engaging in quality development will result in continued enhancement of employee competence and commitment. All employees are involved. It should be noted that the firm addresses the concept of the customer, raising the question of who the customers of a public organization are. In the case of a day-care centre, for example, are they the children, the parents, the people of the community, the staff, or some other group? Thus, PM has no clear definition of the concept of customer. At the same time, the firm also emphasizes that a public organization has (political) objectives of a different nature than those of a private business.

The forceful assertion that the public sector has customers, despite all indications to the contrary, is rather surprising. If there are customers, then 'the market' should be able to control quality, and there would be less need for quality standards to fulfil this function. Paradoxically, in this situation as defined by the standardizers, we should expect the need for quality standards to be the least. In fact, it can as easily be claimed that the public sector needs quality systems, on the very ground that there are no specific customers or markets that might object clearly and vigorously to poor quality. Why then do the standardizers not argue along these lines? One reason may be that the standards that they offer were originally developed for business, and that the basic underlying assumptions were valid in a business context. The concept of the customer is then used simply because customers are essential for a business.

For the benefit of adopters and their customers

A classic argument for standards is that they are beneficial for those who adopt them. It is expected that standards will be followed by the people with an interest in doing so. Standardizers want people to conclude that the standard is good for them. But it adds to the attractiveness of standards if they can be shown to have good effects on others as well. In the cases described here, the standardizers argued that their standards were good both for the public services that were supposed to adopt them and for their 'customers'.

'The Swedish Quality Award emphasizes how a business operates—in other words, how we produce goods and services. We can only change what we are doing when we have become aware of how we are doing it. In this view of quality the focus is on the customer' (SIQ 1996c). Users of services provided by the public sector are considered customers, but taxpayers are not. The standardizers do not justify their standard on the ground that it benefits the citizenry as a whole.

It is claimed that the standards are in the interest of the adopters, on the ground that 'organizations' that follow the standards will be successful—because successful companies use the Swedish Quality Award standard. 'Quality is the distinguishing feature of a successful organization' (SIQ 1996b). The way to make the organization a good one is to use the standard, it is held (SIQ 1996–7).

It is said that ISO 9000 is necessary for the organization. By making unceasing efforts at improvement, SIS maintains, the organization will be able to meet new demands and objectives. ISO 9000 is not supposed to put operations into a steady state. On the contrary: working on quality with ISO 9000 as a model is about 'visions, belief in the future, improvement, decisiveness, security, commitment, and continuing development '(SIS KvalitetsForum 1995). As SIS argues in its brochure, called 'Make the company stronger':

Quality development is intended to result in satisfied customers, efficient company opera-tions, and continuing enhancement of employee competence and commitment. Quality development inspires the confidence of the market. All employees must be committed to quality. There are unlimited opportunities for improvement, so that quality development never ceases. That is precisely what makes quality development so exciting.

SIS sees the existence of virtually total harmony between the interests of the organization and those of the customer: 'Briefly put, quality development means continually increasing the value of the good or service to the customer. Satisfied customers are the companies' most important asset. The long-term trust of cus-tomers is the foundation of profitability. Efficient, customer-oriented control of the business leads to success and lasting profitability' (SIS KvalitetsForum 1995). Quality work based on ISO 9000 is said to fulfil an important function of this nature. 'Quality pays off', SIS repeatedly asserts (SIS ForumCenter 1996, p. 6).

PM, on the other hand, views the interests of the organization somewhat differ-ently. For instance, the objectives set by the political leadership serve as the point of departure in PM's world. PM cites the following as the distinguishing features of its standard: its wide range of applicability, its simplicity, and the link between resources and the objectives of the activity as set by the political leadership. The point is thus to accomplish politically defined objectives. The standard is supposed to heighten awareness of these objectives and facilitate the discussion surrounding them, and also to promote the use of methods for evaluating the quality systems of the organization.

Another line of argument frequently encountered is that the standard encourages economizing and improvements in efficiency. The standardizers seek to persuade the potential adopter that their standards will lead to efficiency in the production of public services, as well as to 'profitability'. The purpose of the standards is to ensure that the quality aspects of production are considered, but using the standard will also make the production more efficient—or profitable (SIQ 1996–7; SIQ 1995, 1996b, 1996c; SIS Forum AB 1994–7; SIS ForumCenter 1996; SIS Kvali-tetsForum 1995).

A business that wins the Swedish Quality Award can be assured of more satisfied customers, and thus a more effective operation, SIQ maintains (SIQ 1996b, 1996c). Direct or indirect reference is made to the need for public sector activities to cut costs and improve efficiency. 'The important thing is to get the most for the money we spend on the operation. We are told this so that we will economize intelli-gently' (Svensson 1993; Svensson and Pihlgren 1989). PM's standard is said to be based on the CQM concept (Commitment Quality Management); the basic phi-losophy of CQM is to permit 'flexible adaptation to complex organizational envi-ronments with multidimensional commitments'. It is claimed that the model is well conceived and that using it will result in solidly supported programmes for contin-ually improving efficiency.

References to others

The third line of the standardizers' arguments is to show that there is support elsewhere for themselves and their standards. The idea is to demonstrate that the standards were developed, influenced, or accepted by other significant and highly regarded actors, adding that the standardizers resemble these actors, engage in similar activities, or are in contact with them. A variation is to show that any party using the standards would be in distinguished company.

The first argument in this category is that the standards have been accepted in other countries. The standards marketed by SIS and SIQ are presented as internationally recognized. PM states in its brochures that it is working with the UN General Assembly on issues relating to quality. It adds that most of its activities are conducted outside Sweden.

SIQ claims that it belongs to an international association for quality development and that the Swedish Quality Award is part of an international trend: there are similar quality awards and incentives for improvement in other parts of the world. SIQ collaborates in various ways with the organizers of these quality awards, who share their experience and ideas. In Japan the Deming Prize has been in existence for more than forty years, SIQ points out. The Malcolm Baldrige National Quality Award has meant, and still means, a great deal to the development of American business, the institute claims. The Swedish Quality Award is based on the American counterpart (SIQ 1996*a*).

The international character of the ISO standard is also emphasized. According to SIS, ISO consists of a number of internationally agreed principles and requirements for managing a business so that it earns the confidence of customers and markets. It emphasizes the truly international nature of ISO 9000. While ISO 9000 is a European standard, it has also been accepted throughout the industrialized world, in countries including the United States, Japan, and Australia. 'The ISO 9000 family is a global one with several generations', states SIS (SIS KvalitetsForum 1995, p. 8).

Secondly, the standardizers point to their connection with academic research. They aim to encourage research. SIQ is charged with 'helping worthy projects at the start' (SIQ 1996*c*). The institute notes that its staff participate in reference and work groups of R&D projects on quality. SIS also stresses its ties with the academic world. MBO models are said to have been conceived and designed by academic researchers. The model used by PM has been described in a number of books which may most accurately be classified as textbooks (Svensson 1993; Pihlgren and Svensson 1989).

Thirdly, those who accept the standard are sometimes offered an opportunity to meet prominent people. Activities in the field of quality are enlivened with numerous contests, prizes, award ceremonies, and conferences. In December each year an impressive ceremony is held in Gothenburg, Sweden: 'Some 100 personally invited guests from Swedish business and government participate in the ceremony' (SIQ 1996*c*). Any organization 'may be the one which the committee of judges selects as an outstanding example and which receives the symbol of the Swedish Quality Award from His Majesty the King' (ibid.).

SIQ was one of the founders of the biennial conference, 'Quality in municipalities, county councils and state agencies'. Here, too, there is an element of competition: a jury selects the best articles in the field of quality, and the authors receive cash awards. One of those conferring the prizes has been the Swedish prime minister (*Kvalitet och Förnyelse* 1997).

Fourthly, official authority is involved, albeit in a somewhat unexpected way. Although SIS and SIQ might have emphasized the role of the government as co-financier or co-founder, they have not done so. Instead they stress their legal status as private organizations, following the example of business in general and industrial companies in particular.

Nevertheless, the standardizers value some kind of official backing for their standards. They have had some success in persuading public commissions and state agencies to recommend the incorporation of the standards in legislation. The Swedish Health and Medical Care Act mandates quality systems, thus opening up a new market for standardizers. Moreover a provision has been added to the Social Services Act requiring quality assurance systems in every work unit: this means that every profit or cost centre must then use a standard. The standardizers also make references to approval by labour unions. It should be noted that the latest collective bargaining agreement for teachers contains a section on development work in schools. The section provides for the use of a model along the lines of SIQ's basic standard.

Arguments that are missing

Several of the 'traditional' arguments in favour of product standardization are not found in the three cases studied. Normally one of the main arguments for standards is that they facilitate communication and exchanges of some kind. In its general promotional material, SIS argues that ISO 9000 makes it possible to speak the same language in international communication and trade, since the principles and requirements are the same the world over. ISO 9000 is described as the global standard that promotes understanding across national boundaries (SIS KvalitetsForum 1995). These arguments are not used in marketing to the public sector, for obvious reasons; schools and day-care centres do not have the same need as businesses for local, regional, nation-wide, or international communication with other organizations of their own kind.

Nor are the traditional arguments in favour of uniformity applicable, now that public services seem more interested in adapting to local conditions or in making a point of their own uniqueness. And in the public sector the argument that standardized organizations are more competitive cannot be used, either; here units are expected not to compete but to promote the common good. Thus the standardizers seem to be observing some differences between private industry and the public sector after all.

PART III

Adopting Standards

9

Following Standards

NILS BRUNSSON AND BENGT JACOBSSON

In Part II we have used some empirical examples in order to discuss how standards in the field of administration are created and how their content is determined. In all the examples given, the standards were produced at considerable distance from those who were supposed to follow them in practice. Also, the standards reflected ideals and popular ideas rather than any actual practice. They were derived from an imagined general case rather from than a specific one. Standardizers tried to convince others to follow their standards by arguing that the follower's specific case was in fact an example of an appropriate general one. But given the role of the standardizers and the character of their standards it is far from clear why people interested in their specific situation should follow standards at all.

The four chapters in this final part of the book deal with these potential followers of standards. In this chapter we discuss what it means to follow a standard and why individual actors do so. The next two chapters concern the ways in which adopters react collectively to standards; there we examine why a number of potential adopters choose to follow the same standard, thus establishing various degrees of uniformity among themselves. In the final chapter we discuss positive and negative effects of standardization and following standards for followers and others.

Following standards by changing practice or presentation

A typical standard consists of a statement about the generally desired qualities of a product, an activity, or a document, for example. The standardizer seeks to regulate the design of these objects or processes. Following a standard means establishing some degree of consistency between the standard and what one does. Such a consistency can be created in two ways: either by changing practice to fit the standard, or by changing the presentation of practice in accordance with the standard.

Practising standards

When practice is changed, we may say that the standard is 'implemented' or practised. The follower performs a translation. The translation involves two aspects, from talk to action—what the standard says is translated into what the follower does—and from the general to the specific—the general requirement of the

standard is translated into the follower's own specific practice. When this translation has taken place, the adopter is practising the standard.

For example, there are standards which recommend that schools conduct self-
evaluations. Implementing or practising this kind of standard means that schools
change their practice to make it more consistent with the standard. They initiate
various evaluation projects: they let pupils say what they think about the teaching;
they ask parents to fill out questionnaires about the work of the school, etc.

Often, however, this is not enough. There are parties besides the standardizers
that are interested in whether the standard is followed or not, and their judgement
may be important to the follower. So the follower finds it important not only to
practise a standard but also to tell others that it does so. Such reporting is sometimes
even required by other parties, such as certifiers of compliance with the standard.
The school in our example is likely to present its new projects, citing them as
examples of evaluation to parties such as politicians, parents, and audit offices.

Such presentations are also the result of a translation, but in the opposite direction to that involved in practising standards. Instead of just translating the standard
into practice, the school also describes its new practice in terms of the standard.
One could say that this new practice is standardized. It involves the translation from
action to talk, from the specific to the general, from own activity to categories that
can be understood by others.

Standardizing practice

Alternatively, following a standard may involve translation in the latter direction
only—from specific action to general talk; the follower of a standard changes its
presentation of its practice, but it does not change the practice. Existing practice is
continued but now described in accordance with the standard. In other words the
follower standardizes its practice but does not practise the standard. This strategy is
likely when the adopter believes that its practice complies reasonably well with the
standard—and there is reason to assume that this belief is shared by relevant others.
Standardizing existing practice is also a way of following standards; in the extreme
case, standards for nomenclature, it fulfils the very purpose of the standardization.

For example, instead of implementing an evaluation standard, a school might
maintain that it has always conducted evaluations by giving pupils examinations. If
the school's claim is credible, it will not have to change its practice; it can still be
considered to follow modern standards that call for evaluations. To show compliance with the standard, it may also be necessary to relabel what is already being
done. Grading, conferences on troublesome pupils, planning days and the like may
now be referred to as forms of evaluation instead of something else. In other situations individuals may have to call taking a walk exercise if they want to convince
themselves and others that they follow certain health standards; organizations may
have to give their planning activities the new name of quality improvement if they
want to show that they follow quality standards; governments' *ad hoc* initiatives in
relation to administration would be termed administrative policy if there were a

standard that such a policy should exist. In all these cases, there would be no change in existing practice, just a change in the way it was presented.

Sometimes, though, standardizing practice may require more than renaming it. The adopter may have to demonstrate that its current practices are *really* evaluations, administrative policy etc. What is done must then be described more precisely. And sometimes the current practice cannot possibly be described in a credible way as consistent with the standard. The follower has then to change, not only presentation but also practice. The school would have to evaluate not only the pupils, but the teachers as well; the individual would have to walk faster and further; the organization would have to establish a special unit for quality development and the government one for administrative policy, for example. In these cases standardizing practice requires practising the standard.

Ambiguity and de-coupling

Exactly how existing practice should be changed by the standard need not be very clear. There are often several possible interpretations of standards and also of practice (Czarniawska and Joerges 1996). As described in Chapter 5 there are a number of ways to provide additional value for the customer under the ISO 9000 standard, and more than one method of operation can be considered to meet this standard. In addition it is generally difficult to do *exactly* what a standard says. The standard is general and abstract, whereas operations are always specific. Practising a standard is mostly about adapting practice so that the standard describes it with reasonable accuracy.

Since it is often unclear what kind of practice may be presented as conforming to a standard, the adopters may have considerable freedom to decide whether or not to change existing practice at all or how much to change it. They can use the standard as an argument for changing their practice, or they can argue that their practice is already in accordance with the standard. In either case they have to convince others that their interpretations are sensible. When adopters think that changing practice would involve sacrifices, they may find it useful to adopt a step-by-step approach to the translation process: first testing whether existing practice can be translated into the standard, and then—only if the translation is not credible enough—taking the trouble to change existing practice. Whatever strategy is chosen, the adopter of the standard will be open to criticism by others who have a different opinion on whether existing practice conforms to the standard. If practice is changed, there may be criticism for attempting to introduce a rehash of old, already well-established principles. If current practice is not changed, there may be criticism for presenting it in a misleading, unduly positive light.

The scope for criticism is also affected by the extent to which practice is of interest to and observable by others than those who decide on adoption, and what authority or power these others possess. In organizations, members often have good insights into and strong interest in practice; they may not accept any interpretation of standards from their leaders. People outside the organization may have a strong interest but less insight. The purpose of various forms of certification and auditing is to provide such outsiders with a reliable basis for determining whether a particular operation conforms to a particular standard.

The scope for interpretation and criticism also depends on the nature of the standard. It is of course futile to maintain that narrow-gauge railway track (891 mm.) can meet the standard for normal gauge (1,435 mm.). To conform to that standard, a railway line using narrow-gauge track will have to change its practice. On the other hand, the same railway line may claim to follow management by objectives (MBO) without having to change its practice at all. Since a variety of practices, from generally having one's objectives in mind to the preparation of specific statements of objectives, may pass as MBO, many can hold that they are already following this standard.

Extensive research on individuals and organizations has shown that there may be substantial differences between presentation and practice, between formal structures and actual operations, and between what people say and what they do (Kaplan 1964; Weick 1976; Meyer and Rowan 1977; Argyris and Schön 1978; Brunsson 1989; Jacobsson 1989; K. Brunsson 1995). Actors have dual systems which are decoupled from each other; they may argue that they follow a standard while not doing so in practice. This is a phenomenon which standardizers seldom appear to notice, or at least seldom discuss seriously in public. Standardizers seem to assume that standards that change presentation always change practice.

For example, as argued in Chapter 5, standardizers in the field of administration seem to have overlooked much of the research on organizations of the last thirty years. They seem to assume that the introduction of administrative standards will have a major impact on the operations of organizations, and on the results achieved. If potential adopters of these standards were to share that view, they would think twice before putting the standards into practice. If a standard has a substantial impact, the consequences will be more severe if the standard proves inappropriate. One reason why administrative standards are followed so extensively is probably that the adopters do not really expect the effects to be as dramatic as the standardizers claim. Even if the standard thereby loses some of the appeal that it possessed in the rhetoric of the standardizers, it may be easier to follow, since it will involve less risk and arouse less resistance. For instance, certification of conformity with ISO 9000 is focused more on documentation than on the operations documented (Walgenbach 1997). The standard is then rather innocuous: if one fears that its implementation is not a good idea, one does not need to let it affect actual operations.

Thus standards may be followed in different ways: by practising standards, by standardizing practice, or by doing both. But why do actors follow standards at all? This question is the subject of the next section.

Why follow standards?

In Chapter 1 we noted that standards are directed at actors—that is, at units capable of acting and of having a will of their own. Standards are directed at those who are able to decide for themselves whether to act according to a standard or not. We identified two kinds of actors: individuals and organizations. However, an actor is only capable of following standards in areas where it truly is an actor—in other words, where it can make choices and take action. An actor may not have the capacity to act in all areas; for example, a small company may not have the resources to follow certain administrative standards which require expensive bureaucratic procedures and a large administrative staff. And in some areas it may make no difference what the actor wants, since there is little or no room for choice; for example, individuals who have to obey certain laws and organizational directives will have no use for standards which tell them to do otherwise.

When able to act and choose, actors' propensity to follow a particular standard will depend on their identity—that is, who they are—and on their situation. Like other rules, standards are intended only for certain kinds of actors and situations. In order to judge whether a standard is relevant one must know and be able to classify oneself and one's own situation. One must be able to answer the three questions we mentioned in Chapter 1: Who am I? What is my situation? What is appropriate for an actor like me in a situation like this one?

Identity

Standards are always addressed to general categories, not to individual adopters. In other words, they are directed at potential adopters who have defined their identity in terms that basically fit the general category indicated by the standard. Anyone who considers himself unique, and thus not belonging to any general category, will find that no standards apply to him. By following standards actors tend to become more like others, but they will not be receptive to standards unless they have seen some similarity between themselves and others in the first place. In other words, standardizers may create some similarity, but they are also dependent on much pre-existing similarity if they are to spread their standards to many (Strang and Meyer 1993).

The identity of an actor is not always clear and immutable. As we discussed in the previous chapter, for example, it is not certain what should be considered an organization. A school, a public administration unit or a municipality is sometimes regarded as such; at other times each is treated as an organization. The latter view appears to have become more common in recent years. Whichever definition prevails will determine which standards the unit will be receptive to: 'schools' are more likely to adopt standards for schools than for organizations and vice versa. And certain definitions, such as that of a public administration unit, a subsidiary, a pupil, or a subordinate, imply that the unit is not a full-fledged actor; it may even lack the authority to decide whether to follow standards.

Standardizers need not passively accept a given identity for a potential adopter. Sometimes they will try to influence an actor's perception of its own identity, attempting to convince it that it is a full-fledged actor capable of adopting standards and that it belongs to a group for which certain standards are relevant. As we noted in the last chapter, standardizers seeking to sell standards to organizations tried to convince leaders that they were in charge of organizations rather than public services, for example. And standardizers offering standards for service enterprises argue that many businesses and public units fall into this category (Furusten 1999).

Certain standards are almost unavoidable if the potential adopter would like to maintain a particular identity. There are standards which constitute a certain kind of actor; if one does not follow certain standards people may doubt that one is really a particular kind of actor. Any individual who wants to be perceived as a gentleman should behave according to the standards for gentlemen provided by etiquette books. Any organization rejecting all the basic administrative standards of the 'POSDCORB' type (referred to in Chapter 5) would risk casting doubt on whether it really was an organization, or at least on whether it was a good one. In order to be viewed as a responsible member of the international community a nation-state has at least to take a position on standards created by UN bodies for labour market and educational policies.

Some standards aim to maintain or accentuate the essential characteristics of the actor. As described in Chapter 1, an actor is an entity possessing independence and sovereignty, autonomous or self-interested goals, rational means and qualities, independent resources, and clear boundaries (Meyer *et al.* 1987). Put differently, an actor is an entity with a clear specific identity, a strong hierarchy (i.e., a system of strong internal control from the top—be it a leader's control of organizational actions or the soul's control over the body), and a high degree of rationality (Brunsson 1996). Many standards consist of prescriptions of how to reinforce identity, hierarchy, and rationality. Many organizational standards deal with how an organization can reinforce its identity by pinpointing its special tasks or defining its business mission, how it can strengthen hierarchy by achieving better internal leadership and control, how it can become more rational by planning more, and the like. Individuals are given general advice on, for example, how they can establish their identity by 'finding themselves', how they can gain greater control over their lives and stop smoking or go on a diet, and how they can become more goal directed and plan ahead. It is difficult for organizations or individuals who think of themselves as actors to reject such standards.

Not only does the identity of a potential adopter affect which standards it will follow. Following standards may also be a way actively to define one's own identity, to show that one is a particular kind of actor (or, for the standards just described, that one is an actor at all). For example, one way for a government to demonstrate that it actually is governing a nation-state is to follow established standards for nation-states. A new nation-state uncertain of its position—one needing to prove that it is a genuine, modern, good state—is likely to be more receptive to such standards than well-established nation-states like the UK or the USA (Meyer 1997). Likewise a public service which has been given the status of a company may have a particular need to show that it really is a business; consequently, it may be much more eager than well-established companies to follow standards for businesses. Contrary to what is assumed in traditional diffusion models (Smith *et al.*

1927), this mechanism makes the periphery more likely to adopt standards than the centre.

Following certain standards and other rules may even be the principal method of acquiring a certain identity. If an individual wants to gain an MBA degree, he or she should of course enrol in a programme which meets the standards for this type of education. If an organization wants to become or remain a member of a standard-based organization, that organization should follow its standards (Chapter 4). One way for a country to improve its chances of admission to the European Union (EU) is to start observing standards and other rules adopted by the EU or generally followed by EU members.

Situation

Standards are intended not only for a certain kind of actor but also for a certain kind of situation. Normally the situation is specified directly or indirectly in the standard. Standards for telephones are relevant to the manufacturer of telephones. Standards for quality assurance, decentralization, and evaluation are intended for situations characterized by poor quality, centralization, and limited knowledge of what has happened.

But like the identity of potential adopters, the nature of the situation is not always evident. This fact is often exploited by standardizers for promoting their standards. One way for standardizers to gain acceptance for their standards is to convince the potential adopter that its situation is relevant. Those who market standards for solving economic problems will refer to an impending economic crisis; those who offer standards to make a business more competitive will warn that competition is likely to increase in the future. Thus, standardizers talk not only about solutions, but also about problems. When standardizers succeed with such efforts, certain problems become fashionable; in other words, many become convinced that they are suffering from these particular problems. Standards which promise solutions to the same problems will then become popular and are likely to be adopted.

Following certain standards may also be a way for the adopter to demonstrate that it is confronting a particular situation. For instance, governments and corporate executives may choose to follow standards for dealing with financial problems in an effort to create or increase citizen or employee awareness of the need for economizing.

Standardization and being an actor

Even though standards are addressed to actors, there is a fundamental contradiction between standardization and being an actor. An actor is an independent individual or organization that is willing and able to make its own choices and to make these choices in a rational way, and a unit that possesses qualities which are special and sometimes unique. Consequently, an actor will not readily follow rules seen as created by outsiders, particularly not directives, which leave the actor no choice. For actors, therefore, standards are more appropriate than directives as a form of rules. Even so, actors may be somewhat suspicious of standards. Conforming to standards means following the advice of others, relinquishing a certain degree of one's freedom of choice and self-control to others, and often becoming more similar to many others as well—none of which is very consistent with the concept of an actor.

We may therefore expect a certain reluctance to follow standards—in particular those that are well known and followed by many—from individuals and organizations seeking to be highly autonomous, innovative, and different. Possibly they will submit to standards in areas of marginal importance; for example, a company aspiring to offer unique products or services may be fairly receptive to administrative standards which apply only to internal operations. It is also easier to follow highly general standards than those specifying exactly what to do.

A special role is played by the standards that aim to reinforce the essential aspects of being an actor, which were described above. Their contents are clearly attractive to those who want to maintain or strengthen their actorhood. At the same time they present a paradox to those who want to be strong actors, since such actors ought not to follow standards, but instead find their own unique solutions (Brunsson 1996).

How voluntary is the standard?

In principle, following a standard is voluntary. The standardizer is not able or willing to force his standard upon others. And even though the identity and situation of an actor may make it appropriate to follow a particular standard, it is not certain that the actor will do so. An actor will require more incentives to adopt a standard. A third party besides the standardizer and the potential adopter may provide such incentives. A third party may want the actor to follow certain standards, or interaction and communication with this third party may be greatly facilitated by following certain standards. If actors are highly dependent on their relations with such third parties, the relevant standards become practically coercive.

For example, customers may want to buy only those products that comply with certain standards or from producers that follow certain quality or environmental standards. It may be hard to find another football team to play with if one does not follow the standard rules for football. It may be difficult to communicate that one's vessels are indeed safe if they are not properly registered and classified by Lloyd's or a similar body. In all these examples the degree of voluntariness is in practice very low: the actor will have no choice but to follow certain standards.

A particular standard may also be coercive in practice because others than the potential adopter generally believe it to be reasonable and that it is important to follow it. In other words, the third party may be public opinion in general or the opinion of groups important to the adopter. For example, when decentralization in organizations is highly fashionable it is difficult for business managers or governments to avoid following standards of decentralization. The options open to leaders may also be limited by pressure from within; if the citizenry of a state or the employees of a company believe that a certain standard is particularly reasonable, natural, and good, the leadership may be virtually compelled to follow it. In a country facing economic problems, the government finds it hard to reject standards that make the budgeting process more rigorous, even if it doubts the value of such standards.

In other cases, an actor may be virtually forced to observe some standard but have a wide range of standards to choose from. For example, a number of different administrative standards may be in vogue. If the management of a certain organization declined to follow any of these standards, it would probably be accused of not being up to date. At the same time, however, it has considerable freedom to choose which specific standard to adopt.

When the degree of voluntariness in following a standard is low, we can expect it to encounter resistance. At least some potential adopters may want to criticize the standard or may even seek to change it. But in contrast to what tends to happen in relation to directives, it is difficult to find either a forum in which to express criticism, or someone to hold responsible, as we pointed out in Part I. So those affected by standards are well advised to show an interest in processes which generate standards. For example, many companies try to join committees that develop product standards of importance to its business, sometimes for the sole purpose of preventing the development of any standard at all. And even if everyone recognizes the value of a particular standard it becomes more difficult to reach agreement when the standard is expected to become coercive in practice. If such standards, coercive but unfavourable, are nevertheless issued, adopters may well seek to minimize their impact. For instance, they may try to ensure that the standards affect presentation rather than practice.

It may seem that those who wish to influence others by standards would always prefer their standards to have a low degree of voluntariness. However, our present discussion would indicate that this is not necessarily true: it becomes harder to create such standards and to ensure that they do affect practice.

Incentives

Of course, adopters are not always forced by others to adopt a standard. Instead they adopt a standard since they believe that it does offer an improvement on the present solution. Adopters are likely to have similar beliefs to those of people in general, and few standards break radically with the generally accepted ideas of their time. In some cases though, a standard may fill a certain knowledge gap between standardizer and adopter: the standard may deal with a problem which adopters have not noticed, or may offer a solution which they did not previously know of or realize to be superior. Potential adopters are more likely to hold this view of standards if they believe that the standardizer generally knows more than they do about what should be done—in other words, if they believe that relevant knowledge can be found at a distance, with distant experts. In issuing standards, standardizers generally assert a claim to such expert knowledge, as we discussed in Chapter 3. The propensity to follow standards will of course be greater if potential adopters fully appreciate the standardizers' expert status; it will be less if potential adopters believe that the necessary knowledge is closer at hand, with themselves or held by people with insights into their specific situation.

Expert authority may also be viewed as something acquired along with the standard. A standard is not just any rule. It is also affected by the authority of the standardizer, which may be considerable. Furthermore, standardizers generally provide arguments for using their standards, including arguments that there is a problem to be solved. If there are already a number of respected adopters of the standard, this fact will serve as an additional argument.

This package of expertise and authority, and the example of other adopters, is useful for someone who wants to promote a certain standard. For example, it is helpful to organizational leadership with little authority: reference to a standard improves the chances that the members will do what the leaders want, or that outside parties will accept what the organization has done. In such cases leaders will try to present their proposals as being in accordance with standards. The expert authority of standards may even be more important to organizational leaders than the exact features of what is done. Even if the standard does not agree exactly with what the leadership would have wished, following it is preferable to frustrating and perhaps fruitless attempts to sell the leadership's own solution to members and outsiders. For instance, management may find it hard to impose its own administrative solution but easier to introduce an internationally recognized administrative standard that comes reasonably close to it. While following a quality standard is complicated and expensive, it may also be a way for a management to gain acceptance for certain changes which it desires and which can be presented as measures to improve quality.

Observing a standard may also be seen as a partial abdication of responsibility; one may reduce one's responsibility somewhat by following in the footsteps of others, rather than going one's own way. We expect that individuals and managements wishing to lighten the burden of their responsibility will be receptive to standards.

Not only the advantages but also the disadvantages of a standard have a bearing on whether an actor will follow it. And there are several disadvantages. For example, limitation of responsibility will be viewed negatively by those who think that assuming responsibility is the right thing to do; someone who wants to show how much he is contributing to the success of his organization will probably prefer his own solutions to standards. Another drawback to standards is that they often prevent an actor from doing or saying exactly what he wants. Finally, changing one's practice in accordance with a standard may be costly, but the more consistent existing practice is with the standard, the less the cost will be. It is easiest to follow standards which can be used to describe one's practice as it already is or as it is planned to be, provided the standards are also consistent with the desired manner of presentation.

When many actors follow the same standards by changing their practice or presentation, many of them will also be doing the same things. In such cases standardization will have led to uniformity. In the next chapter we identify the factors that
must be present for uniformity to result.

10

Standardization and Uniformity

NILS BRUNSSON

Uniformity is typical of today's world. In the eighteenth and nineteenth centuries explorers were still astounded by the vast extent to which people's customs, mores, beliefs, and possessions differed from place to place; at that time much still remained to explore and discover. Nowadays an explorer would be more struck by the similarities everywhere. Automobiles, McDonald's fast food, the organization of government, social problems, what we read in the newspapers, and everyday life in general—all are remarkably alike the world over. There is little left to explore and discover, and for that reason there are not many explorers today, either. Anthropologists wanting to report on something different must seek out increasingly remote and desolate places, or else resign themselves to writing about the substantially smaller differences between the major cultures at centre stage. The unfortunate tourist in search of something new is fed folklore, which bears little or no relation to the prevailing culture; in many cases it is a rather recent invention (Hobsbawm and Ranger 1983).

It is often assumed that standardization will lead to uniformity. In everyday language 'standardized' and 'uniform' are often treated as synonyms. The result of standardization—intended or not—is thought to be that many will resemble each other in appearance and behaviour. To be sure, the production of standards is the cause behind some of the global uniformity that we find today, but it is not the only cause. And standardization may not bring about as much uniformity as expected.

In this chapter we discuss the relationship between standardization and uniformity. While in the preceding chapter we examined the consequences of standards for individual actors, here we discuss standardization in relation to groups of actors. In order to clarify the role of standardization in producing uniformity, we first review several other processes which can also lead to uniformity. We then discuss how standards can contribute to this outcome.

Processes that create uniformity

Uniformity means that many are alike; whatever is of interest—be it products, education, or the form of organization—will be the same. Social scientists seeking to understand why similarities arise have often started with the similarities themselves. They have wondered why a particular practice, form of organization, or other phenomenon has become commonplace. Often a special metaphor is used for this process—that of diffusion.

Uniformity through diffusion

Diffusion is a concept commonly used in the social sciences to describe and explain uniformity (Strang and Meyer 1993). Most often the concept refers to the end result of a process: when a phenomenon is common it is said to be widely diffused. Sometimes, however, the concept is deliberately or unintentionally used to designate the process itself: the similarities are claimed or assumed to have arisen through a process of diffusion. When something is diffusing, it spreads from the centre to the periphery. Diffusion of new ideas, things, or techniques means that these spread to increasingly remote places.

Processes of diffusion may be compared to epidemics, where contagion is an important process (March 1981): individuals, societies, organizations, etc. in close contact with the source of the 'infection' or with other 'infected' units are easily infected themselves; that is, they tend to be receptive to what is being diffused. An infection may also be spread by carriers that show no symptoms. The carrier of a disease may be a rat or a mosquito. In the world of organizations the infection—a new management technique, for instance—may be spread by consultants. These may move from organization to organization, selling their ideas, or they may infect numerous organizations at the same time at major conferences.

An absolute requirement of models which are supposed to explain similarities is that they also can explain differences. In the diffusion model, differences are usually explained by time and distance: those who are (still) different have not yet come in contact with what is being diffused (most probably since they are located at the periphery).

The diffusion model is based on a physical metaphor. The critical explanatory factor is contact with certain others who possess special knowledge. The model has traditionally been used to explain rather slow processes, such as the gradual spread of new agricultural methods from the inventors to increasingly remote places (Smith *et al.* 1927). It is often assumed, implicitly or explicitly, that lack of information about the phenomena being diffused is a major obstacle to uniformity. For example, it takes time for all the peripheral actors to accept a superior new agricultural technique because information about the new technique spreads slowly.

The notion of diffusion seems well adapted to certain physical processes; for example, undesired air pollutants are diffused from a source over large areas. It may also be appropriate for social processes, when information is a scarce resource, as was often the case in older societies: knowledge spread slowly from one place to another.

In modern society, however, there is often no shortage of information. New technologies, new methods of organization, or new clothing fashions are diffused by the mass media with lightning rapidity throughout the world. Almost everyone is 'infected' with this information at virtually the same time. However, not everyone actually becomes like the others. Therefore, the diffusion of information seems to be of limited value in explaining either uniformity or diversity.

A more thorough explanation would seem to require a better understanding of those who receive diffused information. A simple modification to the basic diffusion model is to introduce the concept of immunity: certain individuals or units have intrinsic qualities that protect from infection despite exposure to what is being diffused. For instance, they may be too poor to invest in a new, more expensive agricultural technique. A more radical deviation from the simple diffusion model is to treat the adopters as actors. Unlike the effects of air pollution, social practices are influenced by human beings. So we can assume that if a certain practice is to 'arise' in a new location, an actor has made a deliberate choice to start acting in this particular way (Malinowski 1927; Latour 1986). If we assume that receivers of information are active, and we examine what they do, we will probably find other and perhaps better explanations for uniformity and diversity than those the diffusion model can offer.

A more actor-oriented explanation of uniformity should begin with the processes that determine how the actors will behave. The question will be why a large number of them will behave in the same way. Note that the actors themselves need not know that their behaviour is similar. Nor need they try to resemble one another. With an actor-based approach, we may distinguish three different processes which can give rise to similarities: innovation, imitation and conformity to rules. Following standards falls into the last category.

Uniformity through innovation

Uniformity may arise through innovation, when several actors independently conceive and implement the same ideas. If they are in similar situations and face similar problems, they may find similar solutions. For example, if the employees of many organizations believe strongly in their own individuality and right to decide for themselves (Thomas *et al.* 1987), it may be that numerous employers will adopt similar, more decentralized forms of organization. Or if more and more people begin to see themselves as customers of public organizations rather than citizens, then many of these organizations may adopt the methods of private business in dealing with these new 'customers'.

We should expect innovative processes to result in more similarities among actors, the greater the number of them that share the same view of themselves, their situation, and their problems, and the fewer the possible actions and solutions to the problems. If many would like to get rich but there are few ways to do so, then many will bet on the lottery. If it is commonly held that organizations should be able to respond more flexibly to a varied environment, and decentralization is considered one of the few ways of achieving that, then many organizations will be decentralized. If numerous governments have problems with budget deficits, and it is difficult for them to raise revenue or incur debts, they will propose many cost-cutting programmes. By contrast, responses to innovative processes will vary when actors view their situation or their problems in markedly different ways, or when there are many possible solutions to their problems.

Uniformity through imitation

Unlike innovation, imitation means that actors deliberately copy each other; when you imitate someone, you try to learn how that person acts and then do the same yourself. If imitation is successful, there will be similarity, at least between the imitator and the imitated.

The probability that many will become similar through imitation increases, the more the imitators and the fewer the imitated. A social structure with a small élite and large masses trying to imitate the élite will thus favour uniformity. To take an extreme example, if everyone imitates a single individual, there is a high probability of uniformity among all actors. The fact that children imitate their parents need not result in very great similarities among children from different families, since there are many different parents. On the other hand, when young people imitate world-famous individuals, perhaps in the field of popular culture, the uniformity becomes much greater; there are few such role models and many young people.

Even if those imitated are numerous, imitation may give rise to considerable uniformity if those imitated resemble each other. If the parents who are imitated are similar, then their children will be, too. Thus, a homogeneous culture creates both similar parents and similar children. But in a global perspective, parents are dissimilar because they belong to different cultures. At the same time, there are individuals who are popular throughout the world. In this situation the processes of imitation which we have assumed to exist will tend to make children more alike as they grow older: a kind of global youth culture will emerge.

The number of imitators will depend in turn on how many believe that they already resemble a particular model to begin with. For we tend to imitate those whom we resemble rather than those whom we find different from ourselves. A state is less likely to imitate a sports club than another state; a school is less likely to imitate a hospital than another school. If you consider your company to be a 'knowledge company' you are likely to imitate other such companies that you know to be successful; and processes of imitation will result in more uniformity, the more enterprises there are that see themselves as 'knowledge companies', and the fewer well-known, successful 'knowledge companies' there are to imitate.

However, imitation may fail to achieve the intended similarity (Sevón 1996). Information on what is imitated may be insufficient, and it may be difficult for the imitator to act on it. Further, the imitator is often not interested in perfect imitation but would like to add his own ingredients. Imitation is then mixed with innovation (Malinowski 1927; Latour 1986; Westney 1987; Sahlin-Andersson 1996; Sevón 1996).

In practice it is often difficult to observe directly what the desired object of imitation is doing. What it says—or others say—that it is doing may be all that the would-be imitator has to go on. Such reports may be expressed in rather abstract terms, in which case imitation is not unlike following a standard. Of course, one may also imitate others' reports directly—that is, by saying what they are saying. It is usually much simpler to imitate talk rather than practice, since it is generally easier to hear what is being said than to see what is being done. In such situations imitation tends to produce more uniformity in talk than in action.

When uniformity has been analysed in terms of diffusion models, it has sometimes been thought that diffusion takes place through imitation. We would then have an explanation for why information is considered a scarce resource. Since it may take time to find information on what others are doing, the process of diffusion may be slow, particularly if it involves successive imitation: the original is imitated by an actor, who in turn is imitated by the next actor, and so on.

In the strict sense of the word, imitation of others' actions is probably not the most common way to uniformity, at least not among organizations. As with the diffusion model, there is a danger that researchers may confuse the outcome with what has led up to it. Uniformity as an outcome is sometimes referred to as imitation, even though it may not be due to imitation. Individuals and organizations have limited opportunities to observe what their counterparts are doing in practice; they are thus often in a poor position to imitate each other's actions. They are somewhat more likely to imitate what others are saying about themselves. And, more important, they have access to another kind of talk, namely numerous standards that they may follow.

Uniformity and following standards

Rules and adherence to them may also create uniformity. One may say that uniformity is the purpose or point of rules—a rule expresses the idea that actors of a certain kind should do the same thing in a particular kind of situation. Normally several actors will behave in a similar manner on several occasions.

In Chapter 1 we distinguished three kinds of rules: directives, norms, and standards. There are certain differences among these rules in regard to their consequences for uniformity. Both directives and standards can be used with the explicit purpose of creating uniformity. Unlike standards, directives can be backed up by sanctions; we may assume that the force of the sanctions and the possibility of applying them affects the degree to which directives can lead to uniformity.

The power of norms to establish uniformity depends on their prevalence: that is, on how many believe in them. What factors determine the belief in norms? This question is among the thornier ones in the social sciences. For example, in institutional theories of organizations, uniformity is often explained by the fact that a particular norm has many adherents, but it has been much more difficult to determine why the norm became so prevalent in the first place. Explaining differences has been even harder; for example, why has a particular norm been adopted by most actors of the same kind in the same culture, but not by all?

In many other respects the tendency of directives and norms to create uniformity depends on the same factors as apply in relation to standards. As mentioned in the previous chapter, following standards means that we try to translate a generally formulated rule into terms relevant to our own situation. We do not invent our own solution, nor do we try to imitate anyone else (even though standards are often accompanied by references—true or untrue—to others who have successfully followed them).

Below we discuss what determines whether standards will create uniformity or not; the outcome will depend on the adopters as well as on the standards and the standardizers. As well as considering the factors, mentioned in the previous chapter, that affect whether a standard will be followed, we also discuss some collective phenomena that bear on uniformity and diversity. Bearing in mind that the more people there are that follow a standard, the greater the uniformity, we examine how widespread information about the standards is; to what degree the standards compete with each other; and how similar they are.

Information

A standard should be widely known among potential adopters if it is to produce similarity among many of them. Standards are generally quite easy to recognize. Normally they are published and actively marketed. As has been noted, would-be imitators may have problems in obtaining relevant information; someone wanting to follow standards will seldom have the same difficulty. Standards often figure actively in the public discourse on various phenomena. Relevant actors will normally be familiar with this discourse and may sometimes participate in it. Engineers in telecommunications follow what is written and said by experts, debaters, and standardizers in the telecommunications area; many become actively involved themselves. Those with power to make changes in forms of administration can easily find standards in the literature on management. Makers of government policy on administration will have no trouble finding standards in this field; as we saw in Chapter 7, many of them participate in designing these standards.

Thus, a lack of uniformity is seldom due to insufficient information about standards—contrary to the assumptions of the classic models for diffusion of social phenomena. Even though not all standards are equally perceptible above the roar of the media, some standards are noticed by many, thus making uniformity possible.

The number of actors

A lack of uniformity has more to do with the potential adopters of a standard than with lack of information. Not all of these will find the information about the standard relevant. And the number of potential adopters varies. As we noted in the last chapter, in order to choose whether to follow a standard, one must be free to choose and capable of acting independently; in other words, one must be an actor.

The number of independent actors varies with the degree of centralization in the social system. There are few such actors in extremely centralized systems. A highly centralized organization constitutes a single actor: only central management has the power to decide, for example, which standards the organization will follow. In a decentralized organization there are many units or even individuals that can function as actors. In a centralized dictatorship with a planned economy, there will be considerably fewer actors than in decentralized democratic market economies.

Indeed, the number of actors seems generally to be increasing, as described in Chapter 2. In recent decades it has become more common for people to think of themselves as individuals with the right to choose for themselves rather than having to follow detailed directives from states, families, local communities, or employers. In many areas more decentralized structures have been introduced, making the development of individualism more feasible. More individual actors have been appearing. Similarly, the number of actors in the form of organizations has increased through the recent trend in both the private and the public sector in many countries for large hierarchies to split up into smaller, highly autonomous companies or public services; such 'outsourcing', the forming of separate 'business units', 'privatization', or the forming of public-sector 'organizations' create more organizations that are full-fledged actors (Brunsson and Sahlin-Andersson forthcoming).

When there are more actors, more can follow standards. If the other conditions for uniformity through standardization are met, there may be a high degree of uniformity, sometimes much greater even than in centralized systems (Meyer and Scott 1983). Fads spread quickly to parts of the world where individuals enjoy extensive liberty. Autonomous organizations tend to be receptive to many administrative standards and tend to become similar (Meyer and Rowan 1977; Røvik 1998). When Swedish municipalities decentralized and established fairly autonomous local entities, these entities developed conspicuously similar policies, thereby undermining an important purpose of the decentralization reforms.

Sometimes centralization may even be essential if differences are to be preserved; a central actor can actively try to establish differences within his field of control, for instance by issuing directives in this direction. More totalitarian states have been better than most modern democracies at maintaining economic differences among individuals. In Sweden local governments are highly autonomous actors with comparatively loose connections to the central state: they are more homogeneous than the state agencies that are under direct state control.

Relevance: The identity and situation of the actor

Whether an actor will follow standards depends, as mentioned in the previous chapter, on how that actor defines its own reality. If many actors consider themselves to be basically alike, they tend to find the same standard relevant; if they do, uniformity among them will be more probable. Perceived similarities thus promote further similarities. Standardizers who want to have their standards spread to many are likely to argue that many are similar to each other.

A distinguishing feature of the modern, global world is the existence of extremely large groups of actors that define themselves in the same way the world over—as individuals, organizations, nation-states, physicians, companies, democracies, etc. In other words many consider themselves basically similar to many others. Standards directed to such general actors are likely to be adopted by many (Strang and Meyer 1993). This situation leads readily to a high degree of uniformity. ISO claims that its 9000 series are the world's most widely sold standards. Unlike many other standards ISO 9000 standards are intended for all organizations, not just for particular ones, such as manufacturers of certain kinds of products; both municipalities and manufacturers of separators follow ISO 9000, but only the latter follow the CEN standards for separators. And throughout the world, the greater the number of phenomena classified as organizations, the greater the number to which ISO 9000 is relevant.

As noted in the previous chapter, the situation of the potential adopter is also relevant to the observance of standards. If many actors believe that they are in the kind of situation in which the standard is to apply, uniformity will be more probable; if many have the same problem, many are likely to adopt the standard that is intended to solve that problem. Advice on dealing with economic crises will have more followers if many find that they have economic problems. And in fact, problems tend to be similar for many actors of the same kind. One explanation is that opinions on what the important problems are tend to become world-wide fads. Another may be that certain problems go with being a certain kind of actor: individuals will always have problems in weighing independence against dependence; organizations will always have to find a balance between central control and local freedom; every nation-state has problems in reconciling democracy with efficient government. Standards that are said to solve such problems will always be in demand.

Interpreting standards

If a standard is so abstract or unclear that it can be interpreted in different ways, it may attract more followers, who can adapt their interpretation of the standard to their needs and preferences. But when such adaptations are made there is no guarantee of uniformity, even if there are many followers of a standard; there is little uniformity if followers interpret the standard differently. Since highly abstract standards allow for a variety of different interpretations, there may be substantial variation among actors who try to follow them. The range of possible interpretations is particularly wide when abstract standards are to be translated into practical action.

On the other hand, there is often less room for interpretation of what is to be said. Just as in the case of imitation, standards may produce considerable uniformity in what actors say that they do, but less uniformity in what they actually do. What actors say is more influenced by standards than what they do. This means that many actors talk in one way and act in another. Standardization helps produce 'decoupling' and hypocrisy (Brunsson 1989). For example, at one point many municipalities claimed that they had introduced or were introducing a particular administrative method then in vogue, the purchaser-provider model; at the same time there were indications of substantial variation in the practices of these municipalities (Fernler 1996).

Certification of compliance with standards is intended to ensure that the local interpretations of a given standard do not deviate excessively from what has been defined as correct. Certification should thus prevent the interpretation of a standard from varying too greatly. However, while certification is often intended to investigate what is actually done, it is often in practice based on what is said to be done, thus enforcing uniformity of talk rather than of action.

Implementation

Implementation of standards means attempting to make them affect what is done. Processes of implementation may lead to differences among actors seeking to follow the same standard. Even if the managers of an organization, for example, interpret a particular standard in the same way as other managers do, it is not certain that the practices of their organizations will be very similar. Since the specific circumstances of implementation differ, the practices may differ as well. Those who are to implement a standard may be sceptical about certain aspects of it, and more willing to follow it in some respects than in others. And different aspects of a standard may appeal to different implementors in different organizations.

The implementation of standards may further diminish their effectiveness in establishing uniformity. But the standards can still produce uniformity of presentation in cases when presentation need not be very representative of practice; in situations where hypocrisy is possible. This is often the case in large organizations where few have insights into actual practice. And in polls people may present their actions as following popular standards even if these standards do not govern their actual practice. Following a standard in what we say may be quick and easy, but implementing it in practice often takes longer. As in the case of the purchaser-provider model above, fads or fashions can spread rapidly when there is little requirement for time-consuming implementation or when no one checks whether implementation has occurred.

In many situations there are strict requirements of uniformity in presentation, but much more latitude is allowed in implementation. As we showed in Chapter 5, the ISO 9000 standards are largely about presentation rather than practice. For certification of conformity to the standard, objectives and procedures must be correctly expressed in writing; what is done in practice receives little attention. By the same token, reviewing a company to determine whether it meets its European Union product-safety requirements is actually about whether it claims to have internal procedures to assure safety, and not about the safety of the products themselves (Jacobsson 1993).

The abstract nature of standards means that their effect on the degree of uniformity of presentation and of practice differs. As previously noted, standards that are highly abstract are less likely than more concrete ones to create uniformity in practice. For presentations we should expect the opposite effect, at least in cases when presentations are required to reflect practice with reasonable accuracy. A highly abstract standard may be used for presenting a great variety of practices, without the adopters being accused of misrepresenting reality. A less abstract standard can be used for presenting fewer practices.

Competing standards

The degree of uniformity is also dependent on the number of competing standards available to a particular target group and for a particular area of actitivities. If there are many standards to choose from, those who follow the standards need not become very much alike. In many spheres of standardization, particularly in product standardization, attempts are made to limit the number of competing standards, preferably to a single standard. When these attempts are successful, uniformity is highly probable—in other words, all who are willing to follow standards are likely to act or express themselves in the same way.

Nevertheless, many attempts to set one standard have failed, and there have continued to be competing standards. There are numerous examples of such competing standards, not least in the case of product standards: standards for electrical plugs still differ from country to country; there are still variations in the distance between railway rails and tracks, etc. And there are many administrative standards, each proposing a somewhat different method of organization. Here, in contrast to product standardization, there is rarely any effort to agree on a single standard; on the contrary, it is important to many standardizers to launch new and different standards on a continuing basis. The same is true of many standards that tell individuals how to live their lives.

When there are many competing standards the result may be varying degrees of uniformity and diversity. As we shall see, the significant factors are the similarities among the competing standards and their relative attractiveness.

Although many standardizers in the area of administration seek to differentiate their standards from those of competitors, these efforts are not always successful. As we showed in Chapter 5, there may be fundamental similarities between standards which superficially appear somewhat different: administrative standards are usually based on a particular view of organizations as being clearly defined, manageable units for which planning is feasible and appropriate. When competing standards are similar in this way or others, those who follow them will resemble each other in word or deed, no matter which standards they have adopted. Thus, similarities among the standards will lead to similarities among those standardized. For example, followers of the quality standards described in Chapter 8 will all introduce or maintain procedures for planning and evaluation, or will claim that they have.

When there are several competing standards, there will be greater uniformity if certain standards gain more followers than others. One of the standardizers may command more authority than others, or many actors may find some standards more attractive than others for other reasons. Without such differences among the standards, there will be greater diversity among adopters of the standards.

Another important factor is whether adopters find uniformity desirable. To the extent that they do, they will tend to choose standards that others have adopted. A self-reinforcing process may then result; the outcome may even be that everyone follows the same standard, so that competition among standards virtually ceases, giving way to monopoly. The qwerty standard for typewriter keyboards is hardly optimal, but the need for uniformity is so great that few find it feasible to deviate from this standard.

In other cases the adopters see no point in following the example of others. If they observe a particular standard, their reason for doing so is not that they expect others to do the same. They may even find it to their disadvantage to do as others do; individuals and organizations not uncommonly seek to maintain their own distinctive profile. In such cases competition among standards is more likely to continue than to be replaced by monopoly.

In some areas globalization has led to a larger number of competing standards; in others, to fewer. International standards organizations have sought to reduce the number of competing standards through international standards designed to replace those at the national level. These efforts have contributed to greater uniformity. By contrast, in other areas globalization has encouraged the proliferation of competing standards. For instance when management gurus have reached out to an international audience, companies in all countries have been exposed to more standards than when they listened only to domestic gurus. Foreign food recipes have spread to all countries, and these standards have affected practice, so that we now find Thai, Chinese, French, and almost all other cuisines in restaurants in all the larger cities of the world, instead of just the local cuisine. The diversity within each city has increased.

Standards for diversity

Even where standards give rise to uniformity, they normally allow for some diversity as well. Standards may also make existing diversity more visible. The fact that actors follow standards enables us to see how they differ in some other respects. The world of sport provides one example. When all football teams follow the standards of football, it also becomes clear how they use their non-standardized freedom of action in different ways. Differences that are essential within sport become apparent: we can now tell which is the better team, since we know who has won the game played by the rules. In such cases standards clearly regulate not only what shall be similar but also what shall be different.

The same applies to markets as well, where there is also a combination of standardization and freedom of action. Here, too, competition takes place in the free—that is, non-standardized—zone. If all the technical aspects and components of telephones are standardized and successfully made uniform, diversity will be limited to design, service, and price, and these will be the characteristics that can be used in competition among producers.

The EU has been accused of conducting and encouraging a kind of standardization which permits only price competition, allegedly ruling out competition through development of new and improved products and thus retarding technical progress. Of course, such criticism may be levelled at all far-reaching product standardization. At the same time, however, some degree of standardization facilitates variation in the unregulated sphere. For example, if screw threading is not standardized, exchange between machinery manufacturers and their suppliers will be more complicated; the effect will be to hamper the development of new types of machines.

Components may be standardized while products consist of different combinations of these components. By choosing a unique combination of components, a company is able to offer a unique product. In other cases, the composition of the whole may not be unique. To return to the example of restaurants mentioned above, the diversity among restaurants within each city has increased since they now serve different cuisines. On the other hand, the diversity among the cities has decreased: the set of restaurants within each city is similar to those of other cities: the cities all contain Thai, Chinese, etc. restaurants. Large cities are uniform in the sense that their supply of restaurants is equally varied and varied in roughly the same way.

Product standards may also be intended to establish only a moderate degree of uniformity, so that many different products are compatible with other products without being copies of each other. Standardizing functions instead of form is also a way of limiting the requirements of similarity without doing away with them entirely; such standards specify the function to be fulfilled by the product but not exactly how it is to be designed.

Achieving uniformity through standards

Standards may contribute to uniformity, an effect that standardizers often seek. But as we have shown here, the uniformity that results from standards is often limited. Obviously, for one standard to be accepted and uniformity to occur, it is not enough that people see a benefit from being similar to others. We have argued that the degree of uniformity will depend on the characteristics of the adopters, of the standards, and of the standardizers.

Uniformity is dependent on the adopters in several ways. Uniformity tends to be greater when there are more actors; when actors believe that they belong to few, broad categories of actors and, likewise, when many share views on their situation; and when actors see a benefit in doing as others do. Uniformity of practice is more likely if adopters interpret and implement standards in similar ways; uniformity of talk is more likely if a high degree of hypocrisy is possible.

Uniformity is dependent on several characteristics of the standards. Uniformity will tend to be greater if there are few competing standards, if a few standards are much more competitive than others, or if competing standards are similar. Abstract standards will promote uniformity of talk but will not promote uniformity in practice.

Uniformity is also dependent on standardizers. The number of competing standards and the tendency for certain standards to attract a greater following than others are influenced by the authority of different standardizers and on how effectively information about various standards is spread. When standardizers introduce processes of certification, uniformity will be more probable, particularly of how practice is presented.

Standards organizations like ISO and CEN try to use several of these factors to create situations that will promote uniformity. They make strong efforts to spread information about their standards and they emphasize the benefits of uniformity—the usefulness of everyone following the same standard. Benefits of uniformity are created in a very concrete way when standards organizations succeed in committing central actors to a standard, so that others who want to interact with these have to follow the standard. Most notably standards organizations seek to achieve a monopoly for their standards by establishing a monopoly for their standardizing authority. According to ISO's formal definition (presented in Chapter 1), a standard is to be issued by a 'recognized body'.

If standardizers want their standards to be widely followed, they cannot generally build on their authority only. They should define the adopters and the situations to which their standards apply in broad, inclusive terms, just as standardizers of quality systems have done. As described in Chapter 8, these standardizers defined adopters very broadly as businesses and other organizations regardless of whether they were industrial companies, schools, or something else. And all needed quality systems. The standards focused on presentation rather than practice and were quite abstract. The standards were readily acceptable to organizations, since they were consistent with generally accepted views on how organizations should be presented—largely the conventional wisdom of the popular management culture referred to in Chapter 5. And the standards were also remarkably similar; those who followed them became similar to others no matter which specific quality standard they used. In addition, two of the standardizers discussed in Chapter 8 used a certification procedure to determine whether their standards were being followed. It is no wonder that many units come to have similar systems for quality management or at least that they make similar claims as to what system they have.

Since the standards created by standards organizations are intended to remain in effect over a longer period, they should be fairly stable over time and not readily changeable. Thus, they should provide for uniformity not only over space—over several actors, products, etc.—but over time as well. Uniformity in these two dimensions is the theme of the next chapter.

11

Standardization and Fashion Trends

Nils Brunsson

In the previous chapter we looked at uniformity and diversity in space. It is also possible to speak of uniformity and diversity across time, that is, of stability and change. Actors can talk or act in similar or different ways at different times. There can be different combinations of uniformity and diversity over time and in space.

First, there can be great similarities across both space and time—many things are similar for long periods of time. This can happen, for example, when a standard becomes institutionalized; when it becomes a stabilized mode of action. As mentioned in Chapter 1, using a fork when eating was a standard in the sixteenth century that has long since become a norm and a general practice.

Secondly, there can be great diversity across both time and space. For example, schools may follow changing standards for schools while hospitals follow changing standards for hospitals; when the standards change, so do schools and hospitals, but without becoming similar to each other.

Thirdly, strong uniformity can exist across time while there is much diversity across space—actors can be stable in their differences. It is an eternal truth that some standards apply to Jupiter and some to the ox (*Licet Jovi, non licet bovi*), and in fact they seem to consistently to behave differently.

Finally, there can exist a great uniformity across space but a small one across time; many actors are similar to each other in each period, but the characteristics that are similar are not stable: the similar characteristics are different in different periods. The combination of a high degree of uniformity in space, and diversity or variation across time, is often designated as fashion; here it will be called fashion trend. Fashion trends can characterize clothing styles or car models, and be mainly concerned with aesthetics. But fashion trends also exist in other areas that are usually considered more technical; they can, for example, be about more 'serious' things such as what techniques we use to achieve certain ends in business, politics, or child care (Abrahamson 1996a). Certain methods are extremely popular and common during a particular time but are later replaced by other methods. Many people like the same clothing style and dress the same, many managers believe in the same administrative techniques, and many governments attempt to resolve labour market issues in a similar manner at a certain time, only to later change their preferences and do things differently but still in the same manner as the others. These are the types of events that we examine in this chapter.

Fashions and fashion trends

Theories on fashion do not generally differentiate between what is popular and what is common. In these theories, a fashion designates both what is well known and popular and what is characteristic of what many practise or present (Abrahamson 1996*b*). This definition is too broad for our purposes. Something can be well known and popular without being characteristic of the practice or presentations of the practice of a larger group. *Haute couture* fashion may not always be reflected in many people's way of dressing. And something can be common without being very popular. Smoking was high fashion in the 1930s; but in many countries the percentage of smokers was not higher then than at the beginning of the 1990s, when smoking was definitely not fashionable.

For our purposes 'fashion' designates something that is well known and popular among many and which changes over time; the term 'fashion trend' is used for describing what actors actually do, to designate common and changing behaviour. A *fashion* has to do with what people know, like, and pay attention to. Fashions can consist of ideas, models, or things that are well known and popular. They can also consist of well-established or popular rules. Fashions can consist of standards that are well known and generally liked, of generally shared norms, or even of directives that are generally accepted. Fashion involves changes in attention—that different ideas etc. are attended to at different points in time; what is well known and popular changes over time.

A *fashion trend*, on the other hand, has to do with what people do, their behaviour. A fashion trend has many actors behaving in the same way at the same time, while at a later time, actors will behave in a different way, but in the same way as many others behave at that time. In order for us to be able to use the term 'fashion trend' it is enough that there are differences across time and spatial similarity in several periods. It does not require that the actors who behave similarly are the same in each period. For example, we can talk about a fashion trend if a large proportion of companies, belonging to the same population, for instance an industry, use the same budget technique in one period and an equally large proportion use another budget technique in the next period, even if no company that used the first technique ever uses the second. Often, however, the spatial similarities do include the same actors over several periods of time: at least some of the companies which used the first technique use the second. For instance, this may happen when what actors do in one period affects what they do in the next.

A fashion trend is not necessarily consistent with some previous or current fashion. There are other origins of fashion trends than fashions. Fashion trends may be the result of innovation. As described in the previous chapter, innovative processes may produce uniformity, when many actors encounter similar problems at the same time, and there are only a limited number of ways available to resolve the problems. If the problems shift over time fashion trends are likely. Fashion trends can also arise through imitation, for example through the imitation of a few by the many, and through the fact that the few change how they do things periodically.

In both of these pure cases of innovation and imitation fashion trends arise without any corresponding fashion.

However, fashion trends sometimes occur as the result of fashions—through the fact that certain ideas, standards, norms, and so on are popular during limited periods of time, and that this popularity affects behaviour in the same period or in some period after. The attention paid to some standards tends to follow fashion patterns. Fashions among standards are in turn a common cause of fashion trends, sometimes in combination with innovation and imitation. We now look at standardization as an explanation for fashion trends.

Standardization as the origin of fashion trends

If we are to explain fashion trends as the result of standardization, we must of course point to some relevant standards. We then have to explain uniformity in behaviour across space—that many follow the standard; and the change—that many follow another standard after a time. The causes can be found both in the demand and in the supply: both with the standard adopters and with standardizers.

A high degree of uniformity in space can be explained by one or more of the factors we mentioned in the previous chapter. The factors pertain both to the demand and the supply side. The demand factors, which according to the last chapter can be expected to promote uniformity in space, include: that the adopters are being subject to the same information regarding standards; that they interpret and implement those standards in similar ways; that they determine similar standards to be relevant because they experience their identity and their situations in a similar manner; and that the costs of complying with the relevant standard are small in comparison with the advantages it brings. The supply factors, which can be expected to promote uniformity, include the existence of few competing standards, or that the competing standards are similar.

Change occurs as the result of the tendency of the adopters of standards to begin doing things differently after a time. This also needs to be explained. The cause of change need not be fashions in standards. There can be many other causes, one of which may be that adopters interpret and implement the same standard in different ways in different situations. They can, for example, let the standard affect first their presentations and later their actions. If many start doing so, the behaviour of many actors will change, but will still be similar to that of the others.

Other reasons for change can be that actors follow different standards at different times—even if the general popularity of various standards has not changed—or that they interpret old standards in a new way. One explanation for this, on the demand side, may be that the actors' situation changes and that certain old standards (or old interpretations) no longer fit. Different management principles can fit differently for different businesses under different financial conditions, and, therefore, companies choose to follow new standards when the situation changes. If the conditions change for many companies at the same time, this can give rise to a fashion trend (Barley and Kunda 1992). Although people tend to wear similar clothes, their clothes tend to change with the seasons. The similarity may be driven by fashion but the change is driven more by the weather.

In other cases change is due to fashions among standards. This fashion explanation refers to what we have called the supply side of standardization. According to this explanation some standards are well known and popular, but the set of such standards changes over time: there are fashions in standards. In other words, at any moment, or at least intermittently, there are few competing standards in an area or competing standards are similar, and this situation continues into the next period, although the relevant standards in that period are different. If the actors persistently comply with these fashionable standards, they will be subject to change: what is fashionable shifts, and thereby the behaviour of many actors. Fashion in standards then gives rise to fashion trends.

Sometimes the collective belief in certain standards is so strong that these standards turn into what can be called temporary norms. At a certain time almost everyone may believe that the standard is the only right or sensible solution to what is believed to be an important problem. Later the same standard may become something very far from a norm: it may be considered as another case of 'just a fashion', that is, an irrational and whimsical collective myth. Fashions are more powerful when actors do not perceive them as fashions (Røvik 1993).

Sometimes the demand can affect the supply of standards. This may, in turn, affect both the degree of uniformity and the pattern of change. If many people comply with a standard, it can result in the standard becoming better known and more popular, causing more to follow it. In consequence, the uniformity in behaviour increases. At a later stage or in other circumstances, the effect can be the opposite: those actors, who do not want to be the same as all others, begin to demand a new standard to follow (Røvik 1996); this may result in a new standard becoming popular, and this in turn can eventually lead to the actors changing behaviour while still maintaining a high degree of uniformity: thus there is convergence around a new standard.

As an example of a possible combination of factors, let us apply a standard- and fashion-based explanation to fashion trends regarding clothing. There are standard setters (fashion houses and large producers of garments) with great authority, who create standards that are basically similar to those created by the other fashion houses each year. It is easy for them to spread their standards via shows of standard models and via pictures in mass media. Many find these standards relevant—everybody needs clothes and many want to dress fashionably. Or, whatever people think, there is a third party, the retailers, who follow the standards by buying only fashionable clothes, thus limiting the supply to consumers to such garments. All of this serves to create spatial uniformity—people dress in similar clothes.

But there are also factors that work for change, with the result that, although people continue to dress similarly, a few years later they are all wearing a new style. The fashion houses have a vested interest in creating new models and, in the long term, new fashion houses become authoritative. People find it easy to accept new fashions, since they can afford to buy new clothes and are not compelled by a strong need or strong, stable preferences to have their clothes always follow a certain style (for instance because, within reasonable limits, they do not need to consider the practicality of their clothing). Furthermore, there are those who actively demand new creations since they do not want to wear what everyone else is wearing. All in all, fashion among standards then gives rise to strong fashion trends.

Fashion trends for clothes can be expected to be weaker when there are no fashions: for instance, when there is no central fashion authority or where such an authority is weak: the USA and France are perhaps different in this respect; or when actors have definite and stable preferences for specific solutions, as they may have for work clothes. Fashion trends for clothes can also be expected to be weaker when there is not much striving for originality, for example in such collective cultures as China, which then will contain much uniformity over space but little variation over time.

But this is only one explanation of fashion trends. In other contexts—and indeed for clothing styles—there can be several and other factors which explain the fashion trends. The causes in fashion trends in clothes and in child care may be partially different. Both for clothes and for other fashion trends, there may be different elements of innovation, imitation, and fashion following involved, and standards may be more or less important. Different fashion trends require different explanations. So it may not be very useful to try to formulate a theory for fashion trends that is generally applicable and at the same time much more detailed than the type of descriptions of possible causes and mechanisms that we have given here. Instead it might be more useful to construct explanatory models for various, more specific fashion trend situations.

The focus in all such explanations of fashion trends is on explaining the uniformity in space, and the variation over time. But it is rare that uniformity and variation are total phenomena; it is more usual that many, but not all, follow fashion trends. This also needs to be explained: explanatory models for fashion trends should be able to cover uniformity *and* diversity, spatial similarity *and* spatial variation. And models for fashion trends should be such that they may be used for explaining both change and stability—the fact that we sometimes experience rapid fashion trends and that sometimes actors exhibit stable similarities.

Instead of contributing further generalizations, the rest of the chapter presents an example of a possible more detailed, standard-based explanatory model which has as its aim to explain a specific type of fashion trend pertaining to certain standardizers, standards, and adopters. The model pertains to fashion trends in organizational forms. Fashion is only one of several explanatory factors in the model.

Fashion trends in organizational forms

One area where strong fashion trends occur is in the forms adopted by organizations (Abrahamson 1996a). Organizational forms are formal structures, processes, and ideologies, presented as characteristics of a certain organization. These forms may include, in relation to structures, a matrix organization or a purchaser-provider organization; in relation to processes, zero base budgeting, or management by objectives; and in relation to ideologies, customer service or customer orientation. Many organizations have similar organizational forms, and these have a tendency to change rather quickly.

Fashion trends in organizational forms can perhaps sometimes be explained by innovation processes. Organizations can, for example, choose similar forms because they work with similar things in similar environments, and these change over time. This is, however, contradicted by the fact that organizations in varying fields, and with varying tasks and operations, often exhibit great similarities in form (Meyer and Rowan 1977). Companies in different countries and industries frequently exhibit similar forms, and companies and public sector bodies tend to be increasingly similar.

Fashion trends in organizational forms may also occur by imitation, through the many attempting to imitate the few, changeable others. But this explanation is not very useful in the commonly observed case, when new forms seem to appear at about the same time in many organizations—there does not appear to have been time for imitation.

Fashion trends in forms may also be the result of the fact that organizations have to comply with the same or similar directives. This is sometimes the case. Some organizational forms, such as those of the joint stock company, are legally specified. And legislation is, after all, the same for organizations of a certain type in any given country, and legislation is also being harmonized internationally. When the laws change this can give rise to fashion trends. Similarly, common norms regarding organizational forms and concurrent norm modifications may give rise to fashion trends.

Standardization and fashion in standards may also be important causes of fashion trends in organizational forms. As described in earlier chapters there are many administrative standards for organizational forms and many standardizers in this field, who are able to disseminate their message effectively. Many organizations comply with the same standard at any given time, and the popular standard can be quite rapidly succeeded by another equally popular standard. Certain standards achieve great popularity, at least when they are new. New standards receive attention in, for example, the business press. Organizations are often willing to comply with new standards partly because no one knows for certain what the best form is. Many organizations are active in competitive environments, where it is important to be best, and where a new form can appear to offer a competitive advantage compared to other forms. We may assume that standards and fashion among standards is an important, if not the most important, factor behind fashion trends in organizational forms.

Complex fashion trends

As we have pointed out above, there are strong tendencies toward fashion trends in organizational forms: similarities in space without a parallel correspondence of similarity in time. A form that is common during one period is replaced by an equally common but different form during another period. But the pattern can be more complicated than that. At any given time one or a few standards for organizational form are fashionable. The result should be a high degree of similarity among organizations. This may be the case, but it may be less so than one would expect. A survey of popular standards for organizational forms in Swedish municipalities showed that standards, which were or had been the height of fashion in the media and at conferences, were actually only adopted by anywhere from as little as 6 per cent up to 70 per cent of the municipalities studied (Johansson and Johnsson 1995).

It appears, therefore, that standards with almost unanimous support in public opinion do not necessarily lead to a corresponding degree of uniformity. Organizational forms may still be rather different, even if the organizations are of the same type and nationality and belong to the same organizational field. There is often a combination of uniformity and diversity within a field: even if many organizations comply with a fashionable standard, everyone does not. The existence of one dominant standard does not explain all the different organizational forms. We need to explain both the uniformity and the diversity that occur.

In practice the adoption processes and adoption patterns of an organizational form can be quite complex. One example is the development that has occurred in Swedish municipalities in the past few decades. In the public debate, new standards regarding organizational forms have appeared every few years (Johansson and Johnsson 1994). Most of these standards surfaced at the same time in other countries, both as standards in the public debate and as forms in municipalities and state agencies (Hood 1991; Reichard 1995). The leadership in the different municipalities were very familiar with the public debate (Fernler 1996), and it can be assumed that they had all heard about the new standards at approximately the same time. A new form was implemented in many municipalities in a short period of time, when the form was fashionable in the public debate (Johansson and Johnsson 1994); this means that most of the organizations had no one to imitate when they implemented the new form.

However, as mentioned above, the said forms were implemented in only some of the municipalities, and often only a minority of them. It was also difficult to find any common characteristic between the municipalities that adopted a certain form, for example, characteristics such as size or political majority. Nor could one find a strong connection between the forms an individual municipality accepted: the same organization could reject a standard at one time, only to accept a similar standard at a later time (ibid.). Certain forms even appear to have been invented in several municipalities at approximately the same time (Fernler 1996).

In order to explain such processes, we need an explanatory model that can explain uniformity and rapid change: the fact that a new standard can be adopted very quickly and at the same time by many organizations. It should also be possible to use the model for explaining diversity: the fact that many organizations do not comply with the standard. The model should not be based on the assumption that organizations that become similar in form have had the contacts and time necessary to imitate each other. Explanations should not be based on the assumption that organizations have certain stable characteristics that make them more prone to follow certain standards than others. The model must allow for the fact that similar forms can appear through innovation and not necessarily as products of standard compliance. All in all the model should explain something that we would call 'cropping up', that is to say, the scattered and seemingly random appearance of similar forms in many but far from all organizations at the same time. In the next section we describe one version of such a cropping-up model.

A cropping-up model of organizational forms

The model outlined below is based on many of the factors and arguments presented earlier in this book, particularly in earlier chapters in Part III. The model contains three basic components: organizational forms, reforms, and discourse. The model contains specific assumptions on the nature and dynamics of these components. It is based on the assumption that, fundamentally, organizational forms are not things or practices; rather, they are presentations, which must follow the rules regarding the way we can talk about organizations. The reform processes whereby these forms are introduced require even closer adaptation to these rules. They also require attempts to implement the talk in practice—attempts that are often time-consuming and frustrating. The common component that makes uniformity possible is assumed to be a broad societal discourse on organizations and on standards for organizations.

Standards in vogue—what is popularly talked about—may not be very common as organizational forms, and vice versa. A certain standard may even at a certain time be considered the only way to go; yet not very many organizations—in the extreme case none—may have implemented the standard. The model describes the mechanisms whereby fashionable standards are, or are not, translated into local forms, and the resulting relation between fashion and fashion trends in organizational forms.

Organizational forms

Organizational forms are part of the way organizations are presented to the external world or to their own members by authorized people such as managers. Organizational structures are often displayed in organization charts, while procedures and ideologies appear in various policy documents. These written sources are normally confirmed by oral presentations by management and by labels denoting entities, practices, or ideas. The forms are presented as descriptions of the way the organization actually works, or the way it will be working in the near future. The forms also tend to be highly rationalized, being typically presented as means to legitimate ends or as solutions to important problems. Or at least rationalizations are readily available upon request (Meyer and Rowan 1977).

Organizational forms are ways of talking about an organization. Just as there are rules for action that restrict our freedom to act, so there are rules for talk that restrict the way we can talk, at least if we are to be believed or taken seriously (N. Brunsson 1995). In open societies most of these rules consist of norms and standards rather than directives. In the model it is assumed that this is true of talk about organizations, and thus of organizational forms. Organizations cannot then be presented just anyhow: the presentation must be adapted to ideas about what an organization can and should be. The forms must be such that they can be regarded as possible organizational forms; they should be adapted to what people consider good or at least acceptable. In addition, they should be understandable: excessively complex or ambiguous forms are not likely to be understood.

On the other hand, organizational forms often do not have to be as well adapted to the practice of the individual organization. As mentioned in the preceding chapter, presentation and practice may be quite different; there is some, although seldom unlimited, room for hypocrisy.

Reforms

The processes whereby new forms are launched are referred to below as reforms. Reforms as defined here consist of two basic activities: attempts at convincing people that the new forms should be installed and attempts at getting them to influence practice, getting them implemented. Studies of many such reforms, in a variety of organizations (Brunsson and Olsen 1997), revealed a certain pattern, which is used here in formulating some assumptions about the reform component of the model.

The extent and intensity of talk differed as between existing forms and new ones. Reforms required much more mobilization and talk than existing forms. Typically reforms produced much elaborate talk about the forms to be, and a good deal of rationalizing argument. Reform contents were well adapted to general, aesthetic norms of talk, such as those referring to logic, consistency, and clarity. Reform contents were also adapted to what was generally considered to be a good organization. Reforms promised major improvements in the way the organization functioned. This made it easy to make people in organizations interested in implementing reforms and reforms were common.

At the outset, reforms were described as a set of simple, general, and seemingly very sensible—not to say beautiful—principles, consistent not only with popular standards but also with common and more stable basic norms for organizations; for instance, organizations were to become more goal oriented, everybody's tasks should be clearer and should not overlap with the tasks of others, everyone's freedom to act efficiently should be increased, better planning and evaluation processes should be installed, and so on. The principles contained standards that were popular and not controversial at the time of their introduction, such as decentralization or management by objectives. The situation before the implementation of the reform was described in a less favourable way: it was said to be complicated, tasks were unclear, there were inefficiencies, and lack of local freedom, and so on.

In sum, it seemed that reforms not only produced more talk than existing forms, but also followed norms and standards for talk about organizations more closely. This can be explained by the fact that reforms are future oriented and intentional. The way we can talk about existing forms may be limited to some extent not only by the rules for talk, but also by practice. It may be necessary to adapt talk somewhat to what people actually do, in particular if the talk is directed at the doers themselves. The contents of reforms, on the other hand, can be more easily adapted to the rules geared exclusively for talk, since they are not meant to reflect current practices. Reforms include descriptions of practice: their implementation and their effect on practice is the main argument in their favour. But this practice is still in the future, and can thus easily be presented as consistent with the new forms. But reforms not only *can* but *must* be well adapted to rules for talk about organizations. Reforms contain intentions; the forms presented are those we intend, and they are to lead to the effects we intend. The rules regarding the intentions that we can present are generally stricter than those applying to our presentations; for instance, we may admit to bad results but we are less likely to say that we intended them. This is true of reforms as well: we may present current organizational forms as less than perfect, but it is more difficult not to intend to be as near to perfect as possible. It is particularly difficult to entertain and present intentions that are not consistent with such common norms. Nor are intentions contrary to legitimate directives acceptable. But it is also difficult to present, argue for, and gain acceptance for intentions that are contrary to popular standards in the discourse.

It is not being claimed that all empirical reforms are like those described here, but the model includes this type of reform. It will be assumed that organizations are attracted by such reforms. Since these reforms can be much more 'beautiful' than possible presentations of today's practice, most reform proposals will prevail over the defence of most old forms. But it is still assumed that there is one major obstacle to reforms, namely previous reforms.

Reforms are supposed to be implemented, that is, the principles of the reform should be turned into detailed instructions and should affect organizational behaviour, and even results; and this takes time. It is hard to argue for a new reform until the previous one has been given a serious try, particularly if the reforms concern the same activities.

However, this obstacle is only temporary. When the new forms become existing forms, they have to be adapted somewhat to current practices, and they are therefore likely to become less attractive: a new form will easily appear more attractive and will outcompete the existing form. And a new reform does not necessarily have to wait for the full implementation—or, even less, for the results—of the old reform; the old reform can become relatively unattractive at a much earlier stage. This is because implementation is assumed to be an important threat to reforms. When the beautiful principles are turned into more detailed rules and instructions and are adapted to the special practical conditions of the specific organization, the new forms soon become less beautiful and more like the old ones, thus losing much of their attraction. Their promises do not seem to be being fulfilled.

The new forms may also become more controversial. Further, principles adapted to rules for talk are not necessarily feasible or favourable in practice. This may become obvious long before the reform is regarded as fully implemented—or, even more, before it has given rise to any intended effects on daily practice. So, after a serious attempt at implementation, the reform may fall into disrepute and may well be interrupted by a new reform (Brunsson and Olsen 1997, ch. 3).

When reform processes look as described here, and when there is no lack of new reform ideas, a specific pattern of reform can be established. A reform starts when the previous reform has been in the process of implementation long enough, and it ends when its own implementation has been under way for a while. The organization is almost continuously in the throes of some stage of a reform, but reforms can only be launched at intervals.

The assumption of implementation as a threat to reform and the resulting pattern of reform also reflected the empirical situation in the reforms studied. Reforms easily prevailed over older forms, often over those still being implemented. A common way of ending a reform was to start a new one. In some large organizations reforms were a standard recurring activity. Major reforms occurred often, but not constantly—generally at intervals of a few years. A study of the 125-year history of one large organization showed that major reorganizations took place at intervals of 3–15 years, and that the intervals between them had been shrinking in more recent years (Brunsson *et al.* 1989).

Although it is assumed that reforms easily win over existing forms, a specific reform proposal may meet competition from other reform proposals which also contain attractive principles. It is assumed that such competition will be won by reforms which fit better at a more detailed level with the norms and standards for talk about intended forms, and for which more favourable and less critical arguments are available. Such norms, standards, and arguments are largely produced and reproduced in an arena other than the individual organization, namely in a general public discourse.

Organizational discourse

As demonstrated in this book, it is not only people in individual organizations who talk about the present and future forms in their own case; there are also a great number of standardizers who tell others what organizational forms they should introduce. Standards and other ideas are presented in what can be called a general discourse. Although the discourse varies somewhat from one organizational field or country to another, much of it is very general and treats large groups of organizations as though they were in need of the same standard forms (see Chapters 5 and 8). The discourse is to a large extent international, that is, national borders are not thought to be important and much of the discussion takes place across such borders. Organizational problems and solutions are both discussed.

Although the standards discussed are likely to be based on some common basic conceptions of and norms for organizations (see Chapter 5), they differ in terms of their more detailed aspects. For example, all the standards discussed may be based on the assumption that organizations should be controlled from the top, but they may still differ greatly about the form that is best for bringing this about.

In this discourse only a limited set of standards can be attended to at one time. The standards attended to can be variously controversial, and the level of controversy may change over time. At one time standards may represent temporary common social norms in that almost everyone agrees that they represent the only right ideas. On other occasions the same standard may be challenged and doubted by many, have come into widespread disrepute, or even be considered by many to be a fashion only.

Standards can also differ in their level of abstraction. Very specific organizational forms are sometimes suggested as the 'right' ones. Zero-based budgeting might be an example of this. In other instances the suggested forms are of a more principled and abstract character, more in the nature of slogans than recipes. 'Back to basics', concentrating on the 'core' business, and decentralization are cases in point. At an even higher level of abstraction the discourse may concern problems but no specific solutions: there may be a large measure of agreement in identifying the important and urgent problems, without any very specific suggestion being made about specific standard forms that could perhaps provide a solution. As mentioned above, the attention paid to problems varies just as much as the attention paid to solutions: there are fashions in both. In the 1970s the lack of internal democracy in organizations was a fashionable problem; later, inadequate customer orientation and cost efficiency were among the problems in vogue.

Knowledge of this general discourse is not 'outside' the organizations; people working on the managing and reforming of organizations are aware of the discourse and may even take part in it. In the cropping-up model it is not assumed that knowledge about problems and standards and the discourse in general is a scarce resource. Rather, it is assumed that people interested in organizational issues will hear very quickly about any new standards, regardless of where these originated: they will all be reported widely in the media and interested people follow the media.

This kind of discourse is thus added to our model. We assume that a set of organizations is connected to a common discourse. The discourse provides standards regarding what are acceptable or good organizational forms, arguments in favour of the standards, and problems that require solutions.

The standardizers participating in the discourse have a certain authority that can be referred to when people want to argue for reform in their own organization. The standards in the discourse help to explain which reforms are chosen by individual organizations: they may serve as an important inspiration for reformers who are designing a new reform, and they can determine which of several reform proposals is accepted by an organization.

It is assumed that the discourse evolves continually. New standards are attended to, others become uninteresting and disappear from the agenda. A basic mechanism behind changes in attention may be a focus on novelty: when no further descriptions and arguments can be added to the discourse, there is not much left to discuss and attention can be directed towards a new standard, which has not yet been described in such detail and for which there still are new arguments.

Some standards move from commanding general agreement to becoming highly controversial, others move in the opposite direction or retain a fairly stable element of controversy. Finally, some standards even become generally regarded as bad. The discourse can move towards greater specification: that is, abstract principles are given a more detailed, concrete content; problems are given solutions, or concrete cases are quoted in which principles are said to have been transformed into practice. Or the discourse may move towards more conflict, as counter-arguments are proposed. These two tendencies may be interrelated as they are in the reform processes in individual organizations described above, so that more specification produces more controversy. Specification and controversy may be replaced by new abstract ideas or by compromise, and perhaps by abstraction again.

Model dynamics

The cropping-up model is thus based on specific assumptions about organizational forms, local reforms, and a general discourse. Organizational forms are ways of talking about organizations. Reforms, the presentation of new forms and attempts at implementing them, have to be adapted to the rules for talking about organizations, and particularly to talking about organizational intentions. Some of these rules are provided by a general and continually evolving discourse about organizational forms, containing standards for such forms. Since the reforms are adapted to rules for talk and intentions they are attractive and are difficult to stop. Reforms are easily started. But due to this very connection with talk and discourse, reforms are apt to lead to disappointment when it comes to implementation: what is considered good talk does not necessarily correspond to good or even possible local practice. Moreover, what is good generally may not be good for the individual organization. The result of all this is that standards after a while tend to come into disrepute and new reforms containing new standards are initiated. We get recurring reforms in a continually evolving discourse.

There is thus a certain dynamic. At any one moment we have a set of organizations ripe for reform, namely, organizations which have gone so far in implementing previously popular forms as to create frustration and an interest in new forms. At every such moment all these organizations are exposed to the same discourse, with its specific set of more or less controversial and more or less specific standards.

From the discourse it is possible to gather ideas about standard forms currently attracting attention there, and to find arguments and support for them. Reform proposals implying fairly uncontroversial forms will have the advantage over reform proposals along other lines. The level of attention and of controversy affects not only the organizations' choice of forms, but also to some extent the area—organizational structure, perhaps, or budget procedure—in which they reform, since not all areas are necessarily being attended to or sparking uncontroversial ideas at every point in time. Since the discourse is continually evolving—creating new standards, new controversies, and new specifications—the set of organizations which go in for reform during the next period will not introduce the same set of forms. So what forms a specific organization tries to implement depends on when its reform begins. And when a reform begins depends on how far the previous reform has come.

Processes such as these could explain both uniformity and diversity between organizations. The explanation refers to no attributes of the individual organization apart from the timing of its reform cycles. Organizational reforms are similar in organizations reforming at the same time, and different in organizations reformed at different times.

If the implementation process differs somewhat in length in different organizations, perhaps due to some random external variables, organizations which have embarked on a certain reform simultaneously will not be ripe for a new reform at quite the same time. It is then slightly less likely that these organizations will choose the same reform as the others in the second round. This makes for variation over time as regards the organizations which any specific organization is likely to resemble. In other words it impedes any order among organizations on a cohort basis, and confirms a picture of great variability and randomness.

The model explains how popular standards in the general discourse are translated into local organizational forms. It also demonstrates why fashion does not always produce much uniformity; why fashionable standards are not necessarily reflected in the forms of very many organizations: the standards are adopted only by organizations which happen to be ripe for reform during the period when these standards are popular.

Processes producing uniformity

The processes whereby ideas are translated from the general discourse to local organizational forms should also be specified. The process we have described so far is one of following standards. But another possible process involves innovation, whereby a form is constructed locally. As mentioned above, sometimes there are ideas in the discourse which are much attended to and uncontroversial, but which also are fairly abstract and do not define any particular forms: they consist of slogans or problems rather than very specific standards. Then the individual organization has to invent its own forms. But even if the ideas are abstract, they may be specific enough to make most reformers in most organizations come to very similar conclusions regarding what form to introduce. The forms are invented locally, but are still very similar. There is a parallel here with certain inventions and discoveries in science: oxygen, for example, was discovered by at least two scientists simultaneously (Kuhn 1962). Similarities arising from innovation are particularly likely when there is a strong consensus about what problems are important, but no agreement on specific solutions.

Strictly speaking, local inventions of organizational forms are not examples of standard adoption, but they they may give rise to standards. Organization members may well see their own invented form as something unique at first, only to learn later that it is in fact quite common. In this case they may perceive themselves as the first to introduce it, and perhaps develop a theory about how they have influenced other organizations. The forms are presented as standards in the discourse. These standards have evolved from below, from the group of adopters rather than from professional standardizers.

The purchaser-provider standard that was popular in Swedish local governments in the middle of the 1990s seems to have evolved in this way. Early, many agreed that an important problem was that the politicians tended to represent the employees in the public sector rather than their constituencies. This problem made several local governments and consultants invent and implement the purchaser-provider form (Fernler 1996), and this form then became a fashionable standard stimulating even more local governments to introduce the form.

Dissemination of forms

Given the processes described above, the number of organizations using a particular form will depend mainly on the length of time during which the corresponding general idea, standard, or problem is comparatively important and uncontroversial in the discourse. The longer a standard or problem is considered to be the right one in the discourse or the greater the frequency of its being so considered, the greater will be the number of organizations which will have embarked upon a reform period during this particular discourse, and the greater the number which will have adopted the standard form or invented similar forms. In this way (length of) time translates into (width of) space.

The compass of a particular form also depends on whether or not competing standards or problems appear. If new standards do compete, the old ones are likely to be questioned and ultimately likely to be erased. For instance, an old principle for structuring the whole organization cannot normally be retained when a new such principle is installed. It is hard to be basically centralized *and* basically decentralized. When the competitive aspect is weaker, an old standard can be retained together with new ones, so long as it does not fall into disrepute for other reasons.

A form becomes very common if the standard recommending this form is attractive and remains uncontroversial for a long time, and if competitive standards do not appear for a considerable time after the standard giving rise to the reform has faded away in the discourse. Budgeting can provide a relevant example here. As mentioned in Chapter 1, it became popular for use in the private sector in the middle of the twentieth century, and generated a great deal of literature over a long period. Many companies started using budgets. Even if this technique did not quite deliver what it promised, disappointed users did not meet competing standards but rather standards that were possible to combine with continued budgeting. Thus most organizations still present budgets, although budgeting is no longer receiving much attention in the discourse. Budgeting has even become highly institutionalized and almost a constitutive norm of modern organizations; having formed the basis for special departments or other structures in many organizations, budgeting is now taken for granted and could not be easily questioned in the discourse—or such questioning would not affect organizations very much (Wallander 1994). Similarly, organizations may maintain that they hold 'development talks' with their employees long after everybody except a few specialists have ceased to refer to the technique as important. In this way standards which may once have appeared quite suddenly can give rise to stable norms and sedimental forms, continuing to exist although they are no longer paid much attention (Danielsson 1983).

Cropping up explained

The cropping-up model is not intended for use in explaining all uniformity or diversity in organizational forms, nor for explaining all fashion trends. But it can provide a possible or partial explanation of the more or less simultaneous appearance of similar forms among many, although far from all, organizations which do not necessarily have any contact with each other. And when we use this model for explaining uniformity and diversity, we do not need to know any specific characteristics of any individual organizations apart from their position in the reform cycle. Further, the model can explain situations when the reform processes involve the adoption of standards as well as when they involve innovation.

Interaction between reforms and standards

In the cropping-up model it is assumed that the general discourse affects local reforms. But in reality influence may also work in the opposite direction. Local reforms may influence organizational discourse; experience of local reforms may be generally discussed. Local organizations may in fact reinforce the popularity of certain forms, by reporting their own reforms and proclaiming their success. Organizations which are or have been under reform become standardizers.

But local reforms in line with fashionable standards may also introduce controversy about a particular standard, or even engender agreement on its negative aspects. The standard may then become unfashionable, leaving room for new standards. As in the individual organizations, attempts at implementing reform may make general principles seem less attractive. There may be several reasons for this.

First, reforms can lead the discourse and its standards towards a higher level of specification. As has been noted, local reform generally calls for a more specified version of a general standard, or a general problem must be met by a specific standard. The specifications may vary from one organization to another; if these different specifications appear in the general discourse, there will be a higher risk of controversy than before. Different people may advocate different specifications, which can reduce confidence in any specifications. But this process depends on the way the specifications are reported back in the general discourse. The more general the terms in which they are described, the less impact they have on the discourse. If the discourse is dominated by top managers or their assistants, who

possess little detailed information, or by consultants or researchers skilled in gener-
alization, then the reports are likely to be highly general and controversy is less
likely than if the discourse is joined by people who possess more detailed information and who are less prone to generalize.

Secondly, information about local attempts at implementing reform can be
expected to produce a more mixed discourse on implementation and results.
Without empirical evidence, agreement on any particular standard is based on the
beauty of its principles, the expectation of its relatively easy implementation, and
its positive results. If empirical observations are included in the discussions, there is
a greater risk that information about difficulties and negative results will emerge,
thus producing a less favourable picture which may then increase controversy and
produce many arguments against that particular standard. Difficulties in implementation can be expected to be more threatening than negative results. Assessments of
results tend to be more ambiguous, and hence less obviously negative. On the other
hand in periods of general decline and difficulty, ambiguity about the results of
reform may turn reforms into scapegoats, thereby producing agreement on how
'bad' are the standards on which they are based, thus making room for new ideas.

Thirdly, reforms in the same direction in a large number of organizations may
change perceptions of the standard in question among organizational actors and in
the discourse. When the news spreads that this standard is being implemented in
many organizations of different kinds, the innovation process is no longer possible,
and the ways in which the standard can be introduced become limited. What is
more, the standard may now come to be perceived in some cases as a 'fashion'
rather than a rational solution; its adoption may be criticized as an instance of imitation and passive following of fashion, which is difficult to combine with the normal conception of the organization and its management as rational problem-solvers
(Abrahamson 1996b). It is also difficult to combine following fashions with the
basic idea that organizations should have strong identities of their own, with particular or even unique characteristics and tasks. Seeing a standard as a fashion may
involve negative arguments in the discourse, making it more difficult to implement
that standard locally.

These mechanisms do not always work: in some cases the high frequency of an
organizational form has the opposite effect of reinforcing agreement that it is a good
one. On the other hand, it is not likely that attention will be paid to such a form
in the discourse for much longer.

Fourthly, the discourse may be affected by an active local demand for new forms.
After some time there will be a number of organizations which have failed in the
implementation of a specific reform, or which have recognized the absence of
results and which therefore enter upon a phase of new reform. Previous reforms
have made organizations immune to the standard in question. It will be difficult for
the reformers to produce the same reform again, so they will look for another standard in order to be able to launch a new reform.

In most of these cases local reforms help to create new standards. This in turn
provides a basis for new reforms, which in turn tends to change the discourse again,

and so on. If the factors described above are all strong, the system as a whole becomes very dynamic and highly diversified: the discourse changes at a great rate and individual forms are therefore adopted by few organizations only. The fashions give rise to diversity rather than uniformity.

The range of applicability

The cropping-up model is only one of several possible models, which can be used to describe and explain fashion trends of the 'cropping-up' type. It appears useful when it comes to explaining uniformity and diversity in organizational forms. But it may also be a good explanatory model in other contexts. For instance, there are probably cropping-up processes also among individuals. But if the model is to be applicable, its basic premises must be valid as well.

First, the model presupposes a mechanism for variation over time in regard to popular standards. The cause behind such shifts in fashion can vary, but the important thing is that they are there. Secondly, it must be easy for the adopters to assimilate the new standards. This may, for example, be because many standards have positive effects or, as is the case with organizational forms, because the effects are uncertain and the adopters are easy to convince. It may also be because the adopters value compliance with fashion. Thirdly, the adopters must be open to the standards only at predetermined time intervals. The time intervals must be longer than the intervals between fashions.

These prerequisites can be applicable in many circumstances. In others, they are not. Sometimes the first premise about fashion does not apply: democracy has, for example, for a long time dominated as a standard for government, in the same way that the standard for screw threads has been the same for a long time. Sometimes the second premise is not applicable: the principle of the assembly line in manufacturing may possibly be said to have enjoyed varying degrees of popularity at different times, but there are certain operations that are better suited to assembly line processes than others. This has created a fairly constant difference between, for example, car manufacturing and many service industries. The third premise regarding inertia in acceptance is not applicable to clothes fashions in the West, and, therefore, these fashions tend to create variation over time rather than variation in space. The cropping-up model may apply to clothes fashions in fashion-conscious countries in the Third World, however: if people are poor they cannot buy clothes very often and will wear the clothes that were in fashion at the time they could afford them. The result will be a diversity in space, that is, a much more varied street scene than in fashion-conscious rich countries. A similar diversity between very modern and very antiquated techniques can be seen in many Third World countries in the agricultural and industrial sectors.

There are different combinations of uniformity and diversity, and the processes leading there can look quite different.

12

The Pros and Cons of Standardization— An Epilogue

NILS BRUNSSON AND BENGT JACOBSSON

Standards are attractive. And, as we have seen in the previous chapters, there is no lack of standardizers in the world. There are plenty of people who know what is best for everyone else, often claiming their own experthood. A lot of standardization goes on, but how should it be evaluated? Is standardization useful or even essential, or is it harmful and unnecessary? Will all this standardization lead to too much conformity, or is it a way to achieve co-ordination in situations where other rules are less likely to work? Let us first look at what standardizers say themselves.

Why standards?

Standards and standardization tend to be justified on much the same grounds as rules and regulation in general. One argument is that, just like other rules, standards represent an effective way of transmitting information. If we know that someone is complying with a standard with which we ourselves are familiar, this provides us with a good deal of information, obviating the need to ask questions in every individual case. Alternatively, we may not know very much about the content of a standard, but simply assume that it is desirable. The amount of information we need is then even less than in the first case. If we know that a ship has been classified as conforming to certain safety standards, we are perfectly happy to sail on it, often without knowing anything about the exact content of the standards concerned. If we know that a company is certified according to the ISO standard 14001 for environmental management systems, we are supposed to know that its production is as environmentally sound as possible. If the information-conveying role of a standard is to be fulfilled, it is often necessary that a third party should certify that the standard is being followed. We even tend to have more faith in the certifier than in the certified—more in the ship-classifying organization than in the shipowner.

Another argument in favour of using standards is that they have an important co-ordinating function. Standards are often created with a view to making certain products mutually compatible, so that a plug will fit into a socket, for example. The actions of different actors can also be co-ordinated: if we know that another person is complying with a particular standard, it is easier for us to adjust our actions accordingly. Again this can reduce the amount of information needed. Knowing that the standard exists, and that the other party accepts it, is sufficient: there is no need for the two sides to discuss the details of their actions or products with each other. Often, in fact, we will simply have expected that the other person is going to comply with the standard, which allows us to adjust our action to those of the other party beforehand. Again we recognize the advantages of rules in general.

Standards also result in simplification. They reduce the number of possibilities we have to consider. This can make it easier to get information and to co-ordinate actions. It can also be of value in itself: a chaotic world becomes more ordered, making it easier to orientate ourselves and to understand 'how things are'. This is indicated in official definitions of standards as aiming at the achievement of the 'optimum degree of order' (see Chapter 1).

Standards are also often drawn up on the grounds that they provide the best solution to a problem (or at least a very good solution), perhaps by indicating the form of organization that is most effective or most democratic, or the telephone technology that is best. The implication is that there is no reason not to adhere to the standard, since it is the best to be had. A great many standardizers rely almost exclusively on such arguments, not least all the INGOs that want to improve the world, or the management experts who know 'best' how to improve organizations. The 'best possible solution' argument is also used with the other arguments mentioned above. For instance, there may be several standards that would promote co-ordination, but why not choose the one that provides the best solution?

The argument that standards have a strong tendency to make everyone alike is one that standardizers rarely use. Instead, they tend to emphasize that using standards can actually favour variation. In the computer industry, for instance, it is argued that agreement on certain standards makes it easier to direct efforts at finding new and innovative solutions to problems for which no standards as yet exist. In the same vein many management books offer standards for ways in which companies should improve their competitiveness—standards that are obviously intended to increase variation, although this may be difficult to achieve if many companies all decide to follow the standards.

Another argument, rather similar to the one about standardization producing similarity, is that standardization brings advantages in the shape of large-scale production. This was an argument that flourished in the early days of product standardization, when it was claimed that the production of identical goods was a prerequisite of industrialization. Using standardized sizes for clothing, for example, makes things much easier for the clothing industry, just as the adoption of standard dimensions for bolts is of great benefit to the engineering industry.

All of these arguments—about the more effective use of information, better co-ordination of activities, simplification, and the advantages of large-scale production—can be used to show that a certain amount of international standardization is good for international trade and thus for the achievement of prosperity generally. This is certainly one of the main reasons why standardization issues enjoy such high priority in the European Union.

As we discussed at the beginning of this book, standards may be especially attractive since they offer some order in a potentially chaotic world. Standards are often regarded as highly legitimate rules, even if they are produced by experts who are somewhat divorced from any democratic procedures. Standards and standardization make it possible to achieve co-ordination without a legal centre of authority (that is, a nation-state or a world state). Such tendencies could be seen in the EU, with its increasing use of product standards and 'soft law' as a means to further integration. Standardization is considered an attractive way of bringing about necessary regulation, avoiding both market solutions and the intervention of states.

Arguments against standards and standardization

If people are to believe what the standardizers say, they must be convinced that standards do have all sorts of positive effects. All the same, these effects can be— and indeed have been—questioned on several counts. One might wonder whether the goals ascribed to standardization are desirable, whether standardization does lead to the realization of these goals, and whether there might not be better ways of achieving the goals than by standardization.

Many of the objections to standards and standardization are similar to the objections to rules and regulation in general. Standardization is often seen as an unwelcome, unnecessary, and harmful intrusion into a world of free, distinct individuals and organizations who are wise enough to decide for themselves, or into the world of civil society or free markets. Standardization, it is felt, will mean regulation from outside, whereby actors, things, and conditions are now to be shaped in a uniform manner.

Becoming more alike is often seen as something undesirable, with many present-day actors—organizations or individuals—preferring to be different from one another rather than alike. As described in other chapters, a high degree of similarity produced by standards runs up against theories and conceptions that such actors have about their autonomy and their distinctiveness: states feel they should be steered democratically by their own people, companies that they should be steered by innovation, and individuals that they should be driven by their striving for self-realization—and all of them thus feeling that they should be different.

Standards are also criticized for going too far in stabilizing the world. If everyone does the same thing, what room is there for innovation? If all companies or states are organized in the same way, how can they learn better ways from each other? If all the technical details of a telephone are standardized except for the outer form, will we have anything to expect apart from endless variations in superficial details—telephones looking like bananas, teddy bears, Mickey Mouse, or whatever—without any fundamental innovations in their technical functioning, their quality, or their effectiveness?

Also, can we trust the expertise and goodwill of those who set the rules? How can we know that the standardizers know best what is right for us? If large international corporations play a leading role in standardization, how can we know that their solutions are best for their consumers or employees, rather than simply for the managers or technicians involved or for the company's shareholders? Similarly, in the case of standardizers who develop standards to be used exclusively by others, how can we determine that their standards are really good for us? If the know-alls in the business field who tell others how large corporations should be managed, were as good as they imply they are, why aren't they doing it themselves?

It is easy to find examples of standardization leading to poor solutions, particularly in the case of product standardization. In terms of safety, for instance, traffic lights based on the red-green colour combination are not a particularly good choice, since these two colours are specially difficult for the colour-blind to distinguish. Or again, a standard height of 440 mm. above ground level for car bumpers may be good for cars, but it is less desirable for human beings since this is the average height above the ground of people's kneecaps. The order of letters on a keyboard, qwerty, which became standard for keyboards is yet another example. The order was originally devised to reduce typing speeds, which was an important consideration at the time in order to prevent the typebars from jamming (David 1986). Although the problem no longer exists, the standard is still with us. We fear that many standards as bad as this still lurk in other areas, although they may be more difficult to demonstrate.

Many critics of regulation and standardization prefer markets to standards. Why not let the market decide how products and services should be designed? Buyers can determine this through the purchases they choose to make. Sometimes, however, it may be the critics of regulation who support standardization, seeing it as a promise of greater freedom and less uniformity in areas that have previously been heavily controlled by directives. If the choice is between national law and standards, or between binding international agreements and standards, many critics of regulation can be expected to prefer standards.

But standardization can also be criticized from the opposite angle, as representing too weak a form of regulation, for its weak links with formal organization, and for its inferiority compared with directives. Critics who take this approach may call for more formal organization. They regard standardization as being too important to world development to be relegated to a bunch of private organizations whose status is unclear and whose democratic roots are weak. Critics of this kind can be expected to call for a return to strong nation-states, perhaps some form of world state, or at least for more state intervention. They would argue that it is better to let a democratically elected body than a private organization determine our rules.

Standardization and the procrustean heritage

We have no answer to the question of whether we need more or less standardization. Whatever line one opts for, some convincing arguments are always available. Standardization deserves to be paid a good deal more attention than it has received up to now. As we noted in Chapter 3, standards are very much a reflection of a modern world that began to emerge as long ago as Descartes, a world informed with a strong belief in general, abstract, and timeless ideas, in experts and the knowledge possessed by experts. Going even further back in history, we may have something to learn from the old Greek myths.

In a way, standardizing is the art of constructing a procrustean bed. Procrustes was a legendary bandit in Greek mythology, a bandit who placed his victims on a specially constructed bed. The bed was a pattern and a yardstick intended to create conformity. Any captive who was not tall enough was stretched until he reached the right length, while those who were taller than the bed was long had their protruding limbs lopped off. Procrustes had a very clear idea of what other people should look like, and in that sense he was very like the 'modern bandits' whom we have called 'standardizers' in this book.

There are differences between modern standardizers and this legendary bandit. Modern standardizers are often active in a large—sometimes a global—market where they have to compete against other standardizers. The marauding that occurred in the Theseus myth, to which Procrustes belongs, was limited in regional terms. The standardization imposed in this Greek legend demanded that someone either sought out the bandit or just happened to pass by where he lay in wait, as Theseus did on his way to Athens. This is not the case today, when modern standardizers instead take active steps to disseminate their rules.

The procrustean bed was not made to measure for its own creator. The standard was meant to be imposed not on him but on others. This proved fatal to Procrustes in his meeting with Theseus, who impudently decided to test the standard on the bandit himself. Nor is it unusual for modern standardizers to exclude themselves from the rules that they produce and distribute to others.

In modern societies, procrustean beds are everywhere. Standardizers jostle with one another as they compete for supremacy. As we saw in the earlier chapters in this book, standardizers come in a variety of guises: as management gurus, consultants, academic researchers, organizations formed with the purpose of information exchange, standard-based organizations, or international governmental or nongovernmental organizations. All these individuals or organizations produce rules intended for others. The whole subject of standards—their production, distribution, and adoption—is of central importance in society today and should also be so in the social sciences.

Bibliography

ABBOTT, A., 1988, *The System of Professions. An Essay on the Division of Expert Labor.* Chicago: University of Chicago Press.

ABRAHAMSON, E., 1996a, Management Fashion. *Academy of Management Review*, Vol. 21, No. 1, pp. 254–285.

—— 1996b, 'Technical and Aesthetic Fashion', in Czarniawska, B., and Sevón, G. (eds.), *Translating Organizational Change.* Berlin: Walter de Gruyter.

AHRNE, G., 1994, *Social Organizations.* London: Sage.

AQS-O No. 20-77 (Förslag till ISO från DIN, 1977).

ARGYRIS, C., and SCHÖN, D., 1978, *Theory in Practice.* San Fransisco: Jossey-Bass.

ARISTOTLE (384–322 BC), 1985, *Nicomachean Ethics.* Indianapolis: Hackett.

BARLEY, S., and KUNDA, G., 1992, 'Design and Devotion: Surges of Rational and Normative Ideologies of Control in Managerial Discourse', *Administrative Science Quarterly*, Vol. 37, pp. 363–99.

BARNARD, C., 1938, *The Functions of the Executive.* Cambridge, MA: Harvard University Press.

BERGER, P., and LUCKMANN, T., 1966, *The Social Construction of Reality.* New York: Doubleday.

BODDEWYN, J. J., 1983, 'Advertising self-regulation: Organization Structures in Belgium, Canada, France, Sweden and the United Kingdom'. Working paper presented at the 6th EGOS Colloquium, 'Beyond Bureaucracy', Florence, 3–5 November.

BOSTON, J., MARTIN, J., PALLOT, J., and WALSH, P. (eds.), 1996, *Public Management: The New Zealand Model.* Auckland: Oxford University Press.

Brief notes—1 meeting, ISO/TC176 QA (Notes TC 176, Ottawa, 1980).

BRUNSSON, K., 1995, *Dubbla budskap. Hur riksdagen och regeringen presenterar sitt budgetarbete.* Stockholm: Stockholm University.

BRUNSSON, N., 1985, *The Irrational Organization: Irrationality as a Basis for Organizational Action and Change.* Chichester: John Wiley & Sons.

—— 1989, *The Organization of Hypocrisy—Talk, Decisions and Actions in Organizations.* Chichester: John Wiley & Sons.

—— 1995, 'Ideas and Action, Justification and Hypocrisy as Alternatives to Control', *Research in the Sociology of Organizations*, Vol. 13, pp. 211–35.

—— 1996, 'Institutionalized Beliefs and Practices. The Case of Markets and Organizations', *Score Working Paper 1996*: 6.

—— FORSSELL, A., and WINBERG, H., 1989, *Reform som tradition, Administrativa reformer i Statens Järnvägar.* Stockholm: EFI.

—— and JÖNSSON, S., 1978, *Beslut och handling. Om politikers inflytande på politiken.* Stockholm: Liber.

BRUNSSON, N., and OLSEN, J. P., 1997, *The Reforming Organization*. Bergen: Fagbokforlaget. (Previously published by Routledge, 1993.)

―――― 1998, *Organizing Organizations*. Oslo: Fagbokforlaget.

――― and SAHLIN-ANDERSSON, K., forthcoming, 'Constructing Organizations. The example of public sector reform', *Organization Studies*.

BUNDGARD-PEDERSEN, T., 1997, *The Europeanization of Standardization. Technical Standards and Multi Level Governance in Europe*. Copenhagen: Copenhagen University.

CARLSON, S., 1951/1991, 'Executive Behaviour. Reprinted with Contributions by Henry Mintzberg and Rosemary Stewart', *Acta Universitatis Upsaliensis. Studia Oeconomiae Negotiorum*, No. 32. Stockholm: Almqvist & Wiksell International.

CHEUNG, A., 1996, 'Understanding Public Sector Reforms: Their globalness, diversity, and changes in values and institutional relationships'. Paper presented at the Third International Conference of Administrative Sciences, Beijing, 8–11 October.

CHRISTENSEN, T., and LÆGREID, P., 1998, *Den moderne forvaltning*. Oslo: Tano Aschehoug.

COHEN, M., MARCH, J., and OLSEN, J., 1972, 'A Garbage Can Model of Organizational Choice', *Administrative Science Quarterly*, Vol. 1, pp. 1–25.

COLEMAN, J., 1990, *Foundations of Social Theory*. Cambridge, MA: Harvard University Press.

CZARNIAWSKA, B., and JOERGES, B., 1996, 'Travels of Ideas', in Czarniawska, B., and Sevòn, G. (eds.), *Translating Organizational Change*. Berlin: de Gruyter.

―――― SEVÒN, G. (eds.), 1996, *Translating Organizational Change*. Berlin; de Gruyter.

DANIELSSON, A., 1983, *Företagsekonomi—en översikt*. Lund: Studentlitteratur.

DAVID, P., 1986, 'Understanding the Economics of QWERTY: The Necessity of History', in Parker, W. N., *Economic History and the Modern Economist*. Oxford: Basil Blackwell.

DiMAGGIO, P. J., and POWELL, W. W., 1983, 'The Iron Cage Revisited: Institutional Isomorphism and Collective Rationality in Organizational Fields', *American Sociological Review*, Vol. 48, pp. 147–60.

DRUCKER, P. F., 1954, *The Practice of Management*. New York: Harper & Brothers.

DURKHEIM, E., 1906 (1974), 'The Determination of Social Facts', in Durkheim, E., *Sociology and Philosophy*. New York: Free Press, 1974.

EGEBERG, M., 1978, 'Organisert politisk ulikhet', in Olsen, J. P. (ed.), *Politisk organisering: organisasjonsteoretiske synspunkt på folkestyre og politisk ulikhet*. Bergen: Universitetsforlaget.

ELIAS, N., 1939, *Wandlungen des Verhaltens in den westlichen Oberschichten des Abendlandes*

EN ISO 9000-1:1994, *Kvalitetsstandarder—Del 1: Allmänna riktlinjer för val och användning*. Stockholm: SIS.

EN ISO 9001:1994, *Kvalitetssystem—Kvalitetssäkring vid konstruktion, utveckling, produktion, installation, leverans och underhåll av programvara*. Stockholm: SIS.

EN ISO 9004-1:1994, *Kvalitetsledning och kvalitetssystemelement—Del 1: Allmänna riktlinjer*. Stockholm SIS.

EVANS, P., 1995, *Embedded Autonomy. States and Industrial Transformation*. Princeton, NJ: Princeton University Press.

FELDMAN, M. S., and MARCH, J. G., 1981, 'Information in Organizations as Signal and Symbol', *Administrative Science Quarterly*, Vol. 26, pp. 171–86.

FERNLER, K., 1996, *Mångfald eller likriktning. Effekter av en avreglering*. Stockholm: Nerenius & Santérus.

FINNEMORE, M. G., 1992, *Science, the State, and International Society*. Stanford: Stanford University Press.

——— 1996, *National Interests in International Society*. Ithaca, NY: Cornell University Press.

FURUSTEN, S., 1999, *Popular Management Books. How they are made and what they mean for organizations*. London: Routledge.

——— and TAMM HALLSTRÖM, K., 1996, 'Standards and Standardization—on the Production of Official and Unofficial Management Standards'. Paper presented at EURAS 3rd annual conference, 'Standards and Society', Stockholm, 3–5 May.

GIDDENS, A., 1990, *The Consequences of Modernity*. Stanford: Stanford University Press.

GREENWOOD, R., SUDDABY, R., and HININGS, C. R., 1998, 'The Role of Professional Associations in the Transformation of Institutionalized Fields'. Paper presented at the Scancor workshop, 'Samples of the future', Scancor, Stanford, September.

GRINDLEY, P., 1995, *Standards, Strategy and Policy. Cases and Stories*. Oxford: Oxford University Press.

GUILLET DE MONTHOUX, P., 1981, *Doktor Kant och den oekonomiska rationaliseringen*. Göteborg: Bokförlaget Korpen.

GULICK, L., and URWICK, L. (eds.), 1937, *Papers in the Science of Administration*. New York: Institute of Public Administration, Columbia University.

HAAS, E. B., 1990, *When Knowledge is Power. Three Models of Change in International Organizations*. Berkeley: University of California Press.

HÄGG, I., and JOHANSON, J. (eds.), 1982, *Företag i Nätverk—ny syn på konkurrenskraft*. Stockholm: SNS.

HÅKANSSON, H., 1987, *Industrial Technological Development: A Network Approach*. London: Croom Helm.

——— (ed.), 1982, *International Marketing and Purchasing of Industrial Goods*. New York: John Wiley & Sons.

HARRISON, R. J., and MUNGALL, S., 1990, 'Harmonisation', in Groom, A. J. R., and Taylor, P., 1990, *Frameworks for International Co-operation*. London: Pinter Publishers.

HAWKINS, R., MANSELL, R., and SKEA, J. (eds.), 1995, *Standards, Innovation and Competitiveness. The Politics and Economics of Standards in Natural and Technical Environments*. Aldershot: Edward Elgar.

HERNES, G. (ed.), 1978, *Forhandlingsøkonomi og blandingsadministrasjon*. Oslo: Universitetsforlaget.

178   BIBLIOGRAPHY

HIRSCHMAN, A., 1972, *Sorti eller protest. En fråga om lojaliteter.* Stockholm: Rabén & Sjögren.

HIRST, P., and THOMPSON, G., 1996, *Globalization in Question.* Cambridge: Polity Press.

HOBSBAWM, E., and RANGER, T. (eds.), 1992, *The Invention of Tradition.* Cambridge: Cambridge University Press.

HOOD, C., 1991, 'A public management for all seasons', *Public Administration,* Vol. 69, pp. 3–19.

——1995, 'The New Public Management in the 1980s: Variations on a theme', *Accounting, Organizations and Society,* Vol. 20, No. 2/3, pp. 93–109.

——and JACKSON, M., 1991, *Administrative Argument.* Aldershot: Dartmouth.

HUGEMARK, A., 1994, *Den fångslande marknaden. Ekonomiska experter om välfärdsstaten.* Lund: Arkiv.

HUGHES, T. P., 1987, 'The Evolution of Large Technological Systems', in Bijker, W E., Hughes, T. P., and Pinch, T. J. (eds.), *The Social Construction of Technological Systems.* Cambridge, MA: MIT Press.

HYDÉN, H., 1997, 'Rätten som standardiserad politik. Från 'frusen' politik till upptinade relationer'. Paper presented at a conference in Elfvik, March.

ISO/IEC Directives—Part 1: Procedures, 1992.

ISO/IEC Directives—Part 1: Procedures, 1995.

ISO/TC176/N242 (Draft of 'Vision, Mission, and Key Strategies', November 1995).

ISO/TC176/SC2/SC2CG/N-30 (QA/QM first interim report), 1995.

ISO/TC176/SC2/N298 (Internal strategy document from TC 176, named 'QA/QM report'), 1995.

ISO/TC176/SPAG/N66 (SPAG report), 1995.

ISO/TC176/SC2/N331.

JACOBSSON, B., 1984, *Hur styrs förvaltningen? Myt och verklighet kring departementens styrning av ämbetsverken.* Lund: Studentlitteratur.

——1989, *Konsten att reagera. Intressen, institutioner och näringspolitik.* Stockholm: Carlssons.

——1993, 'Europeiseringen av förvaltningen', *Statsvetenskaplig Tidskrift,* Vol. 96, No. 2, pp. 113–37.

——1997, *Europa och staten. Europeiseringens betydelse för svensk statsförvaltning.* Report to Förvaltningspolitiska kommissionen. SOU 1997: 30.

——and SAHLIN-ANDERSSON, K., 1995, *Skolan och det nya verket. Skildringar från styrningens och utvärderingarnas tidevarv.* Stockholm: Nerenius & Santérus.

JEPPERSON, R. L., 1991, 'Institutions, Institutional Effects, and Institutionalization', in Powell, W. W., and DiMaggio, P. J. (eds.), *The New Institutionalism in Organizational Analysis.* Chicago: University of Chicago Press.

JOHANSON, J., and Associates, 1994, 'Internationalization, Relationships and Networks', *Acta Universitatis Upsaliensis. Studia Oeconomiae Negotiorum,* No. 36. Stockholm: Almqvist & Wiksell International.

JOHANSSON, P., and JOHNSSON, M., 1994, *Är kommunerna slavar under modetrenderna?* Göteborg: Göteborg University, Förvaltningshögskolan.

———— 1995. *Kommunernas sökande i reformernas labyrint*. Göteborg: Göteborg University, Förvaltningshögskolan.

JÖNSON, K. M. C., 1994, *The Evolution of the ISO 9000 Standards. How it started*. Information to CEN/BT/WG81.

JÖNSSON, STEN, NILSSON, L., RUBENOWITZ, S., and WESTERSTÅHL, J., 1999, *The Decentralized City. Democracy, Efficiency, Service*. Göteborg: BAS.

KAPLAN, A., 1964, *The Conduct of Inquiry. Methodology for the Behavioral Sciences*. New York: Chandler.

KEOHANE, R. O., and NYE, J. S., 1977, *Power and Interdependence*. Boston: Little Brown.

KRASNER, S., 1983, *International Regimes*. Ithaca, NY: Cornell University Press.

KUHN, T., 1962, *The Structure of Scientific Revolutions*. Chicago: University of Chicago Press.

Kvalitet och Förnyelse, No. 1–4. Göteborg 1997.

LATOUR, B., 1986, 'The Powers of Association', in Law, J. (ed.), *Power, Action and Belief: A New Sociology of Knowledge*. London: Routledge & Kegan Paul.

———— 1987, *Science in Action*. Bristol: Open University Press.

LAW, J., 1994, *Organizing Modernity*. Oxford: Blackwell.

LERDELL, D., and SAHLIN-ANDERSSON, K., 1997, *Att lära över gränser. En studie av OECDs förvaltningspolitiska samarbete*. Report to Förvaltningspolitiska kommissionen. SOU 1997: 33.

LILJEROS, F., 1996, *Elitinnebandy. Skapandet av en elitidrott*. Stockholm: Stockholm University, Institute of Sociology.

LINDBLOM, C., 1958, 'The Science of Muddling Through', *Public Administration Review*, Vol. 19, pp. 79–88.

LOYA, T., and BOLI, J. (eds.), 1998, *Constructing World Culture. International Nongovernmental Organizations since 1875*. Stanford: Stanford University Press.

MCGREGOR, D., 1960, *The Human Side of Enterprise*. New York: McGraw-Hill.

MALINOWSKI, B., 1927, 'The Life of Culture', in Smith, G. E., Malinowski, B., Spinden, H., and Goldenweiser, A., *Culture. The Diffusion Controversy*. New York: W. W. Norton.

MARCH, J. G., 1981, 'Footnotes to Organizational Change', *Administrative Science Quarterly*, Vol. 26, pp. 563–77.

———— and OLSEN, J. P., 1989, *Rediscovering Institutions: The Organizational Basis of Politics*. New York: Free Press.

———— and Simon, H., 1958, *Organizations*. New York: John Wiley & Sons.

MARKOVITS, A., 1988, 'The Other American Exceptionalism—Why Is There No Soccer in the United States?', *Praxis International*, Vol. 8, No. 2, pp. 125–50.

MARQUARDT, D., Chové, J., JENSEN, K. E., PETRICK, K., PYLE, J., and STRAHLE, D., 1991, 'Vision 2000: The Strategy for the ISO 9000 Series Standards in the 90s', *Quality Progress*, May 1991, pp. 25–31.

MARX, G., 1959, *Groucho and Me*. London: Columbus Books.

MENDEL, P., 1996, 'The Institutional Development of Global Production: the Case of ISO 9000 International Management Standards'. Paper presented at EURAS 3rd annual conference Stockholm, 3–5 May.

MEYER, J. W., 1987, 'The World Polity and the Authority of the Nation-State', in Thomas, G. M., Meyer, J. W., Ramirez, F. O., and Boli, J., *Institutional Structure: Constituting State, Society, and the Individual*. Newbury Park, CA: Sage.

—— 1994, 'Rationalized Environments', in Scott, W. R., and Meyer, J. W., *Institutional Environments and Organizations: Structural Complexity and Individualism*. London: Sage.

—— 1996, 'Otherhood: The Promulgation and Transmission of Ideas in the Modern Organizational Environment', in Czarniawska, B., and Sevón, G. (eds.), *Translating Organizational Change*. Berlin: Walter de Gruyter.

—— 1997, 'Cultural Conditions of Standardization'. Paper presented at a SCAN-COR/SCORE seminar on standardizing, Arild, 18–20 September.

—— and JEPPERSON, R. L., 1996, 'The Actors of Modern Society: Cultural Rationalization and the Ongoing Expansion of Social Agency'. Paper presented at the conference Institutional Analysis, the University of Arizona, March.

—— and ROWAN, B., 1977, 'Institutionalized Organizations: Formal Structure as Myth and Ceremony', *American Journal of Sociology*, Vol. 83, pp. 364–85.

—— and SCOTT, R., 1983, 'Centralization and the Legitimacy Problems of Local Government', in Meyer, J. W., and Scott, W. R., *Organizational Environments, Ritual and Rationality*. Beverly Hills, CA: Sage.

—— BOLI, J., and THOMAS, G., 1987, 'Ontology and Rationalization in the Western Cultural Account', in Thomas, G. M., Meyer, J. W., Ramirez, F. O., and Boli, J., *Institutional Structure: Constituting State, Society, and the Individual*. Newbury Park, CA: Sage.

MILLER, P., 1999, 'Governing the Enterprise: The Hidden Face of Accounting', in Porter, T., and Ross, D. (eds.), *The Cambridge History of Science*, Vol. 7: Modern Social and Behavioural Sciences. Cambridge: Cambridge University Press.

MINTZBERG, H., 1973, *The Nature of Managerial Work*. New York: Harper & Row.

—— 1978, 'Patterns in Strategy Formation', *Management Science*, Vol. 24, pp. 934–48.

—— 1991, 'Managerial Work: Forty Years Later', in Carlson, S., 'Executive Behaviour. Reprinted with contributions by Henry Mintzberg and Rosemary Stewart', *Acta Universitatis Upsaliensis. Studia Oeconomiae Negotiorum*, No. 32, pp. 97–111. Stockholm: Almqvist & Wiksell International.

MÖRTH, U., 1996, *Vardagsintegration—la vie quotidienne—i Europa: Sverige i EUREKA och EUREKA i Sverige*. Stockholm: SU Stockholm Studies in Politics No. 54.

NORMANN, R., 1975, *Skapande företagsledning*. Lund: Aldus.

OLSEN, J. P., and PETERS, B. G., 1996, *Lessons From Experience: Experiental Learning in Administrative Reforms in Eight Democracies*. Oslo: Scandinavian University Press.

OLSON, O., GUTHRIE, J., and HUMPHREY, C., 1998, *Global Warning, Debating*

International Developments in New Public Financial Management. Cappelen: Akademisk Forlag.

OSBORNE, D., and GAEBLER, T., 1993, *Reinventing Government—How the Entrepreneurial Spirit is Transforming the Public Sector*. New York: Plume.

——and PLASTRIK, P., 1997, *Banishing Bureaucracy—The Five Strategies for Reinventing Government*. New York: Addison-Wesley.

OUCHI, W. G., 1980, 'Markets, Bureaucracies and Clans', *Administrative Science Quarterly*, Vol. 25, pp. 129–41.

PARSONS, T., 1937, *The Structure of Social Action*. New York: McGraw-Hill.

PERSSON, L., 1992, 'Konkurrens och makt', in Brunsson, N., and Hägg, I. (eds.), *Marknadens makt*. Stockholm: SNS Förlag.

PETERS, T., and WATERMAN, R., 1982, *In Search of Excellence*. New York: Random House.

PINCH, T., and BIJKER, W. E., 1984, 'The social construction of facts and artefacts: or how the sociology of science and the sociology of technology might benefit each other', *Social Studies of Science*, Vol. 14, pp. 399–441.

POLLITT, C., 1993, *Managerialism and the Public Services: Cuts or Cultural Change in the 1990s?* (2nd edition). Oxford: Blackwell.

POWER, M., 1997, *The Audit Society. Rituals of Verification*. Oxford: Oxford University Press.

POWELL, W. W., and DiMAGGIO, P. J. (eds.), 1991, *The New Institutionalism in Organizational Analysis*. Chicago: University of Chicago Press.

PUMA, 1995, *Governance in Transition. Public Management Reforms in OECD Countries*. OECD.

REED, M. I., 1996, 'Expert Power and Control in Late Modernity: An Empirical Review and a Theoretical Synthesis', *Organization Studies*, Vol. 17, pp. 573–97.

REICHARD, C., 1995, 'New Steering Models as the German Variant of New Public Management Concepts'. Paper presented at the EGPA conference in Rotterdam.

RHENMAN, E., 1969, *Företaget och dess omvärld. Organisationsteori för långsiktsplanering*. Stockholm: Bonniers.

ROBERTSON, R., 1992, *Globalization. Social Theory and Global Culture*. London: Sage.

ROMBACH, B., 1991, *Det går inte att styra med mål!* Lund: Studentlitteratur.

——and SAHLIN-ANDERSSON, K., 1996, *Från sanningssökande till styrmedel. Moderna utvärderingar i offentlig sektor*. Stockholm: Nerenius & Santérus.

ROVIK, K.-A., 1993, *De-institutionalization and the Fashion Mechanism*. Tromsø: University of Tromsø.

——1996, 'Deinstitutionalization and the Logic of Fashion', in Czarniawska, B., and Sevón, G. (eds.), *Translating Organizational Change*. Berlin: de Gruyter.

——1998, *Moderne Organisasjoner*. Bergen: Fagbokforlaget.

SAHLIN-ANDERSSON, K., 1996, 'Imitating by Editing Success: The Construction of Organizational Fields', in Czarniawska, B., and Sevón, G. (eds.), *Translating Organizational Change*. Berlin: Walter de Gruyter.

SASSEN, S., 1998, *Globalization and its Discontents. Selected Essays*. New York: New Press.

SCHMIDT, S., and WERLE, R., 1998, *Coordinating Technology. Studies in the International Standardization of Telecommunications*. Cambridge, MA: MIT Press.

SCOTT, R., 1998, *Organizations. Rational, Natural, and Open Systems* (4th edition). New Jersey: Prentice-Hall, Inc.

SEVÓN, G., 1996, 'Organizational Imitation in Identity Transformation', in Czarniawska, B., and Sevón, G. (eds.), *Translating Organizational Change*. Berlin: de Gruyter.

SIKKA, P., and WILLMOTT, H., 1995, 'The Power of "Independence": Defending and Extending the Jurisdiction of Accounting in the United Kingdom', *Accounting, Organizations and Society*, Vol. 20, No. 6, pp. 547–81.

SIQ, 1995, 'Kriterier och anvisningar för Utmärkelsen Svensk Kvalitet—ett verktyg för verksamhetsutveckling'. Göteborg.

SIQ, 1996*a*, 'Arbetshäfte för ständiga förbättringar'. Göteborg.

SIQ, 1996*b*, 'Institutet för Kvalitetsutveckling'. Göteborg.

SIQ, 1996*c*, 'Vägvisare för vinnare'. Göteborg.

SIQ, 1996–7, 'Kundorienterat. Nyhetsbrev från Institutet för Kvalitetsutveckling'. Göteborg.

SIS, 1994, 'Framtid med kvalitet—en introduktion till verksamhetsstyrning med ISO 9000 som modell'. Stockholm: SIS Kvalitetsforum, Utgåva 1, September.

SIS Forum AB, 1994–7, 'Nytt om niotusen. Aktuell information om kvalitet och ISO 9000'. Göteborg.

SIS Forum AB, 1996, 'Gör företaget starkare'. Göteborg.

SIS ForumCenter, 1996, 'Kvalitet framför allt—en introduktion till verksamhetsstyrning med ISO 9000 som modell'. Utgåva 2, November.

SIS KvalitetsForum, 1995, 'Framtid med Kvalitet 9000—en introduktion till verksamhetsstyrning med ISO 9000 som modell. 2:a upplagan'. Stockholm.

SJÖSTEDT, G., 1973, *OECD-samarbetet: Funktioner och effekter*. Stockholm: SU, Statsvetenskapliga institutionen, Stockholm Political Studies No. 3.

SMITH, G. E., MALINOWSKI, B., SPINDEN, H., and GOLDENWEISER, A., 1927, *Culture. The Diffusion Controversy*. New York: W. W. Norton.

SOU 1997:57. *I medborgarnas tjänst. En förvaltningspolitik för staten*. Betänkande av Förvaltningspolitiska kommissionen.

SS—EN 45020, 1999, *Allmänna termer och rekommendationer avseende standardisering och därmed sammanhängande områden* (ISO/IEC Guide 2: 1996). Utgåva 2: SIS.

SS-ISO 9004-2, *Kvalitetssystem—Del 2: Allmänna riktlinjer för tjänster*. Stockholm: SIS.

STRANG, D., and MEYER, J. W., 1993, 'Institutional Conditions for Diffusion', *Theory and Society*, Vol. 22, pp. 487–511.

STREECK, W., 1996, 'Neo-Voluntarism: A New European Social Policy Regime?', in Marks, G. *et al.*, *Governance in the European Union*. London: Sage.

STUURMAN, C., 1995, 'Technical Standards and the Law', Doctoral thesis. Amsterdam: Vrije Universiteit.

SVENSSON, A., 1993, *Målstyrning i praktiken*. Stockholm: Liber.

——and PIHLGREN, G., 1989, *Målstyrning: 90-talets ledningsform för offentlig verksamhet*. Stockholm: Liber.

TAMM HALLSTRÖM, K., 1996a, 'Den växande standardiseringen—framväxten av ISO 9000-standarder'. Score (thesis research proposal).

——1996b, 'The Production of Management Standards', *Revue d'Economie Industrielle*, No. 75, 1st Quarter, pp. 61–76.

TARSCHYS, D., 1988, 'Den kluvna människan', in Tarschys, D., and Hägg, I. (eds.), *I välståndets rävsax*. Stockholm: SNS.

THOMAS, A., 1989, 'One-Minute Management Education: A Sign of the Times', *Management Education and Development*, Vol. 20, pp. 23–38.

THOMAS, G., MEYER, J., RAMIREZ, J. W., and BOLI, J., 1987, *Institutional Structure: Constituting State, Society and the Individual*. Beverly Hills: Sage.

THOMPSON, J., 1967, *Organizations in Action*. New York: McGraw-Hill.

TOULMIN, S., 1990, *Cosmopolis. The Hidden Agenda of Modernity*. Chicago: University of Chicago Press.

WALGENBACH, P., 1997, 'Between "Show Business and Galley"—On the Use of the ISO 9000 Standards in Companies'. Paper presented at a SCANCOR/SCORE seminar on standardizing, Arild, 18–20 September.

WALLANDER, J., 1994, *Budgeten—ett onödigt ont*. Stockholm: SNS Förlag.

WEBER, M., 1964, *The Theory of Social and Economic Organization*. New York: Oxford University Press.

WEICK, K. E., 1976, 'Educational Organizations as Loosely Coupled Systems', *Administrative Science Quarterly*. Vol. 21, pp 1–19.

WESTNEY, D. E., 1987, *Imitation and Innovation: The Transfer of Western Organizational Patterns to Meiji Japan*. Cambridge, MA: Harvard University Press.

VON WRIGHT, G., 1993, *Myten om framsteget*. Stockholm: Bonniers.

Index

Printed in the United States
By Bookmasters